# Focus on
# Grammar 4A

**Marjorie Fuchs**
**Margaret Bonner**

with Jane Curtis

**Focus on Grammar 4: An Integrated Skills Approach, Fifth Edition, Volume A**

Pearson Education, 221 River Street, Hoboken, NJ 07030

**Staff credits:** The people who made up the *Focus on Grammar 4, Fifth Edition, Volume A* team, representing content creation, design, manufacturing, marketing, multimedia, project management, publishing, rights management, and testing, are Pietro Alongi, Rhea Banker, Elizabeth Barker, Stephanie Bullard, Jennifer Castro, Tracey Cataldo, Aerin Csigay, Mindy DePalma, Dave Dickey, Warren Fischbach, Pam Fishman, Nancy Flaggman, Lester Holmes, Gosia Jaros-White, Leslie Johnson, Barry Katzen, Amy McCormick, Julie Molnar, Brian Panker, Stuart Radcliffe, Jennifer Raspiller, Lindsay Richman, Robert Ruvo, Alexandra Suarez, Paula Van Ells, and Joseph Vella.

**Text design and layout:** Don Williams
**Composition:** Page Designs International
**Project supervision:** Bernard Seal
**Contributing editors:** Françoise Leffler and Bernard Seal

**Cover image:** Andy Roberts / Getty Images

Printed in the United States of America
ISBN 10: 0-13-413278-5
ISBN 13: 978-0-13-413278-5

# Contents

# WELCOME TO
# FOCUS ON GRAMMAR
## FIFTH EDITION

BUILDING ON THE SUCCESS of previous editions, *Focus on Grammar* continues to provide an integrated-skills approach to engage students and help them understand, practice, and use English grammar. Centered on thematic instruction, *Focus on Grammar* combines comprehensive grammar coverage with abundant practice, critical thinking skills, and ongoing assessment, helping students accomplish their goals of communicating confidently, accurately, and fluently in everyday situations.

## New in the Fifth Edition

### New and Updated Content
*Focus on Grammar* continues to offer engaging and motivating content that appeals to learners from various cultural backgrounds. Many readings and activities have been replaced or updated to include topics that are of high interest to today's learners.

### Updated Charts and Redesigned Notes
Clear, corpus-informed grammar presentations reflect real and natural language usage and allow students to grasp the most important aspects of the grammar. Clear signposting draws attention to common usage, the difference between written and spoken registers, and common errors.

### Additional Communicative Activities
The new edition of *Focus on Grammar* has been expanded with additional communicative activities that encourage collaboration and the application of the target grammar in a variety of settings.

### Expanded Writing Practice
Each unit in *Focus on Grammar* now ends with a structured "From Grammar to Writing" section. Supported by pre-writing and editing tasks, students engage in activities that allow them to apply the target grammar in writing.

### New Assessment Program
The new edition of *Focus on Grammar* features a variety of new assessment tools, including course diagnostic tests, formative and summative assessments, and a flexible gradebook. The assessments are closely aligned with unit learning outcomes to inform instruction and measure student progress.

### Revised MyEnglishLab
The updated MyEnglishLab offers students engaging practice and video grammar presentations anywhere, anytime. Immediate feedback and remediation tasks offer additional opportunities for successful mastery of content and help promote accuracy. Instructors receive instant access to digital content and diagnostic tools that allow them to customize the learning environment to meet the needs of their students.

# The *Focus on Grammar* Approach

At the heart of the *Focus on Grammar* series is its unique and successful four-step approach that lets learners move from comprehension to communication within a clear and consistent structure. The books provide an abundance of scaffolded exercises to bridge the gap between identifying grammatical structures and using them with confidence and accuracy. The integration of the four skills allows students to learn grammar holistically, which in turn prepares them to understand and use English more effectively.

**STEP 1: Grammar in Context** integrates grammar and vocabulary in natural contexts such as articles, stories, dialogues, and blog posts. Students engage with the unit reading and theme and get exposure to grammar as it is used in real life.

**STEP 2: Grammar Presentation** presents the structures in clear and accessible grammar charts and notes with multiple examples of form and meaning. Corpus-informed explanations and examples reflect natural usage of the target forms, differentiate between written and conversational registers whenever appropriate, and highlight common errors to help students avoid typical pitfalls in both speaking and writing.

**STEP 3: Focused Practice** provides numerous and varied contextualized exercises for both the form and meaning of the new structures. Controlled practice ensures students' understanding of the target grammar and leads to mastery of form, meaning, and use.

**STEP 4: Communication Practice** provides practice with the structures in listening exercises as well as in communicative, open-ended speaking activities. These engaging activities provide ample opportunities for personalization and build students' confidence in using English. Students also develop their critical thinking skills through problem-solving activities and discussions.

Each unit now culminates with the **From Grammar to Writing** section. Students learn about common errors in writing and how to recognize them in their own work. Engaging and motivating writing activities encourage students to apply grammar in writing through structured tasks from pre-writing to editing.

## Recycling

Underpinning the scope and sequence of the *Focus on Grammar* series is practice that allows students to use target structures and vocabulary many times, in different contexts. New grammar and vocabulary are recycled throughout the book. Students have maximum exposure, leading them to become confident in using the language in speech and in writing.

## Assessment

Extensive testing informs instruction and allows teachers and students to measure progress.

- **Unit Reviews** at the end of every unit assess students' understanding of the grammar and allow students to monitor their own progress.

- **Diagnostic Tests** provide teachers with a valid and reliable means to determine how well students know the material they are going to study and to target instruction based on students' needs.

- **Unit Review Tests, Mid- and End-of-Term Review Tests, and Final Exams** measure students' ability to demonstrate mastery of skills taught in the course.

- The **Placement Test** is designed to help teachers place students into one of the five levels of the *Focus on Grammar* course.

## The Importance of Context

A key element of *Focus on Grammar* is presenting important grammatical structures in context. The contexts selected are most relevant to the grammatical forms being introduced. Contextualized grammar practice also plays a key role in improving fluent use of grammar in communicative contexts. It helps learners to develop consistent and correct usage of target structures during all productive practice.

## The Role of Corpus

The most important goal of *Focus on Grammar* has always been to present grammar structures using natural language. To that end, *Focus on Grammar* has incorporated the findings of corpus linguistics,* while never losing sight of what is pedagogically sound and useful. By taking this approach, *Focus on Grammar* ensures that:

- the language presented reflects real, natural usage
- themes and topics provide a good fit with the grammar point and elicit the target grammar naturally
- findings of the corpus research are reflected in the syllabus, readings, charts, grammar notes, and practice activities
- examples illustrate differences between spoken and written registers, and formal and informal language
- students are exposed to common errors in usage and learn how to recognize and avoid errors in their own speech and writing

## *Focus on Grammar* Efficacy

The fifth edition of *Focus on Grammar* reflects an important efficacy initiative for Pearson courses—to be able to demonstrate that all teaching materials have a positive impact on student learning. To support this, *Focus on Grammar* has been updated and aligned to the **Global Scale of English** and the **Common European Framework** (CEFR) to provide granular insight into the objectives of the course, the progression of learning, and the expected outcomes a learner will be able to demonstrate upon successful completion.

To learn more about the Global Scale of English, visit www.English.com.

# Components

**Student Books with Essential Online Resources** include access codes to the course audio, video, and self-assessment.

**Student Books with MyEnglishLab** offer a blended approach with integration of print and online content.

**Workbooks** contain additional contextualized practice in print format.

**Digital Teacher's Resources** include printable teaching notes, GSE mapping documents, answer keys, audio scripts, and downloadable tests. Access to the digital copy of the student books allows teachers to project the pages for whole-class instruction.

***FOG Go* app** allows users to access the student book audio on their mobile devices.

* A principal resource has been Douglas Biber et al, *Longman Grammar of Spoken and Written English*, Harlow: Pearson Education Ltd., 1999.

# The *Focus on Grammar* Unit

*Focus on Grammar* introduces grammar structures in the context of unified themes. All units follow a four-step approach, taking learners from grammar in context to communicative practice. Thematic units add a layer to learning so that by the end of the unit students will be able to discuss the content using the grammar points they have just studied.

## STEP 1    GRAMMAR IN CONTEXT

**Before You Read** activities create interest and elicit students' knowledge about the topic.

**Vocabulary** exercises help students improve their command of English.

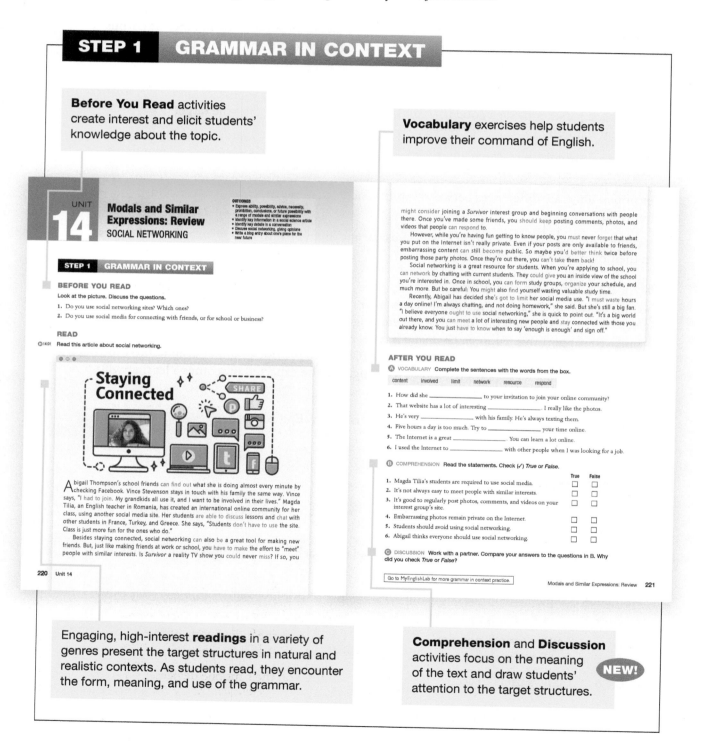

Engaging, high-interest **readings** in a variety of genres present the target structures in natural and realistic contexts. As students read, they encounter the form, meaning, and use of the grammar.

**Comprehension** and **Discussion** activities focus on the meaning of the text and draw students' attention to the target structures.

**NEW!**

**Grammar Charts** present the structures in a clear, easy-to-read format.

### STEP 2   GRAMMAR PRESENTATION

**FUTURE**

**Affirmative Statements**

| | |
|---|---|
| We are going to take | |
| We will take | the airship at 9:00. |
| We are taking | |
| We take | |

**Negative Statements**

| | |
|---|---|
| We are not going to take | |
| We will not take | the airship at 10:00. |
| We are not taking | |
| We don't take | |

**Yes/No Questions**

| | |
|---|---|
| Is she going to take | |
| Will she take | the airship at 9:00? |
| Is she taking | |
| Does she take | |

**Short Answers**

| | Affirmative | | Negative |
|---|---|---|---|
| Yes, | she is. | No, | she isn't. |
| | she will. | | she won't. |
| | she is. | | she isn't. |
| | she does. | | she doesn't. |

**Wh- Questions**

| | |
|---|---|
| When is she going to take | |
| When will she take | the airship? |
| When is she taking | |
| When does she take | |

**FUTURE PROGRESSIVE**

**Statements**

| Subject | Be (not) going to/ Will (not) | Be + Base Form + -ing | |
|---|---|---|---|
| People | are (not) going to will (not) | be traveling | to Mars by 2050. |

**Yes/No Questions**

| Be/Will | Subject | Going to | Be + Base Form + -ing | |
|---|---|---|---|---|
| Are Will | they | going to | be traveling | to Mars? |

**Short Answers**

| Affirmative | | Negative | |
|---|---|---|---|
| Yes, | they are. they will. | No, | they're not. they won't. |

**Wh- Questions**

| Wh- Word | Be/Will | Subject | Going to | Be + Base Form + -ing | |
|---|---|---|---|---|---|
| When | are will | they | going to | be traveling | to Mars? |

Future and Future Progressive    71

**NEW!**

The newly designed **Grammar Notes** highlight the main point of each note, making navigation and review easier. Simple corpus-informed **explanations** and **examples** ensure students' understanding.

**GRAMMAR NOTES**

**1 Simple Present**

Use the simple present to show that something **happens regularly** or for **unchanging facts**.

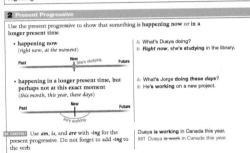

- **happens regularly**
  (always, usually, often, sometimes, rarely)

  People **always** call him Joe.
  We **usually** prefer first names.
  Dusya **sometimes** uses nicknames.

- **unchanging facts**

  She **comes** from Moscow. It's the capital.

**BE CAREFUL** Remember to add **-s** or **-es** to third-person singular (he, she, it) of simple present verbs. Use **do/does** in questions and **do not/does not** in negative sentences.

Dusya **lives** in Toronto. She **doesn't live** in Ottawa.
NOT Dusya ~~live~~ in Toronto. She ~~don't live~~ in Ottawa.

**USAGE NOTE** We often use **adverbs of frequency** (always, usually, etc.) with verbs in the simple present. The adverb usually goes **before the verb**. If the verb is **be**, the adverb goes **after be**. **Sometimes** and **usually** can also go at the **beginning** of the sentence.

Dusya **always** gets home at 7:00 p.m.
She **usually** finishes her work on time.
She is **never** late for class.

We **sometimes** eat lunch together.
**Sometimes** we eat lunch together.

**2 Present Progressive**

Use the present progressive to show that something is **happening now** or in a **longer present time**.

- **happening now**
  (right now, at the moment)

  A: What's Dusya doing?
  B: **Right now**, she's **studying** in the library.

- **happening in a longer present time**, but perhaps not at this exact moment
  (this month, this year, these days)

  A: What's Jorge doing these days?
  B: He's **working** on a new project.

**BE CAREFUL** Use **am**, **is**, and **are** with **-ing** for the present progressive. Do not forget to add **-ing** to the verb.

Dusya **is working** in Canada this year.
NOT Dusya ~~is work~~ in Canada this year.

**USAGE NOTE** We often use **time expressions** (right now, this month, these days, etc.) with verbs in the present progressive. The time expression can go at the **beginning or end** of the sentence. **Now** can also go **after be**.

**These days**, Dusya **is looking** for a new job.
Dusya **is looking** for a new job **these days**.

**Now**, she **is preparing** for a job interview.
She **is preparing** for a job interview **now**.
She **is now preparing** for a job interview.

Simple Present and Present Progressive    7

**NEW!**

**Clear signposting** provides corpus-informed notes about common usage, differences between spoken and written registers, and common errors.

**PRONUNCIATION NOTE**

**07:02 Intonation of Tag Questions**

In tag questions, our **voice rises** at the end when we expect another person to give us **information**.

A: You're not moving, **are you?**
B: Yes. I'm returning to Berlin.

Our **voice falls** at the end when we are making a comment and expect the other person to agree.

A: Seoul is interesting, **isn't it?**
B: Yes, it is.

Go to MyEnglishLab to watch the grammar presentation.

**Pronunciation Notes** are now included with the grammar presentation to highlight relevant pronunciation aspects of the target structures and to help students understand authentic spoken English.

**NEW!**

**Discover the Grammar** activities develop students' recognition and understanding of the target structures before they are asked to produce them.

**Controlled practice activities** lead students to master form, meaning, and use of the target grammar.

---

STEP 3   FOCUSED PRACTICE

### EXERCISE 1   DISCOVER THE GRAMMAR

GRAMMAR NOTES 1–4   **Read the statements. Check (✓) Active or Passive.**

| | Active | Passive |
|---|:---:|:---:|
| 1. The first *National Geographic* magazine was published in October 1888. | ☐ | ☑ |
| 2. Today, millions of people read the magazine. | ☐ | ☐ |
| 3. The magazine is translated from English into forty other languages. | ☐ | ☐ |
| 4. My cousin reads the Russian edition. | ☐ | ☐ |
| 5. Some of the articles are written by famous writers. | ☐ | ☐ |
| 6. *Young Explorer*, another publication, is written for kids. | ☐ | ☐ |
| 7. The publication is known for its wonderful photography. | ☐ | ☐ |
| 8. A *National Geographic* photographer took the first underwater color photos. | ☐ | ☐ |
| 9. Photographers are sent all over the world. | ☐ | ☐ |
| 10. The articles show a lot of respect for nature. | ☐ | ☐ |
| 11. That picture was taken by Reza Deghati. | ☐ | ☐ |
| 12. *National Geographic* is sold at newsstands. | ☐ | ☐ |

### EXERCISE 2   ACTIVE OR PASSIVE

GRAMMAR NOTES 1–4   **The chart shows some of the forty language editions that *National Geographic* publishes. Use the chart to complete the sentences. Some sentences will be active; some will be passive.**

| Language | Number of Speakers* |
|---|:---:|
| Arabic | 240 |
| Chinese (all varieties) | 1,200 |
| English | 340 |
| Japanese | 130 |
| Korean | 77 |
| Russian | 110 |
| Spanish | 410 |
| Turkish | 71 |

*first-language speakers in millions

1. Spanish *is spoken by 410 million people.* _____
2. Around 110 million people *speak Russian* _____
3. Arabic _____
4. _____ Chinese.

---

### EXERCISE 2   RELATIVE PRONOUNS AND VERBS

GRAMMAR NOTES 3–6   **Complete the statements in the personality quiz. Circle the correct words. (In Exercise 9, you will take the quiz.)**

## Personality Quiz

Do you agree with the following statements? Check (✓) *True* or *False*.

| | TRUE | FALSE |
|---|:---:|:---:|
| 1. People (who) / which talk a lot tire me. | ☐ | ☐ |
| 2. On a plane, I always talk to the stranger who take / takes the seat next to me. | ☐ | ☐ |
| 3. I'm the kind of person that / which needs time to recover after a social event. | ☐ | ☐ |
| 4. My best friend, that / who talks a lot, is just like me. | ☐ | ☐ |
| 5. I prefer to have conversations which focus / focuses on feelings and ideas. | ☐ | ☐ |
| 6. I am someone whose favorite activities include / includes reading and doing yoga. | ☐ | ☐ |
| 7. People whose / their personalities are completely different can be close friends. | ☐ | ☐ |
| 8. I'm someone that always see / sees the glass as half full, not half empty. | ☐ | ☐ |
| 9. Difficult situations are often the ones that provide / provides the best opportunities. | ☐ | ☐ |
| 10. Introverts, that / who are quiet, sensitive, and creative, are perfect friends. | ☐ | ☐ |

### EXERCISE 3   IDENTIFYING ADJECTIVE CLAUSES

**A**   GRAMMAR NOTES 1–4, 6   **We often use identifying adjective clauses to define words. First, match the words on the left with the descriptions on the right.**

| | | | |
|---|---|---|---|
| _h_ | 1. difficulty | a. | This situation gives you a chance to experience something good. |
| ___ | 2. extrovert | b. | This attitude shows your ideas about your future. |
| ___ | 3. introvert | c. | This ability makes you able to produce new ideas. |
| ___ | 4. opportunity | d. | This person usually sees the bright side of situations. |
| ___ | 5. opposites | e. | This person requires a lot of time alone. |
| ___ | 6. optimist | f. | This money was unexpected. |
| ___ | 7. outlook | g. | This person usually sees the dark side of situations. |
| ___ | 8. pessimist | h. | This problem is hard to solve. |
| ___ | 9. creativity | i. | These people have completely different personalities. |
| ___ | 10. windfall | j. | This person requires a lot of time with others. |

A **variety of exercise types** engage students and guide them from recognition and understanding to accurate production of the grammar structures.

---

**Editing** exercises allow students to identify and correct typical mistakes.

### EXERCISE 5   EDITING

GRAMMAR NOTES 1–7   **Read this post to a travelers' website. There are ten mistakes in the use of embedded questions. The first mistake is already corrected. Find and correct nine more. Don't forget to check punctuation.**

WORLDWIDE TRAVEL

Email this page to someone!    New Topic    Post a Poll    Post Reply

Subject: **Tipping at the Hair Salon in Italy**
Posted April 10 by Jenna Thompson

   *if or whether*
I wonder you can help clarify some tipping situations for me. I never know what doing at the hair salon. I don't know if I should tip the person who washes my hair? What about the person who cuts it, and the person who colors it? And what happens if the person is the owner. Do you know do I still need to tip him or her? That doesn't seem logical. (And often I'm not even sure who is the owner!) Then I never know how much to tip or where should I leave the tip? Do I leave it on the counter or in the person's hands? What if somebody's hands are wet or have hair color on them? Can I just put the tip in his or her pocket? It all seems so complicated! I can't imagine how do customers figure all this out? What's the custom? I really need to find out what to do—and FAST! My hair is getting very long and dirty.

**Listenings** in a variety of genres allow students to hear the grammar in natural contexts.

---

**STEP 4    COMMUNICATION PRACTICE**

### EXERCISE 6  LISTENING

**A** Claudia Leggett and her son, Pietro, are flying from Los Angeles to Hong Kong. Listen to the announcements they hear in the airport and aboard the plane. Read the statements. Then listen again and check (✓) *True* or *False*.

|  | True | False |
|---|---|---|
| **Announcement 1:** Claudia has two pieces of carry-on luggage, and Pietro has one. They can take them all on the plane. | ☐ | ☑ |
| **Announcement 2:** Look at their boarding passes. They can board now. | ☐ | ☐ |

| **Announcement 3:** Look at their boarding passes again. They can board now. | ☐ | ☐ |
|---|---|---|
| **Announcement 4:** Pietro is only ten years old. Claudia should put his oxygen mask on first. | ☐ | ☐ |
| **Announcement 5:** Claudia is sitting in a left-hand window seat. She can see the lights of Tokyo. | ☐ | ☐ |
| **Announcement 6:** Passengers who are taking connecting flights can get this information on the plane. | ☐ | ☐ |

**B** Work with a partner. Listen again to the announcements. Discuss your answers.

EXAMPLE:  A: OK. So, why is the answer to number 1 *False*?
B: The announcement says if you have more than one piece of carry-on luggage, you must check the extra pieces at the gate.
A: Right. And they have three pieces, so they can't take them all on the plane with them. Now, what did you choose for number 2?

*Passengers on Flight 398 to Hong Kong*

---

In the **listening activities**, students practice a range of listening skills. A **new step** has been added in which partners complete an activity that relates to the listening and uses the target grammar.

**NEW!**

---

Engaging **communicative activities** (conversations, discussions, presentations, surveys, and games) help students synthesize the grammar, develop fluency, and build their problem-solving skills.

---

### EXERCISE 7  WHAT ABOUT YOU?

CONVERSATION  Work in a group. Talk about your hobbies and interests. What did you do in the past with your hobby? What have you been doing lately? Find out about other people's hobbies.

EXAMPLE:  A: Do you have any hobbies, Ben?
B: Yes. Since I was in high school, my hobby has been running. . . . Recently, I've been training for a marathon. What about you? Do you have a hobby?
C: I collect sneakers. I got my first pair of Nikes when I was ten, and I've been collecting different kinds of sneakers ever since. . . .

### EXERCISE 8  DONE, DONE, NOT DONE

**A** INTERVIEW  What did you plan to do last month to develop your hobbies and personal interests? Make a list. Include things you did and things that you still haven't done. Do not check (✓) any of the items. Exchange lists with a partner.

*Buy a new pair of running shoes.*
*Research healthy snacks for marathon runners.*

**B** Now ask questions about your partner's list. Check (✓) the things that your partner has already done. Answer your partner's questions about your list. When you finish, find out if the information that you recorded on your partner's list is correct.

EXAMPLE:  A: Have you bought your new running shoes yet?
B: Yes, I have. I bought them last week.
A: And what about the research on healthy snacks?
B: I haven't done it yet.
A: OK. I think we've talked about everything on our lists. Let's make sure our answers are correct.

---

# FROM GRAMMAR TO WRITING

A **From Grammar to Writing** section, now in every unit, helps students confidently apply the unit's grammar to their own writing.

**NEW!**

## FROM GRAMMAR TO WRITING

**A** BEFORE YOUR WRITE  Diplomats are people who officially represent their country in a foreign country. Imagine that you are going to attend a school for future diplomats. Complete the information about some of the features of your ideal school.

Courses required: _____

Language(s) spoken: _____

Living quarters provided: _____

Food offered: _____

Trips taken: _____

Electronic devices provided: _____

**B** WRITE  Use your information to write one or two paragraphs about your ideal school for diplomacy. Use the passive with modals and similar expressions. Try to avoid some of the common mistakes in the chart.

EXAMPLE:  I think the ideal school for diplomacy should teach a lot about cross-cultural understanding. Courses should be required in . . . More than one official language should be spoken. Classes could be offered in . . .

**Common Mistakes in Using the Passive with Modals and Similar Expressions**

| Use *be* + past participle after the modal. Do not leave out *be*. | Language classes **should** be required.<br>NOT Language classes ~~should required~~. |
| Use the **past participle** after *be*. Do not use the base form of the verb after *be*. | A lot could be *learned*.<br>NOT A lot could be ~~learn~~. |

**C** CHECK YOUR WORK  Read your paragraph(s). Underline the passive with modals and similar expressions. Use the Editing Checklist to check your work.

**Editing Checklist**

Did you use . . . ?

☐ *be* + past participle to form the passive after modals or similar expressions

☐ *will* or *be going to* for certainty in the future

☐ *can* for present ability

☐ *could* for past ability or future possibility

☐ *may, might,* and *can't* for future possibility or impossibility

☐ *should, ought to,* and *had better* for advice

☐ *must* and *have (got) to* for necessity

**D** REVISE YOUR WORK  Read your paragraph(s) again. Can you improve your writing? Make changes if necessary. Give your writing a title.

Go to MyEnglishLab for more writing practice.

The Passive with Modals and Similar Expressions  **299**

The **Before You Write** task helps students generate ideas for their writing assignment.

In the **Write** task, students are given a writing assignment and guided to use the target grammar and avoid common mistakes.

**Check Your Work** includes an Editing Checklist that allows students to proofread and edit their compositions.

In **Revise Your Work**, students are given a final opportunity to improve their writing.

# UNIT **REVIEW**

**Unit Reviews** give students the opportunity to check their understanding of the target structures. Students can check their answers against the Answer Key at the end of the book. They can also complete the Review on MyEnglishLab.

## UNIT 21  **REVIEW**

Test yourself on the grammar of the unit.

**A** Match each condition with its result.

| Condition | Result |
|---|---|
| _____ 1. If it rains, | a. you might have good luck. |
| _____ 2. Unless you study, | b. I could pay you back tomorrow. |
| _____ 3. If you cross your fingers, | c. I may not buy it. |
| _____ 4. Unless they lower the price, | d. I'll take an umbrella. |
| _____ 5. If you lend me $10, | e. you could rent one. |
| _____ 6. If you don't own a car, | f. you won't pass. |

**B** Complete the future real conditional sentences in these conversations with the correct form of the verbs in parentheses.

1. A: Are you going to take the bus?

   B: No. If I _____ the bus, I _____ late.
   a. (take)                b. (be)

2. A: What _____ you _____ if you _____ the job?
   a. (do)                  b. (not get)

   B: I _____ in school unless I _____ the job.
   c. (stay)              d. (get)

3. A: If I _____ the test, I _____
   a. (pass)             b. (celebrate)

   B: Good luck, but I'm sure you'll pass. You've studied really hard for it.

   A: Thanks!

**C** Find and correct six mistakes. Remember to check punctuation.

It's been a hard week, and I'm looking forward to the weekend. If the weather will be nice tomorrow Marco and I are going to go to the beach. The ocean is usually too cold

xii  The *Focus on Grammar* Unit

**MyEnglishLab**

**MyEnglishLab** delivers rich online content to engage and motivate **students**.

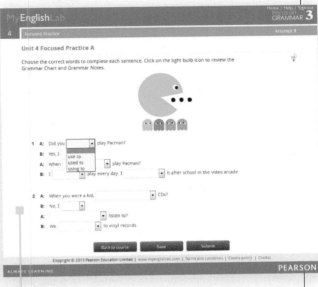

Grammar Coach videos give additional grammar presentations.

**NEW!**

**MyEnglishLab** provides students with:

- rich interactive practice in grammar, reading, listening, speaking, and writing
- immediate and meaningful feedback on wrong answers **NEW!**
- remediation activities
- grade reports that display performance and time on task

**MyEnglishLab** delivers innovative teaching tools and useful resources to **teachers**.

With **MyEnglishLab**, teachers can:

- view student scores by unit and activity
- monitor student progress on any activity or test
- analyze class data to determine steps for remediation and support

**MyEnglishLab** also provides teachers with:

- a digital copy of the student book for whole-class instruction
- downloadable assessments, including the placement test, that can be administered on MyEnglishLab or in print format
- printable resources including teaching notes, suggestions for teaching grammar, GSE mapping documents, answer keys, and audio scripts

# Scope and Sequence

| LISTENING | SPEAKING | WRITING | VOCABULARY |
|---|---|---|---|
| **A conversation about people**<br>■ Can identify people, based on descriptions in a conversation | ■ Can ask people for personal details and introduce them to others<br>■ Can narrate a video, describing what people are doing<br>■ Can discuss naming customs in different countries | ■ Can write a detailed paragraph about oneself | adjustment AWL<br>consist of AWL<br>convince AWL<br>identity AWL<br>in style AWL<br>provide |
| **A personal narrative**<br>■ Can identify the order of events in a recorded description | ■ Can describe one's first meeting with someone<br>■ Can ask and answer questions about important life events<br>■ Can create a story and present it to the class | ■ Can write two paragraphs describing past events in an important relationship | accomplish<br>cover (v)<br>influential<br>pursue AWL<br>recover AWL<br>research (n) AWL |
| **A conversation about hobbies**<br>■ Can recognize key ideas and details in a discussion about hobbies and personal interests | ■ Can talk about hobbies and personal interests<br>■ Can discuss routine accomplishments<br>■ Can research an interesting hobby and present findings to the class | ■ Can write a detailed paragraph about a recent trend | alternative (n) AWL<br>experiment (v)<br>motivation AWL<br>passion<br>survive AWL<br>trend (n) AWL |
| **An interview on a radio show**<br>■ Can understand the order of events in a radio program about career and life choices | ■ Can ask and answer questions about past events and personal achievements<br>■ Can discuss one's schedule for the previous day<br>■ Can research a famous child prodigy and present findings to the class<br>■ Can compare two similar scenes and discuss differences | ■ Can write two paragraphs about a famous person's career and personal life | conduct (v) AWL<br>contract (n) AWL<br>ethnic AWL<br>inspire<br>participate AWL<br>transform AWL |

AWL = Academic Word List item

| UNIT | GRAMMAR | READING |
|---|---|---|

| LISTENING | SPEAKING | WRITING | VOCABULARY |
|---|---|---|---|
| **A discussion about a conference**<br>■ Can follow a group discussion, identifying important details such as the speakers' schedules and plans | ■ Can discuss schedules, reaching agreement on plans<br>■ Can offer a detailed opinion about a controversial topic relating to technology | ■ Can write two paragraphs about a hypothetical scenario that is set in the future | challenge (n) AWL<br>individual (n) AWL<br>innovative AWL<br>technology AWL<br>vehicle AWL<br>vertical (adj) |
| **A conversation about entrepreneurship**<br>■ Can follow a fast-paced conversation about professional aspirations, identifying key details | ■ Can talk about someone's future goals and accomplishments<br>■ Can discuss personal long-term goals and how to achieve them | ■ Can write a detailed paragraph about a classmate's future goals and what that person is doing to achieve these goals | affordable<br>convert (v) AWL<br>corporate (adj) AWL<br>initiative AWL<br>meanwhile<br>status AWL |

| | | | |
|---|---|---|---|
| **On-the-street conversations**<br>■ Can identify important details from fast-paced conversations | ■ Can interview a classmate, asking questions and checking information<br>■ Can discuss details about cities around the world, asking questions and checking information | ■ Can write an interview transcript about a classmate's home city, commenting on and checking information | attracted (adj)<br>constant (adj) AWL<br>extremely<br>originally<br>structure (n) AWL<br>supply (v) |
| **A first-date conversation**<br>■ Can identify key details about people in a conversation | ■ Can discuss similarities and differences between two people<br>■ Can conduct online research about twins separated at birth and report findings<br>■ Can discuss the controversial topic of nature vs. nurture and give own opinion | ■ Can write two paragraphs about the similarities and differences between two people | complex (adj) AWL<br>factor (n) AWL<br>identical AWL<br>image AWL<br>investigate AWL<br>reserved (adj) |

AWL = Academic Word List item

| UNIT | GRAMMAR | READING |
|---|---|---|
| **PART 4**<br><br>**Gerunds, Infinitives, and Phrasal Verbs**<br><br>**9**<br>**Gerunds and Infinitives: Review and Expansion**<br>Page 136<br>THEME Fast Food | ■ Can use a gerund as the subject or the object of a verb<br>■ Can use a range of verbs followed by a gerund or an infinitive<br>■ Can use a gerund after a preposition or a phrasal verb, and an infinitive after certain adjectives or nouns<br>■ Can use infinitives to express purpose<br>■ Can use gerunds and infinitives to make general statements | Social Science Article:<br>*Fast Food in a Fast World*<br>■ Can recognize significant points and ideas in an article about a popular trend |
| **10**<br>***Make, Have, Let, Help, and Get***<br>Page 152<br>THEME Zoos and Marine Theme Parks | ■ Can use *make, have, get,* or *let* to show how someone causes or allows another person/animal to do something<br>■ Can use *help* to show that someone makes things easier for another person/animal | Opinion Article:<br>*That's Entertainment?*<br>■ Can recognize significant points and arguments in an opinion article on a controversial topic |
| **11**<br>**Phrasal Verbs: Review and Expansion**<br>Page 165<br>THEME Telemarketing | ■ Can use a range of phrasal verbs<br>■ Can use transitive phrasal verbs with or without separated objects<br>■ Can use intransitive phrasal verbs<br>■ Can use phrasal verbs with preposition combinations | Magazine Article:<br>*Welcome Home!*<br>■ Can identify specific information in a linguistically complex article |
| **PART 5**<br><br>**Adjective Clauses**<br><br>**12**<br>**Adjective Clauses with Subject Relative Pronouns**<br>Page 182<br>THEME Personality Types and Friends | ■ Can use sentences with adjective clauses beginning with subject relative pronouns such as *who, that, which,* or *whose* to identify or give additional information about nouns<br>■ Can use identifying and nonidentifying adjective clauses<br>PRONUNCIATION Identifying and nonidentifying adjective clauses | Psychology Article:<br>*Extroverts and Introverts*<br>■ Can identify specific information in a linguistically complex article |
| **13**<br>**Adjective Clauses with Object Relative Pronouns**<br>Page 199<br>THEME The Immigrant Experience | ■ Can use adjective clauses beginning with object relative pronouns such as *who(m), that, which,* or *whose* to identify or give additional information about nouns<br>■ Can use adjective clauses beginning with *where* or *when*<br>■ Can use identifying and nonidentifying adjective clauses<br>■ Can use adjective clauses as objects of verbs and prepositions | Online Book Review:<br>*Stories of a New Generation of Immigrants*<br>■ Can identify specific information in a book review |

| LISTENING | SPEAKING | WRITING | VOCABULARY |
|---|---|---|---|
| **A conversation about school food services**<br>■ Can identify key details in a conversation | ■ Can complete a questionnaire and discuss results<br>■ Can make cross-cultural comparisons about a familiar topic<br>■ Can conduct online research on fast food and report findings | ■ Can write two paragraphs describing plusses and minuses of a certain type of food | appealing (adj)<br>consequence AWL<br>convenience<br>globe AWL<br>objection<br>reliability AWL |
| **A conversation between a student and a teacher**<br>■ Can recognize how one speaker influences the other and gets that person do something | ■ Can describe how someone has influenced one's life<br>■ Can contribute to a group discussion about a controversial topic | ■ Can write three paragraphs about a controversial topic, giving arguments for and against and stating one's personal opinion | cruel<br>former<br>humane<br>physical AWL<br>rebel (v)<br>reinforcement AWL |
| **A phone conversation with a telemarketer**<br>■ Can identify key details in a conversation | ■ Can justify and sustain views clearly by providing relevant explanations and arguments<br>■ Can analyze and discuss advertisements | ■ Can write two paragraphs describing a personal experience and what one learned from the experience | authorities AWL<br>eliminate AWL<br>equivalent AWL<br>feature (n) AWL<br>firmly<br>tactic |
| **A conversation between friends at a high-school reunion**<br>■ Can identify the people described in a conversation | ■ Can take a personality quiz and discuss the results<br>■ Can give an opinion and examples in response to a literary quote or an international proverb<br>■ Can complete a questionnaire and discuss the answers | ■ Can write two paragraphs describing the ideal friend and one's best friend | contradict AWL<br>require AWL<br>sensitive<br>tendency<br>trait<br>unique AWL |
| **A description of a childhood room**<br>■ Can follow a personal narrative well enough to identify specific details | ■ Can conduct online research about a successful immigrant and report findings<br>■ Can give an opinion and examples in response to a literary quote | ■ Can write a description of a place from one's childhood and why the place was important | compelling (adj)<br>encounter (v) AWL<br>generation AWL<br>issue (n) AWL<br>poverty<br>struggle (v) |

AWL = Academic Word List item

| LISTENING | SPEAKING | WRITING | VOCABULARY |
|---|---|---|---|
| **A conversation about Facebook**<br><br>■ Can identify key details in a conversation | ■ Can discuss social networking websites, giving opinions<br><br>■ Can take a quiz and compare answers with classmates<br><br>■ Can discuss the advantages and disadvantages of social networking | ■ Can write a blog entry about plans and events in the near future | content (n)<br>involved (adj) AWL<br>limit (v)<br>network (v) AWL<br>resource AWL<br>respond AWL |
| **A personal narrative about regrets**<br><br>■ Can follow a personal narrative well enough to identify specific details | ■ Can take a survey and discuss the results<br><br>■ Can discuss a situation, examining people's actions and giving opinions as to what the people should have done | ■ Can write three paragraphs describing a past problem and evaluating what should or shouldn't have been done | examine<br>exhausted (adj)<br>paralyzed (adj)<br>perceive AWL<br>strategy AWL<br>unrealistic |
| **Conversations between archaeology students**<br><br>■ Can identify key details in conversations and match each conversation with a picture | ■ Can discuss ancient objects, speculating on what they are and what they might have been used for<br><br>■ Can discuss and speculate on new facts found about the Iceman | ■ Can write a detailed paragraph speculating about an unsolved mystery | assume AWL<br>decade AWL<br>indicate AWL<br>preserve (v)<br>speculation<br>victim |
| **An academic lecture about Haiti**<br><br>■ Can follow an academic lecture well enough to identify key details and complete notes | ■ Can discuss and interpret an international proverb<br><br>■ Can engage in an extended conversation about geographical locations and resources found there<br><br>■ Can take a quiz and compare answers with classmates | ■ Can write an essay about a country one knows well | edition AWL<br>explorer<br>inhabitant<br>mission<br>publication AWL<br>respect (n) |
| **Conversations from a science-fiction movie dialog**<br><br>■ Can follow conversations well enough to identify key details | ■ Can discuss rules for group living in close quarters<br><br>■ Can make recommendations for improvement of one's environment<br><br>■ Can discuss the pros and cons of investing money in space projects | ■ Can write one or two paragraphs describing the ideal school for diplomacy | assemble AWL<br>benefit (v) AWL<br>concern (n)<br>cooperate AWL<br>perspective AWL<br>undertaking AWL |

AWL = Academic Word List item

| UNIT | GRAMMAR | READING |
|------|---------|---------|
| ▼ PART **7** CONTINUED | | |
| **19** **The Passive Causative** Page 301 THEME Personal Services | ■ Can use the passive causative to describe services people arrange for someone to do for them ■ Can use the passive causative with *by* + agent when the agent is new or important information | Fashion Magazine Article: *Body Art* ■ Can identify specific information in an article on a familiar topic |
| **20** **Present Real Conditional Sentences** Page 316 THEME Shopping | ■ Can use present real conditional sentences with *if/when* to describe real conditions and results that are certain, such as general truths and habits ■ Can use modals or similar expressions in the result clause to express possibility, advice, or necessity ■ Can use an imperative in the result clause to express instructions, commands, or invitations | Information Article: *Pick and Click: Shopping@Home* ■ Can identify specific information in an article on a familiar topic |
| **21** **Future Real Conditional Sentences** Page 331 THEME Cause and Effect | ■ Can use future real conditional sentences with *if/unless* to describe real conditions and results that are certain ■ Can use modals or similar expressions in the result clause to express possibility, advice, or necessity | Magazine Article: *Knock on Wood!* ■ Can identify specific information in an article on a familiar topic |
| **22** **Present and Future Unreal Conditional Sentences** Page 344 THEME Wishes | ■ Can use present and future unreal conditional sentences to describe unreal conditions and results that are untrue, imagined, or impossible ■ Can use *might* or *could* in the result clause to express possibility ■ Can give advice using *If I were you* ■ Can use *wish* to express wishes related to the present or future | Fairy Tale: *The Fisherman and His Wife* ■ Can identify specific information in a story |
| **23** **Past Unreal Conditional Sentences** Page 359 THEME Alternate Histories | ■ Can use past unreal conditional sentences to describe past unreal conditions and results that are untrue, imagined, or impossible ■ Can use *might have* or *could have* in the result clause to express possibility ■ Can use *wish* + past perfect to express regret or sadness | Information Article: *What if . . . ?* ■ Can extract specific information from a linguistically complex article |

PART **8**

**Conditional Sentences**

| LISTENING | SPEAKING | WRITING | VOCABULARY |
|---|---|---|---|
| A conversation between father and daughter<br>■ Can identify key details in a conversation about tasks on a To Do list | ■ Can talk about plans and preparations for a trip to another country<br>■ Can compare *Before* and *After* pictures of a person and discuss changes in appearance<br>■ Can discuss steps people from different cultures take to improve their appearance | ■ Can write one or two paragraphs describing preparations for a future event | caution (n)<br>expand AWL<br>option AWL<br>permanent (adj)<br>risk (n)<br>temporary (adj) AWL |
| Announcements in an airport and aboard a plane<br>■ Can infer correct information from public announcements | ■ Can discuss and complete an online order form<br>■ Can discuss shopping in different places<br>■ Can compare the advantages and disadvantages of shopping in stores and shopping online | ■ Can write a short article describing things to do and see in one's city or town | consumer AWL<br>dispute (v)<br>policy AWL<br>precaution<br>secure (adj) AWL<br>site (n) AWL |
| An interview with a candidate for student council president<br>■ Can follow an animated conversation well enough to identify details | ■ Can discuss common problems and possible solutions<br>■ Can discuss superstitions, giving opinions and making cross-cultural comparisons | ■ Can write a short speech about what one will do if elected class or school president | anticipate AWL<br>attitude AWL<br>confident<br>insight AWL<br>percent AWL<br>widespread AWL |
| A modern fairy tale<br>■ Can follow a recorded story well enough to identify key details | ■ Can discuss common problems and give advice<br>■ Can discuss hypothetical questions and wishes | ■ Can write a detailed paragraph describing a wish one has for oneself or society, and what might happen if it came true | consent (v) AWL<br>embarrassed (adj)<br>enchanted (adj)<br>furious<br>grant (v) AWL<br>regular (adj) |
| Conversations about past events<br>■ Can follow animated conversations well enough to identify key information about past events | ■ Can speculate about past events or hypothetical situations<br>■ Can analyze past situations and evaluate the decisions made<br>■ Can talk about a past decision one regrets and about what one wishes had happened and why | ■ Can write one or two paragraphs speculating about what would have happened if an important event hadn't taken place | alternate (adj) AWL<br>dominate AWL<br>occur AWL<br>outcome AWL<br>parallel (adj) AWL<br>version AWL |

AWL = Academic Word List item

| LISTENING | SPEAKING | WRITING | VOCABULARY |
|---|---|---|---|
| **Conversations between friends and coworkers**<br>■ Can follow animated conversations well enough to identify key details | ■ Can have a discussion about lying<br>■ Can give an opinion and examples in response to a literary quote or international proverb<br>■ Can complete a questionnaire and compare answers with classmates | ■ Can write one or two paragraphs about a past conversation, reporting what was said using direct and indirect speech | aware **AWL**<br>justify **AWL**<br>majority **AWL**<br>nevertheless **AWL**<br>reveal (v) **AWL**<br>survey (n) **AWL** |
| **A conversation about a recent weather report**<br>■ Can identify key details in a discussion about a weather report | ■ Can conduct a simple interview and report the other person's answers<br>■ Can do an online search about an extreme weather event and report findings | ■ Can write two paragraphs about an extreme weather event, reporting another person's experience | devastation<br>exceed **AWL**<br>extreme<br>inevitable **AWL**<br>shelter (n)<br>whereas **AWL** |
| **A conversation about a visit to a headache clinic**<br>■ Can identify key details in a conversation about medical advice | ■ Can discuss health problems and possible home remedies<br>■ Can report on how someone followed instructions | ■ Can write one or two paragraphs describing a health problem one had and reporting the advice one received | astonishing<br>fatigue (n)<br>interfere<br>monitor (v) **AWL**<br>persist **AWL**<br>remedy (n) |
| **A conversation about a job interview**<br>■ Can identify key details in a conversation about a job interview | ■ Can role-play a job interview and discuss with classmates<br>■ Can talk about a personal experience with a job interview<br>■ Can complete a questionnaire about work values, discuss answers, and report conversations | ■ Can write a report on a job interview | appropriate (adj) **AWL**<br>candidate<br>evaluation **AWL**<br>handle (v)<br>potential (adj) **AWL**<br>pressure (n) |
| **A call-in radio show about tipping**<br>■ Can understand a call-in radio program well enough to identify information | ■ Can discuss tipping around the world, giving opinions<br>■ Can talk about problems encountered during first-time experiences<br>■ Can role-play a conversation between a hotel clerk and a guest asking for information | ■ Can write a detailed paragraph about a confusing or surprising situation | clarify **AWL**<br>custom<br>depend on<br>logical **AWL**<br>ordinary<br>ultimate **AWL** |

**AWL** = Academic Word List item

# About the Authors

**Marjorie Fuchs** has taught ESL at New York City Technical College and LaGuardia Community College of the City University of New York and EFL at Sprachstudio Lingua Nova in Munich, Germany. She has a master's degree in Applied English Linguistics and a certificate in TESOL from the University of Wisconsin-Madison. She has authored and co-authored many widely used books and multimedia materials, notably *Crossroads 4*; *Top Twenty ESL Word Games: Beginning Vocabulary Development*; *Families: Ten Card Games for Language Learners*; *Focus on Grammar 3* and *4* (editions 1–5); *Focus on Grammar 3* and *4, CD-ROM*; *Longman English Interactive 3* and *4*; *Grammar Express Basic*; *Grammar Express Basic CD-ROM*; *Grammar Express Intermediate*; *Future 1: English for Results*; *OPD Workplace Skills Builder*; workbooks for *Crossroads 1–4*; *The Oxford Picture Dictionary High Beginning* and *Low Intermediate*, (editions 1–3); *Focus on Grammar 3* and *4* (editions 1–5); and *Grammar Express Basic*.

**Margaret Bonner** has taught ESL at Hunter College and the Borough of Manhattan Community College of the City University of New York, at Taiwan National University in Taipei, and at Virginia Commonwealth University in Richmond. She holds a master's degree in library science from Columbia University, and she has done work toward a PhD in English literature at the Graduate Center of the City University of New York. She has authored and co-authored numerous ESL and EFL print and multimedia materials, including textbooks for the national school system of Oman; *Step into Writing: A Basic Writing Text*; *Focus on Grammar 3* and *4* (editions 1–5); *Focus on Grammar 4 Workbook* (editions 1–5); *Grammar Express Basic*; *Grammar Express Basic CD-ROM*; *Grammar Express Basic Workbook*; *Grammar Express Intermediate*; *Focus on Grammar 3* and *4, CD-ROM*; *Longman English Interactive 4*; and *The Oxford Picture Dictionary Low Intermediate Workbook* (editions 1–3).

**Jane Curtis** teaches in the English Language Program at Roosevelt University in Chicago. She has also taught at the Universitat de Barcelona in Barcelona, Spain, and at Wuhan University in Wuhan, China. She holds a master's degree in Spanish from the University of Illinois at Urbana-Champaign and a master's degree in Applied Linguistics from Northeastern Illinois University. She has authored materials for *Longman Academic Writing Series 3: Paragraphs to Essays*, Fourth Edition; *Future 4: English for Results*; and the workbook for *Focus on Grammar 4* (editions 3 and 4).

# Acknowledgments

Before acknowledging the many people who have contributed to the fifth edition of *Focus on Grammar*, we wish to express our gratitude to the following people who worked on the previous editions and whose influence is still present in the new work: **Joanne Dresner**, who initiated the project and helped conceptualize the general approach of *Focus on Grammar*; our editors for the first four editions: **Nancy Perry**, **Penny Laporte**, **Louisa Hellegers**, **Joan Saslow**, **Laura LeDrean**, **Debbie Sistino**, and **Françoise Leffler**; and **Sharon Hilles**, our grammar consultant for the first edition.

In the fifth edition, *Focus on Grammar* has continued to evolve as we update materials and respond to valuable feedback from teachers and students who use the series. We are grateful to the following editors and colleagues:

- **Gosia Jaros-White** for overseeing with skill and sensitivity a complex series while never losing sight of the individual components or people involved in the project. She offered concrete and practical advice and was always mindful of learners' needs.

- **Bernard Seal**, of Page Designs International, who joined the *Focus on Grammar* team with a great deal of experience, expertise, energy, and enthusiasm. With his hands-on approach, he was involved in every aspect of the project. He read all manuscript, raising pertinent questions and offering sage advice.

- **Don Williams**, also of Page Designs International, for creating a fresh, new look, which is as user-friendly as it is attractive.

- **Françoise Leffler**, our editor *extraordinaire*, with whom we had the great fortune and pleasure of being able to continue our long collaboration. She provided both continuity and a fresh eye as she delved into another edition of the series, advising us on all things—from the small details to the big picture.

- **Jane Curtis** for her excellent contributions to the first half of this book. Her involvement went beyond her fine writing and choice of engaging topics. She also brought enthusiasm, dedication, and many years of invaluable classroom experience using the series.

- Series co-authors **Irene Schoenberg** and **Jay Maurer** for their suggestions and support, and Irene for sharing her experience in teaching with earlier editions of this book.

- **Julie Schmidt** for her helpful presentation of information and for her input in Part 9.

- **Sharon Goldstein** for her insightful and practical suggestions, delivered with wisdom and wit.

- **Cindy Davis** for her classroom-based recommendations at the very beginning of this edition.

Finally, as always, Marjorie thanks **Rick Smith** for his unswerving support and excellent suggestions. He was a steadfast beacon of light as we navigated our way through our fifth *FOG*.

MF and MB

> *To the memory of my parents, Edith and Joseph Fuchs—MF*
> *To my parents, Marie and Joseph Maus, and to my son, Luke Frances—MB*

# Reviewers

We are grateful to the following reviewers for their many helpful comments:

**Susanna Aramyan**, Glendale Community College, Glendale, CA; **Homeretta Ayala**, Baltimore Co. Schools, Baltimore, MD; **Barbara Barrett**, University of Miami, Miami, FL; **Rebecca Beck**, Irvine Valley College, Irvine, CA; **Crystal Bock Thiessen**, University of Nebraska-PIESL, Lincoln, NE; **Janna Brink**, Mt. San Antonio College, Walnut, CA; **Erin Butler**, University of California, Riverside, CA; **Joice Cain**, Fullerton College, Fullerton, CA; **Shannonine M. Caruana**, Hudson County Community College, Jersey City, NJ; **Tonya Cobb**, Cypress College, Cypress, CA; **David Cooke**, Mt. San Antonio College, Walnut, CA; **Lindsay Donigan**, Fullerton College, Fullerton, CA; **Mila Dragushanskya**, ASA College, New York, NY; **Jill Fox**, University of Nebraska, Lincoln, NE; **Katalin Gyurindak**, Mt. San Antonio College, Walnut, CA; **Karen Hamilton**, Glendale Community College, Glendale, CA; **Electra Jablons**, International English Language Institute, Hunter College, New York, NY; **Eva Kozlenko**, Hudson County Community College, Jersey City, NJ; **Esther Lee**, American Language Program, California State University, Fullerton, CA; **Yenlan Li**, American Language Program, California State University, Fullerton, CA; **Shirley Lundblade**, Mt. San Antonio College, Walnut, CA; **Thi Thi Ma**, Los Angeles City College, Los Angeles, CA; **Marilyn Martin**, Mt. San Antonio College, Walnut, CA; **Eve Mazereeuw**, University of Guelph English Language Programs, Guelph, Ontario, Canada; **Robert Mott**, Glendale Community College, Glendale, CA; **Wanda Murtha**, Glendale Community College, Glendale, CA; **Susan Niemeyer**, Los Angeles City College, Los Angeles, CA; **Wayne Pate**, Tarrant County College, Fort Worth, TX; **Genevieve Patthey-Chavez**, Los Angeles City College, Los Angeles, CA; **Robin Persiani**, Sierra College, Rocklin, CA; **Denise Phillips**, Hudson County Community College, Jersey City, NJ; **Anna Powell**, American Language Program, California State University, Fullerton, CA; **JoAnna Prado**, Sacramento City Community College, Sacramento, CA; **Mark Rau**, American River College, Sacramento, CA; **Madeleine Schamehorn**, University of California, Riverside, CA; **Richard Skinner**, Hudson County Community College, Jersey City, NJ; **Heather Snavely**, American Language Program, California State University, Fullerton, CA; **Gordana Sokic**, Douglas College, Westminster, British Columbia, Canada; **Lee Spencer**, International English Language Institute, Hunter College, New York, NY; **Heather Stern**, Irvine Valley College, Irvine, CA; **Susan Stern**, Irvine Valley College, Irvine, CA; **Andrea Sunnaa**, Mt. San Antonio College, Walnut, CA; **Margaret Teske**, Mt. San Antonio College, Walnut, CA; **Johanna Van Gendt**, Hudson County Community College, Jersey City, NJ; **Daniela C. Wagner-Loera**, University of Maryland, College Park, MD; **Tamara Williams**, University of Guelph, English Language Programs, Guelph, Ontario, Canada; **Saliha Yagoubi**, Hudson County Community College, Jersey City, NJ; **Pat Zayas**, Glendale Community College, Glendale, CA

# Credits

## PHOTO CREDITS

**2–3:** Africa Studio/Shutterstock; **4:** El Nariz/Shutterstock; **5:** Daniel M Ernst/Shutterstock; **11:** Anna Khomulo/Fotolia; **12:** Argus/Fotolia; **13:** (bottom center) Corepics/Fotolia, (bottom left) Olgavolodina/Fotolia, (bottom right) Pavelkubarkov/Fotolia, (center) Alex.pin/Fotolia, (top center) Viorel Sima/Fotolia, (top left) Peter Atkins/Fotolia, (top right) BillionPhotos/Fotolia; **18:** Warner Bros. Television/Everett Collection; **19:** (bottom) Album/Newscom, (top) Prisma/Newscom; **25:** ProStockStudio/Shutterstock; **26:** Dragon Images/Shutterstock; **30:** Chagin/Fotolia; **33:** Innovated Captures/Fotolia; **38:** (bottom) Riccardo Savi/Stringer/Getty Images, (background) zephyr_p/Fotolia; **39:** Amy Harris/Invision/AP Images; **41:** Dmilovanovic/Fotolia; **43:** Brainsil/Fotolia; **44:** Jenner/Fotolia; **45:** Zukovic/Fotolia; **48:** David Rochkind/MCT/Newscom; **54:** Andrey Kuzmin/Fotolia; **56:** Peter Schenider/EPA/Newscom; **57:** Belinsky Yuri Itar-Tass Photos/Newscom; **59:** Dmitry Vereshchagin/Fotolia; **60:** iPhoto Inc./Newscom; **61:** Zhu Difeng/Fotolia; **62:** Chris Walker/KRT/Newscom; **66–67:** Marekuliasz/Shutterstock; **68–69:** Best View Stock/Getty Images; **75:** Luca Oleastri/Fotolia; **78:** (left) Yossarian6/Fotolia, (right) Tatiana Shepeleva/Shutterstock; **79:** (bottom) Kilroy79/Fotolia, (top) Sdecoret/Fotolia; **80:** (bottom) Costazzurra/Shutterstock, (background) Alexzaitsev/Fotolia; **81:** Alex/Fotolia; **82:** Viacheslav Iakobchuk/Fotolia; **86:** (bottom) Bloomberg/Contributor/Getty Images, (top) Naiauss/Fotolia; **92:** (bottom) Rodrusoleg/Fotolia, (background) Hollygraphic/Fotolia; **93:** Michaeljung/Fotolia; **95:** Bits and Splits/Fotolia; **96:** Photo_Ma/Fotolia; **100–101:** Lopolo/Shutterstock; **102:** Ekaterina_belova/Fotolia; **103:** (bottom) Josef Hanus/Shutterstock, (center) Hit1912/Shutterstock, (top) eFesenko/Shutterstock; **109:** Pavel dudek/Shutterstock; **112:** (left) Akg-images/Newscom, (right) Goodween123/Fotolia; **113:** 123dartist/Fotolia; **115:** (bottom) CPQ/Fotolia, (background) Weedezign/Fotolia; **118:** AP Images; **119:** Yonhap News/YNA/Newscom; **125:** Yuttana590623/Fotolia; **126:** Olga Yatsenko/Shutterstock; **127:** Luismolinero/Fotolia; **128:** (bottom) Drobot Dean/Fotolia, (background) Vvoe/Fotolia; **131:** Bruce Gilbert/MCT/Newscom; **134–135:** Wavebreakmedia/Shutterstock; **136:** Mindscape studio/Shutterstock; **136–137:** 123dartist/Fotolia; **137:** Kzenon/Shutterstock; **143:** Alexzaitsev/Fotolia; **146:** Route66/Fotolia; **147:** Alexander Gogolin/Fotolia; **148:** Paladin1212/Fotolia; **152:** Mike Price/Shutterstock; **153:** Andrew Kelly/Reuters; **156:** Jonathonm/Stockimo/Alamy Stock Photo; **158–159:** Menno Schaefer/Shutterstock; **160:** Zap Ichigo/Fotolia; **161:** Andrey Armyagov/Shutterstock; **162:** Byrdyak/Fotolia; **165:** Peter C. Vey/The New Yorker Collection/The Cartoon Bank; **165–166:** Fade in photography/Fotolia; **171:** Srckomkrit/Fotolia; **173:** Highwaystarz/Fotolia; **174:** (bottom) SFerdon/Shutterstock, (top) Gstudio Group/Fotolia; **175:** Phovoir/Shutterstock; **177:** Sam72/Shutterstock; **180–181:** Blend Images/Shutterstock; **189:** (background) Yuttana590623/Fotolia, (top center) Drobot Dean/Fotolia, (top left) Phasuthorn/Fotolia, (top right) Julief514/Fotolia; **190:** Scisetti Alfio/Fotolia; **193:** Talashow/Fotolia; **196:** Donatas1205/Fotolia; **199:** Jayzynism/Fotolia; **200:** StockstudioX/E+/Getty Images; **207:** Jayzynism/Fotolia; **208:** Yusei/Fotolia; **208–209:** Paladin1212/Fotolia; **210:** (bottom) Drew Altizer/Sipa USA/Newscom, (background) Dmlid/Fotolia; **212:** Vvoe/Fotolia; **214:** Janet Mayer/Splash News/Newscom; **215:** 1000 Words/Shutterstock; **218–219:** Siempreverde22/Fotolia; **220:** (left) Marco Antonio Fdez/Fotolia, (right) Raftel/Fotolia; **226:** Gudo/Fotolia; **228:** (bottom) Andy Dean/Fotolia, (top) Marco Antonio Fdez/Fotolia; **229:** (bottom) Marco Antonio Fdez/Fotolia, (top) Giideon/Fotolia; **230:** Uniyok/Fotolia; **231:** Weedezign/Fotolia; **233:** (bottom center) Jcomp/Fotolia, (bottom left) Yayoicho/Fotolia, (bottom right) 12ee12/Fotolia, (center left) Dalibor Sevaljevic/Shutterstock, (center right) Pearson Education, Inc., (top) Marco Antonio Fdez/Fotolia; **234–235:** 12ee12/Fotolia; **242:** Chamille White/Shutterstock; **238:** Photographee.eu/Fotolia; **244:** Brian Jackson/Fotolia; **245:** Pixelrobot/Fotolia; **246:** DW labs Incorporated/Fotolia; **247:** Zephyr_P/Fotolia; **249:** VIPDesign/Fotolia; **253:** (left) Plus69/Fotolia, (right) Martin Shields/Alamy Stock Photo; **258:** Rene Ruprecht/dpa/picture-alliance/Newscom; **262:** (bottom) Valet/Fotolia, (background) Zephyr_P/Fotolia; **264:** (bottom right) The Metropolitan Museum of Art/ Art Resource, New York, (center right) The Metropolitan Museum of Art/Art Resource, New York, (top right) Martha Avery/Corbis Historical/Getty Images; **265:** (bottom) Derek Bayes/Lebrecht/The Image Works, (top) The Image Works; **268–269:** Zea_lenanet/Fotolia; **270:** Webistan Photo Agency; **275:** (left) Pavalena/Shutterstock, (right) Byelikova Oksana/Fotolia;

**276–277:** Anankkml/Fotolia; **278:** (bottom) Galyna Andrushko/Shutterstock, (top) Vvoe/Fotolia; **279:** Macknimal/Shutterstock; **280:** IBO/SIPA/Newscom; **281:** (bottom) Lesniewski/Fotolia, (top) Picsfive/Fotolia; **282:** R Nagy/Shutterstock; **283:** (bottom right) Dovla982/Shutterstock, (center) Manstock007/Fotolia, (top) Paul Stringer/Shutterstock; **284:** (bottom) Nata777_7/Fotolia, (top) Nata777_7/Fotolia; **287:** NASA; **288–289:** NASA; **292:** NASA; **293–294:** Farland9/Fotolia; **294:** NASA; **296:** NASA; **301–303:** Thaporn942/Fotolia; **301:** (bottom) Lane Oatey/Blue Jean Images/Getty Images, (top) Kutukupret/Fotolia; **302:** (bottom right) Tatyana Gladski/Fotolia, (center) Tanee/Shutterstock, (top right) Halfpoint/Shutterstock; **303:** Michael Jung/Shutterstock; **306:** Scrapitsideways/Fotolia; **307:** Photomelon/Fotolia; **309:** (bottom) Alan Poulson Photography/Shutterstock, (top) Dakonta/Fotolia; **310:** (left) Dragon Images/Fotolia, (right) Polkadot_photo/Shutterstock; **311:** Coprid/Fotolia; **314–315:** Lightspring/Shutterstock; **316:** Africa Studio/Shutterstock; **321:** (bottom) Rafael Ramirez Lee/Shutterstock, (background) Locotearts/Fotolia; **323:** (bottom) Sahachat/Fotolia, (center bottom) Seqoya/Fotolia, (center top) Yevgen Belich/Fotolia, (top) Sahachat/Fotolia; **324:** (center) Anshar/Shutterstock, (top) ChameleonsEye/Shutterstock; **326:** Blend Images/Shutterstock; **327:** Skarin/Fotolia; **328:** David Sipress/The New Yorker Collection/The Cartoon Bank; **337:** Matthew Benoit/Fotolia; **339:** Vjom/Fotolia; **340:** Bramgino/Fotolia; **341:** Di Studio/Shutterstock; **344–346:** Pakhnyushchyy/Fotolia; **351:** Dimashiper/Fotolia; **353:** Africa Studio/Shutterstock; **354:** Scisetti Alfio/Fotolia; **356:** Tommaso Lizzul/Shutterstock; **359–361:** Weedezign/Fotolia; **359:** (background) Stepan Popov/Fotolia, (right) Maimu/Fotolia; **360:** (bottom) JSlavy/Shutterstock, (top) Vintagio/Shutterstock; **365:** Everett Collection; **366:** Scisetti Alfio/Fotolia; **367:** (bottom) Jochen Tack/Alamy Stock Photo, (center) Rido/Fotolia, (top) DragonImages/Fotolia; **368:** AF archive/Alamy Stock Photo; **369:** Fotos 593/Fotolia; **370:** Anyaberkut/Fotolia; **374–375:** Patpitchaya/Shutterstock; **376:** Fabiana Ponzi/Shutterstock; **381:** Torsakarin/Fotolia; **382:** (bottom) Richgano/Getty Images, (top) Zephyr_p/Fotolia; **385:** Photka/Fotolia; **386:** Aopsan/Fotolia; **387:** Everett - Art/Shutterstock; **388:** Goir/Fotolia; **389:** Billion Photos/Shutterstock; **392:** Niccolò Ubalducci Photographer - Stormchaser/Moment/Getty Images; **392–393:** Cultura RM Exclusive/Jason Persoff Stormdoctor/Getty Images; **398:** Mark Winfrey/Shutterstock; **400–401:** Samuel D Barricklow/Getty Images; **402:** (bottom) Jacques Palut/Fotolia, (center) Ajr_images/Fotolia, (top) Pathdoc/Fotolia; **403:** (bottom) Scisetti Alfio/Fotolia, (top left) Eldarnurkovic/Fotolia; **405:** STOCK4B GmbH/Alamy Stock Photo; **408:** Nadya Lukic/Shutterstock; **415:** (bottom) Michael Crawford/The New Yorker Collection/The Cartoon Bank, (top) Happy person/Shutterstock; **416:** (bottom right) Africa Studio/Fotolia, (top left) Pablo Calvog/Shutterstock; **417:** Scisetti Alfio/Fotolia; **420:** Photographee.eu/Shutterstock; **427:** Tashatuvango/Fotolia; **428:** Weedezign/Fotolia; **429:** AntonioDiaz/Fotolia; **430:** Goodween123/Fotolia; **431:** Di Studio/Shutterstock; **432:** (bottom left) Showcake/Fotolia, (center) Nuruddean/Fotolia; **433:** Mountainscreative/Fotolia; **434:** A & B Photos/Shutterstock; **443:** Radius Images/Getty Images; **444:** Goodween123/Fotolia; **445:** Fabiomax/Fotolia; **447:** (bottom) Syda Productions/Shutterstock, (top) Ustas/Fotolia; **449:** Pcruciatti/Shutterstock; **486:** (left) Amadeustx/Fotolia, (background) Weedezign/Fotolia; **487:** (bottom right) Dovla982/Shutterstock, (center right) Manstock007/Fotolia, (top) Paul Stringer/Shutterstock

## ILLUSTRATION CREDITS

Aptara – pages 263, 283
Steve Attoe – pages 28, 182, 194, 331, 332
ElectraGraphics – pages 63, 417
Chris Gash – pages 383, 437
David Klug – page 438
Jock MacRae – page 213
Suzanne Mogensen – page 144
Andy Myer – pages 351, 355
Dusan Petricic – pages 248, 298
Steve Schulman – page 311
Susan Scott – pages 260–261
Meryl Treatner – pages 92, 130

# Present and Past: Review and Expansion

PART **1**

**OUTCOMES**
- Describe actions, states, and situations that happen regularly, and unchanging facts
- Describe actions that are happening now
- Identify key information in a social science article
- Identify people based on recorded descriptions
- Describe people, what they do and are doing
- Discuss names in different countries
- Write a detailed paragraph about oneself

**OUTCOMES**
- Describe actions and situations that were completed, or were in progress, in the past
- Describe one past action interrupted by another, or two past actions in progress at the same time
- Identify the order of events in a description
- Describe one's first meeting with someone
- Create a story and present it to the class
- Write about past events in an important relationship

**OUTCOMES**
- Recognize when to use the simple past, the present perfect, or the present perfect progressive
- Show that something was not completed, using *for* or *since* and time expressions
- Identify key details in a reading or a recording
- Discuss hobbies and interests
- Research an interesting hobby and present findings to the class
- Write about a recent trend

**OUTCOMES**
- Describe events that happened, or were in progress, before a specific time in the past
- Show the order of two past events, using adverbs and expressions with *by*
- Identify the order of events in a biographical article and in a radio interview
- Discuss talents and past achievements
- Discuss one's schedule for the previous day
- Write about a famous person's life and career

# Simple Present and Present Progressive
## NAMES

**OUTCOMES**
- Describe actions, states, and situations that happen regularly, and unchanging facts
- Describe actions that are happening now
- Identify key information in a social science article
- Identify people based on recorded descriptions
- Describe people, what they do and are doing
- Discuss names in different countries
- Write a detailed paragraph about oneself

## STEP 1  GRAMMAR IN CONTEXT

### BEFORE YOU READ

Look at the title of the article. Discuss the questions.

1. What do you think the title means?

2. What are some common first and last names in your native language?

3. Do you have a nickname? If yes, what is it? How did you get it?

### READ

01|01  Read this article about names.

# What's in a Name?

Names are different from culture to culture. As a result, students in English language classrooms sometimes need to make adjustments. Yevdokiya Ivanovna Detrova and Jorge Santiago García de Gonzalez provide two interesting examples.

Yevdokiya Ivanovna Detrova is from Russia, but this year she's working and studying in Canada. Yevdokiya is an old-fashioned name, but it's coming back in style. Because her classmates find it difficult to pronounce her name, they use Yevdokiya's nickname—Dusya. In Russia, students always call their teachers by their first name and middle name, for example Viktor Antonovich or Katya Antonovna. A Russian middle name is a *patronymic*—it comes from the father's first name and means "son of . . ." or "daughter of. . . ." So Antonovich means "son of Anton" and Antonovna means "daughter of Anton." Russian students don't use titles like *Mr., Mrs., Miss, Ms.,*[1] or *Professor*. Now, Dusya sometimes hears these titles in class. In addition, several of her English teachers actually prefer to be called by just their first name. Dusya says, "In the beginning, this was very hard for me to do. It still seems a little disrespectful,[2] but I'm getting used to it."

---

1 *Ms.:* (pronounced "miz") used in front of a woman's family name and similar to *Mr.*—it doesn't show if the woman is married or not

2 *disrespectful:* not polite

Jorge Santiago García de Gonzalez comes from Mexico City. He's currently taking English classes at a language institute in the United States. Jorge is his first, or given, name and Santiago is his middle name. His last name consists of not one but two family names. García is from his father's family and Gonzalez is from his mother's family. Unfortunately, people in the United States often think his name is Mr. Gonzalez, but it's actually Mr. García. To avoid the confusion, Jorge is now planning to use García only. His friends are always trying to convince him to use the English name "George" instead of Jorge. However, he doesn't feel comfortable with an English name. He says, "I like my name, and I don't want to lose my identity."

Names have a clear connection to culture and personal identity. What does your name say about you? It probably says a great deal about where you are from and who you are.

## AFTER YOU READ

**A** VOCABULARY  Choose the word or phrase that best completes each sentence.

1. When you make an **adjustment**, you make a _____.
   **a.** promise        **b.** change        **c.** mistake

2. Examples **provide** details. They _____ specific information.
   **a.** ask for        **b.** understand        **c.** give

3. If a name is **in style**, many young people _____ it.
   **a.** have        **b.** don't like        **c.** have to spell

4. In some countries, names **consist of** more than one part. They _____ two or more words.
   **a.** connect        **b.** take out        **c.** include

5. If you **convince** a person, that person will _____ with you.
   **a.** meet        **b.** agree        **c.** argue

6. Your name is part of your **identity**. It shows you are _____ others.
   **a.** different from        **b.** the same as        **c.** friendly with

**B** COMPREHENSION  Read the statements. Check (✓) *True* or *False*.

|  | True | False |
|---|---|---|
| 1. Yevdokiya is now in Russia. | ☐ | ☐ |
| 2. Her classmates call her by her nickname. | ☐ | ☐ |
| 3. In Russia, she calls her teachers by their first name only. | ☐ | ☐ |
| 4. Jorge has a first name, a middle name, and a last name. | ☐ | ☐ |
| 5. Jorge's last name is confusing for many people in the United States. | ☐ | ☐ |
| 6. Jorge is going to change his first name. | ☐ | ☐ |

**C** DISCUSSION  Work with a partner. Compare your answers in B. Why did you check *True* or *False*?

## SIMPLE PRESENT

### Affirmative Statements

They **live** in Mexico.
She always **works** here.

### Negative Statements

They **don't live** in Mexico.
She **doesn't work** here.

### Yes/No Questions

**Do** they **live** in Mexico?
**Does** she **work** here?

### Short Answers

**Yes**, they **do**.
**Yes**, she **does**.

**No**, they **don't**.
**No**, she **doesn't**.

### Wh- Questions

Where **do** they **live**?
Why **does** she **work** so hard?
Who **teaches** that class?

## PRESENT PROGRESSIVE

### Affirmative Statements

They**'re living** in Mexico now.
She**'s working** here today.

### Negative Statements

They **aren't living** in Mexico now.
She **isn't working** here now.

### Yes/No Questions

**Are** they **living** in Mexico now?
**Is** she **working** here now?

### Short Answers

**Yes**, they **are**.
**Yes**, she **is**.

**No**, they **aren't**.
**No**, she **isn't**.

### Wh- Questions

Where **are** they **living** these days?
Why **is** she **working** so hard?
Who**'s teaching** that class now?

# GRAMMAR NOTES

## 1 Simple Present

Use the **simple present** to show that something **happens regularly** or for **unchanging facts**.

- **happens regularly**
  (*always, usually, often, sometimes, rarely*)

- **unchanging facts**

| | |
|---|---|
| **BE CAREFUL!** Remember to add *-s* or *-es* to third-person singular (*he, she, it*) of simple present verbs. Use *do/does* in questions and *do not/does not* in negative sentences. | |

**USAGE NOTE** We often use **adverbs of frequency** (*always, usually,* etc.) with verbs in the simple present. The adverb usually goes **before the verb**. If the verb is *be*, the adverb goes **after be**.

*Sometimes* and *usually* can also go at the **beginning** of the sentence.

---

People *always* **call** him Joe.
We *usually* **prefer** first names.
Dusya *sometimes* **uses** nicknames.

She **comes from** Moscow. It**'s** the capital.

Dusya **lives** in Toronto. She **doesn't live** in Ottawa.
NOT Dusya ~~live~~ in Toronto. She ~~don't live~~ in Ottawa.

Dusya *always* **gets** home at 7:00 p.m.
She *usually* **finishes** her work on time.
She **is** *never* late for class.

We *sometimes* **eat** lunch together.
*Sometimes* we **eat** lunch together.

## 2 Present Progressive

Use the present progressive to show that something is **happening now** or **in a longer present time**.

- **happening now**
  (*right now, at the moment*)

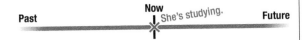

- **happening in a longer present time, but perhaps not at this exact moment**
  (*this month, this year, these days*)

| | |
|---|---|
| **BE CAREFUL!** Use *am*, *is*, and *are* with *-ing* for the present progressive. Do not forget to add *-ing* to the verb. | |

**USAGE NOTE** We often use **time expressions** (*right now, this month, these days,* etc.) with verbs in the present progressive. The time expression can go at the **beginning or end** of the sentence. *Now* can also go **after be**.

---

A: What's Dusya doing?
B: *Right now*, she**'s studying** in the library.

A: What**'s** Jorge **doing** *these days*?
B: He**'s working** on a new project.

Dusya **is working** in Canada this year.
NOT Dusya ~~is work~~ in Canada this year.

*These days*, Dusya **is looking** for a new job.
Dusya **is looking** for a new job *these days*.

*Now*, she **is preparing** for a job interview.
She **is preparing** for a job interview *now*.
She **is** *now* **preparing** for a job interview.

## 3 Non-Action Verbs

Use non-action verbs to describe **states** or **situations**, but not actions.

Non-action verbs describe:

- **emotions** (*love, hate*)
- **mental states** (*remember, understand*)
- **possession** (*have, own*)
- **wants** (*need, want*)
- **senses** and **perceptions** (*hear, see, look, seem*)

I **hate** my nickname.
**Do** you **remember** her name?
Diego **has** two family names.
Jan **wants** to change her name.
You **don't look** happy today.

**BE CAREFUL!** Use the **simple present** with most **non-action verbs**. Do not use the present progressive—even when the verb describes a situation that exists at the moment of speaking.

I **want** to have a special name.
NOT I'm wanting to have a special name.

**USAGE NOTE** In **informal conversation**, some people use the **present progressive with non-action verbs** such as *be, hear, like, love, miss,* and *see* to show that **a situation is temporary or changing**.

Why **are** you **being** impolite today?
I**'m loving** this class.
I**'m** really **missing** my friend Jorge.
I**'m hearing** a lot of unusual names now.

**USAGE NOTE** There is both **an action and a non-action meaning** for some verbs such as *have, come from, think, taste, smell, feel,* and *look*.

| NON-ACTION | ACTION |
|---|---|
| She **has** a nickname. (*It's her name.*) | She **is having** lunch. (*She is eating lunch.*) |
| I **come from** Mexico. (*My country of origin is Mexico.*) | I**'m coming** from school. (*I'm on my way from school.*) |

## 4 Other Uses of the Simple Present

Use the simple present for **situations that are not connected to time**—for example, scientific facts and physical laws.

Water **freezes** at 0°C (32°F).
The Earth **orbits** the sun.

Writers often use the simple present in **book or movie reviews**, in **newspaper reports**, and **descriptions of sporting events**.

This book **gives** information about names.
The movie **takes place** in Paris in 1945.

## 5 Present Progressive with *Always*

You can use the present progressive with *always* to describe a **repeated action**. *Always* usually goes **after** *be*.

She**'s** *always* **smiling**. That's why we call her "Sunshine." It's her nickname.

**USAGE NOTE** We often use the present progressive to describe a **situation that causes a negative reaction**.

He**'s** *always* **calling** me "Sweetie." I really hate that name.

# REFERENCE NOTES

For **spelling rules** for the third-person singular of the **simple present**, see Appendix 22 on
  page 463.

For **pronunciation rules** for the **simple present**, see Appendix 30 on page 467.

For **spelling rules** on forming the **present progressive**, see Appendix 23 on page 463.

For a list of **non-action verbs**, see Appendix 2 on page 454.

## STEP 3    FOCUSED PRACTICE

### EXERCISE 1   DISCOVER THE GRAMMAR

GRAMMAR NOTES 1–5   Read this book review. Circle the simple present verbs and
underline the present progressive verbs.

## Kiss, Bow, or Shake Hands: How to Do Business in Sixty Countries

Book Review

Are you living or working in a foreign country? Do you worry about making
a mistake with someone's name or title? You are right to be concerned.
Naming systems vary a lot from culture to culture, and people often have
strong feelings about their names. Well, now help is available in the form
of an interesting and practical book by Terri Morrison. *Kiss, Bow, or Shake
Hands: How to Do Business in Sixty Countries* consists of communication
tips, information on cross-cultural naming customs, and much more. It also
provides excellent real-world examples. However, it's not just for business
people. In today's shrinking world, people are always traveling to and from
foreign countries. They're flying to all corners of the world, and they're
exchanging emails with people they've never actually met. If you're doing
business abroad or making friends across cultures, I recommend this book.

## EXERCISE 2 ACTION AND NON-ACTION VERBS

GRAMMAR NOTES 1–3 Complete the sentences. Use the correct form of the verbs in parentheses. Use the present progressive where possible.

1. Many parents in the United States _____ *are choosing* _____ baby names such as Emma and
   (choose)
   Olivia for girls and Noah and Liam for boys these days.

2. At the moment, Jean Twenge _____ research at San Diego State University.
   (do)
   Dr. Twenge _____ that a child's name can have a powerful effect later in life.
   (believe)

3. Some parents _____ to give their children names that are currently in style.
   (want)
   These parents _____ names that their children will like as teens and adults.
   (look for)

4. In her research, Dr. Twenge _____ a change in baby names. More and more
   (notice)
   parents _____ their children names such as Moon, Hershey,[1] and Audi.[2]
   (give)

5. These days, children _____ names with unusual spellings like Mykel (Michael)
   (have)
   or Jayceson (Jason). According to researchers, these names _____ identity
   (cause)
   problems because the children _____ why people can't spell their
   (not know)
   names correctly.

---

1 *Hershey:* a U.S. company that makes chocolate candy
2 *Audi:* a popular car made in Germany

## EXERCISE 3 STATEMENTS AND QUESTIONS

GRAMMAR NOTES 1–5 Complete the conversations. Use the correct form of the verbs in parentheses—the simple present or the present progressive.

**Conversation 1**

MARIO: I _____ *'m trying* _____ to find Greg Costanza. _____ you _____ him?
                1. (try)                                                      2. (know)

BELLA: Greg? Oh, you _____ Lucky. That's his nickname. Everyone around here
                          3. (mean)
       _____ him Lucky because he _____ things.
            4. (call)                                5. (always win)

**Conversation 2**

LOLA: So you and Anya _____ a baby. That's great! Have you decided on a name yet?
                          1. (expect)

VANYA: We _____ names related to music. Tell me. What _____ you
                  2. (look for)
       _____ "Mangena"? It means "melody" in Hebrew.
            3. (think of)

LOLA: It _____ pretty. How _____ you _____ it?
            4. (sound)                                      5. (spell)

## Conversation 3

IANTHA: Hi, I'm Iantha.

ALAN: Nice to meet you, Iantha. I'm Alan, but my friends _____call_____ me Al. Iantha is an
       **1.** (call)

unusual name. Where _____ it _____? Is it Latin or Greek?
                       **2.** (come from)

IANTHA: It's Greek. It _____ "violet-colored flower."
              **3.** (mean)

ALAN: That's pretty. What _____ you _____, Iantha?
                        **4.** (do)

IANTHA: Well, I usually _____ computer equipment, but right now
                 **5.** (sell)

I _____ at a flower shop. My uncle _____ it.
  **6.** work                              **7.** (own)

ALAN: You _____! I _____ it's true that names _____
      **8.** (joke)       **9.** (guess)             **10.** (influence)

our lives!

## Conversation 4

ROSA: Dr. Ho, _____ your family name _____ a special meaning in Chinese?
                             **1.** (have)

DR. HO: Yes. *Ho* _____ "goodness."
           **2.** (mean)

ROSA: Speaking of goodness, how about a nice cup of tea? The water _____. By the
                               **3.** (boil)

way, Dr. Ho, why _____ water _____ so quickly here?
                        **4.** (boil)

DR. HO: In the mountains, water _____ at a lower temperature. It's a law of nature.
                      **5.** (boil)

# EXERCISE 4  EDITING

GRAMMAR NOTES 1–5  Read this post to a class blog. There are eleven mistakes in the use of the simple present and the present progressive. The first mistake is already corrected. Find and correct ten more.

## Futura Language School

**CLASS BLOG**  English 047

**POSTED SEPTEMBER 16, 2016, AT 15:30:03**

Hi, everybody. ~~I write~~ *I'm writing* this note to introduce myself to you, my classmates in English 047. Our teacher is wanting a profile from each of us. At first, I was confused because my English dictionary is defining *profile* as "a side view of someone's head." I thought, "Why does she wants that? She sees my head every day!" Then I saw the next definition: "a short description of a person's life and character." Now I understand what to do, so this is my profile:

My name is Peter Holzer. Some of my friends are calling me Pay-Ha because that is how my initials actually sounding in German. I am study English here in Miami because I want to attend the Aspen Institute of International Leadership in Colorado. Maybe are you asking yourself, "Why he wants to leave Miami for Colorado?" The answer is snow! Of course that means adjustments in my life, but good ones. I am coming from Austria, so I love to ski. It's part of my identity. In fact, my nickname in my family is Blitz (lightning) because always I'm trying to improve my speed.

## EXERCISE 5  LISTENING

01|02  **A** You are going to listen to two friends discuss these photos. Their conversation is divided into six parts. Listen to each part. Label each photo with the correct name(s) from the box. Then listen again and check your answers.

| ~~Alex~~ | Bertha | "Bozo" | Karl | Red | "Sunshine" | Vicki |
|---|---|---|---|---|---|---|

a. _____  b. _____  c. _Alex_____

d. _____  e. _____  f. _____ and _____

01|02  **B** Listen to each part of the conversation again. Then work with a partner. Discuss your answers in A. Give reasons for your answers.

EXAMPLE:  A: OK. How do we know that the little girl in picture C is Alex?
B: Well, Janine says that Alex is her niece.
A: Right. She also says parents are now giving names like Alex to girls.
B: OK. So now, who's Red?

**C** Work with a partner. Talk about three favorite photos of your family or friends. Use traditional print photos or digital pictures from your phone or a social media page such as Facebook.

EXAMPLE:  A: Who's this?
B: It's Carolina. She's my best friend.
A: This photo is beautiful. Where is she?
B: She's walking in the mountains near Rio de Janeiro. Carolina loves the fresh air and trees.

## EXERCISE 6 GETTING TO KNOW YOU

**Ⓐ** GAME  Write down your full name on a piece of paper. Your teacher will collect all the papers and redistribute them. Walk around the room. Introduce yourself to other students and try to find the person whose name you have on your piece of paper.

EXAMPLE:  A: Hi. I'm Jelena.
B: I'm Eddy.
A: I'm looking for Kadin Saleh. Do you know him?
B: I think that's him over there.

**Ⓑ** When you find the person you are looking for, find out where he or she comes from and ask about his or her name. You can ask some of the questions below.

EXAMPLE:  A: Kadin, where do you come from?
B: I come from Dubai.
A: What does *Kadin* mean?
B: It means "friend" or "companion" in Arabic.

• Where do you come from?
• What does your name mean?
• Which part of your name is your family name?
• Do you use a title? (for example, *Ms., Miss, Mrs., Mr.*)

• What do your friends call you?
• Do you have a nickname?
• What do you prefer to be called?
• How do you feel about your name?
• Other: _____

**Ⓒ** Finally, introduce your classmate to the rest of the class.

EXAMPLE:  This is Kadin Saleh. Kadin comes from Dubai. His name means "friend" or "companion" in Arabic...

## EXERCISE 7 REAL STUDENTS, REAL LIFE

**Ⓐ** PROJECT  Work with a partner. Choose a busy place at your school where students spend time before and after class. Stay there for five minutes and watch what's happening. Then use the camera on your phone to make two 30-second videos. In the videos, show and explain what students are doing.

EXAMPLE:  A: This student is doing homework.
B: The student next to her is using Facebook and posting information for his friends.
A: These students are having a conversation.
B: We don't know what they're talking about, but they look very serious.

**B** Talk to the students who appear in your videos. Ask for permission to show the videos in class. Then ask the students about their typical activities for that day and time.

EXAMPLE:  A: You're in our video. Is it OK to use the video in our English class?
          B: Sure.
          A: My name is Salvador, and this is May. What's your name?
          B: Andy.
          A: Hi, Andy. What do you usually do on Tuesday at this time?
          B: I always come here. I like to check my Facebook before math class.

**C** Work in a group. Use your phone to share your videos with your classmates. Then talk about typical activities that students at your school do before and after class.

EXAMPLE:  A: What does this person usually do on Tuesday before class?
          B: He always goes to the cafeteria and checks his Facebook.
          C: And what about this student? What does she do?

## EXERCISE 8  A WORLD OF NAMES

**A** SURVEY  Complete this chart with information about your country. Then find out about other countries. Talk to people who are not in your class or do an Internet search. Get information from three additional countries.

| Country | How many family names do people use? | What are three typical family names? | Is the order first name + family name, or family name + first name? |
|---|---|---|---|
| Your Country: | | | |
| Country #1: | | | |
| Country #2: | | | |
| Country #3: | | | |

**B** Work in a group. Compare your answers with those of your classmates. What do you notice about family names around the world?

EXAMPLE:  A: Which countries are in your chart?
          B: I have Brazil, Spain, Thailand, and Nigeria.
          C: Do people in those countries use one or two family names?

# FROM GRAMMAR TO WRITING

**A** BEFORE YOU WRITE Think about how to introduce yourself. Include information about your name, a typical day in your life, and something special that is going on in your life right now. Give details to show your identity. Complete the outline.

Name: _____  From: _____

Information About My Name: _____

My Typical Day: _____

Something Special in My Life Now: _____

**B** WRITE Use your outline to write a paragraph that describes who you are. Use the simple present and the present progressive. Try to avoid the common mistakes in the chart.

EXAMPLE:     My name is Thuy Nguyen. I come from Vietnam. My Vietnamese name is difficult to pronounce, so my friends always use Tina. . . . For me, a typical day begins at 6:00 a.m. I usually . . . These days, I'm looking for a new apartment. That means I'm . . .

## Common Mistakes in Using the Simple Present and Present Progressive

| | |
|---|---|
| Use the **simple present** to describe what **happens regularly** and to give **facts**. Do not use the present progressive. | A typical day **begins** at 6:00 a.m. NOT A typical day ~~is beginning~~ at 6:00 a.m. |
| Use the **simple present** with most **non-action verbs**. Do not use the present progressive. | I **want** to explain. NOT I ~~am wanting~~ to explain. |
| Except with non-action verbs, use the **present progressive** to describe what is happening **now**. Do not use the simple present. | Right now, **I'm looking** for a new apartment. NOT Right now, I ~~look~~ for a new apartment. |

**C** CHECK YOUR WORK Read your paragraph. Underline once the verbs in the simple present. Underline twice the verbs in the present progressive. Circle the adverbs of frequency and the time expressions. Use the Editing Checklist to check your work.

## Editing Checklist

Did you use . . . ?

☐ the simple present to describe what happens regularly and to give facts

☐ the present progressive to describe what is happening right now or in a longer present time

☐ the simple present with non-action verbs such as *be*, *like*, *seem*, and *want*

☐ adverbs of frequency and time expressions in the correct position

**D** REVISE YOUR WORK Read your paragraph again. Can you improve your writing? Make changes if necessary. Give your paragraph a title.

# UNIT 1 REVIEW

**Test yourself on the grammar of the unit.**

**A** Circle the correct words to complete the sentences.

1. Ekaterina study / studies until 10:00 every night.
2. Names like Sarah and Rebekah are coming / come back in style now.
3. How are / do you spell your last name?
4. I don't understanding / understand how to pronounce this name. Can you help me?
5. We often use / are using nicknames with our friends.

**B** Complete the conversation with the simple present or present progressive form of the verbs in parentheses.

ANA: Hi, Kim! I _____ Jeff Goodale. Is he here?
               **1.** (look for)

KIM: I _____ he's here somewhere.
     **2.** (think)

ANA: He _____ a cell phone today, so I _____ to give him a
       **3.** (not carry)                  **4.** (need)
     message from Lynn.

KIM: I _____ him! He _____ next to Kevin.
     **5.** (see)            **6.** (stand)

ANA: Jeff, hi. Call Lynn, OK? She _____ for your call right now.
                     **7.** (wait)

JEFF: That _____ serious! Can I use your phone?
      **8.** (sound)

ANA: Sure. I _____ it's an emergency. She just _____ you to buy
       **9.** (not believe)             **10.** (want)
     a new cell phone.

**C** Find and correct five mistakes.

Hi Leda,

How do you do these days? We're all fine. I'm writing to tell you that we not living in California anymore. We just moved to Oregon. Also, we expect a baby! We're looking for an interesting name for our new daughter. Do you have any ideas? Right now, we're thinking about *Gabriella* because it's having good nicknames. For example, *Gabby*, *Bree*, and *Ella* all seem good to us. How are those nicknames sound to you? We hope you'll write soon and tell us your news.

Love,
Samantha

**Now check your answers on page 475.**

# Simple Past and Past Progressive
## FIRST MEETINGS

**OUTCOMES**
- Describe actions and situations that were completed, or were in progress, in the past
- Describe one past action interrupted by another, or two past actions in progress at the same time
- Identify the order of events in a description
- Describe one's first meeting with someone
- Create a story and present it to the class
- Write about past events in an important relationship

---

## STEP 1    GRAMMAR IN CONTEXT

### BEFORE YOU READ

Look at the title of the article and at the photos. Discuss the questions.

1. Which couples do you recognize?
2. What do you know about them?
3. Do you know how they met?

### READ

▶02|01    Read this article about three famous couples.

# Super Couples

It's a bird, . . . it's a plane, . . . it's Superman! Disguised as Clark Kent, this world-famous character met Lois Lane while the two were working as newspaper reporters for the *Daily Planet*. At first, Lane wasn't interested in mild-mannered[1] Kent—she wanted to cover stories about "The Man of Steel." In time, she changed her mind. When Kent proposed, Lane accepted. (And she didn't even know he was Superman!)

Superman and Lois Lane are certainly not the only super couple. What were other power couples doing when they met? What did they accomplish together? Let's find out.

---

1 *mild-mannered:* behaving in a quiet, gentle way

**Marie and Pierre Curie in their lab**

When she was twenty-four, Maria Sklodowska left Poland and moved to Paris. While she was studying at the Sorbonne,[2] she met physicist Pierre Curie. She was planning to return to Poland after her studies, but the two scientists fell in love and got married. While they were raising their daughters, they were also doing research on radioactivity. In 1903, the Curies won the Nobel Prize in physics. Then, in 1906, a horse-drawn carriage hit and killed Pierre while he was out walking. When Marie recovered from the shock, she was able to pursue the couple's work. In 1911, she received her second Nobel Prize. She was the first person to ever receive two Nobel Prizes.

Frida Kahlo first met Diego Rivera in 1922 while she was studying at the National Preparatory School in Mexico City. Rivera was already a well-known artist. He came to the National Preparatory School to paint one of his famous murals.[3] Three years later, at the age of eighteen, Kahlo received serious injuries in a bus accident. While she was recovering, she started painting from bed. One day, she went to see Rivera to ask him for career advice. He was very impressed with her work. Kahlo and Rivera fell in love and got married. Today, they are considered two of Mexico's greatest, most influential artists.

**Frida Kahlo and Diego Rivera in their studio**

---

2 *Sorbonne:* the University of Paris, in Paris, France
3 *murals:* paintings on a wall

## AFTER YOU READ

Ⓐ VOCABULARY **Complete the sentences with the words from the box.**

| accomplish | cover | influential | pursue | recover | research |
|---|---|---|---|---|---|

1. He was doing _____ to learn more about Mexican art.

2. After she graduated from college, she decided to _____ her interest in painting.

3. Successful people _____ a lot during their lifetime.

4. The man was having some psychological problems. It took him many months to _____ from his illness.

5. After that, he became a very _____ writer. He changed people's opinions about mental illness.

6. Newspapers want to _____ important stories.

**B** COMPREHENSION Circle the word that best completes each sentence.

1. Clark Kent met Lois Lane <u>before / during / after</u> his time at the *Daily Planet*.

2. Lane found out Kent was Superman <u>before / during / after</u> Kent's marriage proposal.

3. Maria Sklodowska met Pierre Curie <u>before / during / after</u> her move to Paris.

4. <u>Before / During / After</u> her marriage, Sklodowska wanted to return to Poland.

5. Frida Kahlo met Diego Rivera <u>before / during / after</u> the time he spent at her school.

6. Rivera began painting murals <u>before / during / after</u> his project at the school.

7. Kahlo began painting <u>before / during / after</u> her recovery from her bus accident.

**C** DISCUSSION Work with a partner. Compare your answers in B. Why did you choose *before*, *during*, or *after*?

---

**STEP 2    GRAMMAR PRESENTATION**

## SIMPLE PAST

| Affirmative Statements |
| --- |
| Maria Sklodowska **studied** in Paris. |

| Negative Statements |
| --- |
| Lois **didn't plan** to marry Clark at first. |

| Yes/No Questions | Short Answers |
| --- | --- |
| **Did** he **teach**? | **Yes**, he **did**. <br> **No**, he **didn't**. |

| Wh- Questions |
| --- |
| What **did** they **do** in their lab? <br> Who **worked** in their lab? |

| Simple Past + Simple Past |
| --- |
| She **painted** it when she **recovered**. |

| Simple Past + Past Progressive |
| --- |
| She **met** him while she **was studying**. |

## PAST PROGRESSIVE

| Affirmative Statements |
| --- |
| She **was studying** in Paris in 1891. |

| Negative Statements |
| --- |
| She **wasn't planning** to get married. |

| Yes/No Questions | Short Answers |
| --- | --- |
| **Was** he **teaching**? | **Yes**, he **was**. <br> **No**, he **wasn't**. |

| Wh- Questions |
| --- |
| What **were** they **doing** in their lab? <br> Who **was working** in their lab? |

| Past Progressive + Past Progressive |
| --- |
| She **was painting** it while she **was recovering**. |

| Past Progressive + Simple Past |
| --- |
| She **was studying** when she **met** him. |

# GRAMMAR NOTES

## 1 Simple Past

Use the simple past to show that something happened and was **completed in the past**. The focus is on the **completion** of the action or situation.

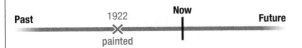

Diego Rivera **painted** his first mural *in 1922*.
  *(He completed his first mural in 1922.)*

Rivera and Kahlo **met** in that same year.

## 2 Past Progressive

Use the past progressive to show that something was **in progress at a specific time in the past**. The action or situation began before the specific time and may have continued after that time. The focus is on the **duration** of the action or situation, not its completion.

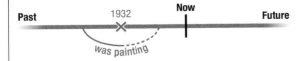

***During 1932**, Diego Rivera **was painting** murals for the Detroit Institute of Arts.
  *(During 1932, he continued painting murals for the Detroit Institute of Arts.)*

Kahlo and Rivera **were living** in Detroit then.

USAGE NOTE These **action verbs** (*come, do, get, go, look, make, say, try,* and *work*) are the most common verbs in the past progressive. They are common both in speaking and in writing.

What **were** Rivera and Kahlo **doing** in Detroit?
They **were working** on their art.

BE CAREFUL! **Non-action verbs** are not usually used in the progressive.

Kahlo **had** a terrible accident.
NOT Kahlo ~~was having~~ a terrible accident.

## 3 Past Progressive + Simple Past

Use the past progressive with the simple past to show that **one action interrupted another action in the past**. Use the **simple past** for the **interrupting action**.

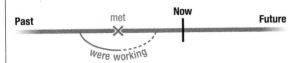

Lois Lane and Clark Kent **met** while they **were working** at the *Daily Planet*.

Use *while* to introduce the action in the **past progressive**.

Use *when* to introduce the action in the **simple past**.

***While** Kent **was going** to the *Daily Planet*, he **saw** a car accident.

Kent **was going** to the *Daily Planet* ***when** he **saw** a car accident.

USAGE NOTE We can also use *when* to introduce the action in the past progressive.

The accident occurred ***while** the driver **was making** a left turn.
The accident occurred ***when** the driver **was making** a left turn.

## 4 Past Progressive + *While* or *When*

Use the past progressive with *while* or *when* to show **two actions in progress at the same time in the past**. Use the past progressive in both clauses.

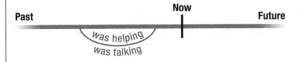

*While* Superman **was helping** people, Lois Lane **was talking** to the police.
*When* Superman **was helping** people, Lois Lane **was talking** to the police.

## 5 Simple Past + Simple Past, or Simple Past + Past Progressive

A sentence with two clauses in the simple past has a very **different meaning** from a sentence with one clause in the simple past and one clause in the past progressive.

- both clauses in the **simple past**

When Kent **arrived** at the newspaper office, Lane **wrote** a report about Superman.
*(First he arrived. Then she wrote the report.)*

- one clause in the **simple past**, the other clause in the **past progressive**

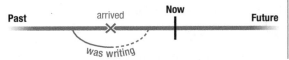

When Kent **arrived** at the newspaper office, Lane **was writing** a report about Superman.
*(First she started writing the report. Then he arrived at the office.)*

## 6 Position of the Time Clause

The **time clause** (the part of the sentence with *when* or *while*) can come **at the beginning or the end of the sentence**. The meaning is the same.

- at the **beginning**

*While* **he was flying**, Superman carried Lois Lane in his arms.

- at the **end**

Superman carried Lois Lane in his arms *while* **he was flying**.

**IN WRITING** Use a **comma after the time clause** when it comes at the **beginning** of the sentence. Do not use a comma after the main clause when the main clause comes first.

*When* **they met,** they were covering the news.
They were covering the news *when* **they met.**
NOT They were covering the news*,ₓ* when they met.

# REFERENCE NOTES

For **spelling rules of regular past verbs**, see Appendix 24 on page 464.
For a list of **irregular past verbs**, see Appendix 1 on page 453.
For **spelling rules** on forming the **past progressive**, see Appendix 23 on page 463.
For a list of **non-action verbs**, see Appendix 2 on page 454.

## EXERCISE 1  DISCOVER THE GRAMMAR

GRAMMAR NOTES 1–6  Read these people's descriptions of how they met important people in their lives. Decide if the statement that follows is *True (T)* or *False (F)*.

1. LUCKY:   I was riding home on my bike when I saw Elena on a park bench.

   __F__  Lucky saw Elena before he got on his bike.

2. ROD:   I was climbing a mountain when I met my best friend, Ian.

   _____  Ian was on the mountain.

3. MARIE:   How did I meet Philippe? I was sitting at home when the phone rang. When I answered, it was the wrong number, but we spoke for an hour!

   _____  Marie knew Philippe before they spoke on the phone.

4. DON:   When I first met Ana, I was working at the school library. Ana was there doing research.

   _____  Don started his library job after he met Ana.

5. TONY:   How did I meet my wife? Actually, my cousins invited her to dinner while I was living at their place. After dinner, we started talking and never stopped!

   _____  Tony moved in with his cousins after he met his wife.

6. MONICA:   I was taking an English class while Dania was taking Spanish. We met in the hall during a break.

   _____  Monica and Dania were students at the same time.


## EXERCISE 2  SIMPLE PAST OR PAST PROGRESSIVE

Ⓐ GRAMMAR NOTES 1–6  Complete the conversations. Circle the correct verb forms.

**Conversation 1**

JASON:  Are you OK, Erin? (Were) / Did you (crying) / cry?
                                1.              2.

ERIN:  Yes, but how were / did you knowing / know? I wasn't crying / didn't cry when you
                     3.              4.                    5.

   were coming / came in.
          6.

JASON:  Your eyes are red.

ERIN:  The movie *Frida* was on TV. It's about the Mexican painter Frida Kahlo. It's so sad. When I

   was watching / watched it, I was thinking / thought about her life. She had so many health
            7.                          8.

   problems and she never really was recovering / recovered from them.
                                              9.

**Conversation 2**

LILY:  You won't believe it! I was seeing / saw David and Victoria Beckham in London last week.
                                    1.

TONY:  London? What were / did you doing / do in London?
                        2.              3.

LILY: I was there on a business trip, but of course I was finding / found some time for shopping.

4.

When I was going / went into Harrods, the Beckhams were walking / walked in the door

5.                                                                 6.

right in front of me.

TONY: That's awesome! You were asking / asked them if you could take a selfie with them when

7.

you were getting / got inside the store, right?

8.

LILY: No, I wasn't wanting / didn't want to look like a crazed fan.

9.

TONY: OK, so what was happening / happened next?

10.

LILY: When I was going / went to the Women's Department, Victoria was looking / looked at

11.                                                                      12.

jeans. I couldn't control myself anymore, so I was taking / took a photo. Here it is!

13.

## Conversation 3

TARO: How were / did you hurting / hurt your foot?

1.            2.

YOSHI: It was an accident. I was falling / fell on my way to class yesterday. I was slipping / slipped

3.                                                           4.

while I was climbing / climbed the stairs to the third floor.

5.

TARO: That's too bad!

YOSHI: Not really. I was feeling / felt sorry for myself when I was sitting / sat in the emergency room,

6.                                                    7.

but suddenly things were changing / changed. I was meeting / met a cool girl who was at the

8.                                         9.

hospital with her sister. We're going out for pizza tonight.

02|02 **B** LISTEN AND CHECK **Listen to the conversations and check your answers in A.**

# EXERCISE 3  SIMPLE PAST OR PAST PROGRESSIVE

**A** GRAMMAR NOTES 1–6 **Complete the conversations. Use the simple past or the past progressive form of the verbs in parentheses. See Appendix 1 on page 453 for help with irregular verbs.**

## Conversation 1

PAZ: What _____were_____ you _____looking_____ at just then? You _____.

1. (look)                                    2. (smile)

EVA: I _____ the video of Nicole's wedding. She _____ so happy.

3. (watch)                                              4. (look)

PAZ: How _____ she and Matt _____?

5. (meet)

EVA: At my graduation party. Matt almost _____ because he was out of town. He

6. (not come)

_____ a big story for the newspaper. Luckily, his plans _____.

7. (cover)                                                                    8. (change)

The rest is history.

## Conversation 2

DAN: I _____ your Superman website while I _____ for some
_1. (find)_ _2. (look)_

information online. It's great.

DEE: Thanks. When _____ you _____ a Superman fan?
_3. (become)_

DAN: Years ago. I _____ a comic book one day when I _____ to marry
_4. (read)_ _5. (decide)_

Lois Lane! No, just kidding. I _____ to _draw_ Lois Lane and Superman.
_6. (want)_

DEE: I _____ a career in graphic arts when I _____ my Superman site.
_7. (pursue)_ _8. (start)_

The website _____ me get my first job.
_9. (help)_

DAN: So it looks like Superman was influential in _both_ our lives!

## Conversation 3

LARA: _____ Jason _____ you when he _____ to see you
_1. (surprise)_ _2. (come)_

last night?

ERIN: Yes! I _____ my apartment when he _____ on the door. When I
_3. (clean)_ _4. (knock)_

_____, we _____ to Fishbone Café. While we
_5. (finish)_ _6. (go)_

_____, Jason _____ me to marry him!
_7. (eat)_ _8. (ask)_

LARA: Congratulations!

ERIN: How much _____ you already _____ about this?
_9. (know)_

LARA: I _____ all the details. But
_10. (not have)_

Jason _____ his plans
_11. (mention)_

when I _____ him
_12. (see)_

yesterday afternoon.

▶ 02|03   **B** LISTEN AND CHECK
**Listen to the conversations
and check your answers in A.**

# EXERCISE 4 CONNECTING CLAUSES WITH *WHEN* OR *WHILE*

GRAMMAR NOTES 3–6 This timeline shows some important events in Monique's life. Use the timeline and the words in parentheses to write sentences about her. Use *when* or *while* and the simple past or past progressive. There is more than one way to write some of the sentences.

| born in Canada | moves to Australia | meets Paul | starts medical school | marries | gets medical degree | gets first job | starts practice at Lenox Hospital | has son; starts book | finishes book; does TV interview | book becomes a success; quits job |
|---|---|---|---|---|---|---|---|---|---|---|
| 1983 | 1998 | 1999 | 2005 | 2006 | 2009 | 2010 | 2012 | 2013 | 2014 | 2015 |

1. *She met Paul when she moved to Australia.*
   (moves to Australia / meets Paul)

2. *She got married while she was studying medicine.*
   (gets married / studies medicine)

3. _____
   (lives in Australia / gets married)

4. _____
   (completes her medical degree / gets a job)

5. _____
   (practices medicine at Lenox Hospital / has her son)

6. _____
   (writes a book / works at Lenox Hospital)

7. _____
   (does a TV interview / finishes her book)

8. _____
   (leaves her job / her book becomes a success)

# EXERCISE 5 EDITING

GRAMMAR NOTES 1–6  Read Monique's email to a friend. There are eleven mistakes in the use of the simple past and the past progressive. The first mistake is already corrected. Find and correct ten more.

Hi Crystal,

I was writing Chapter 2 of my new book when I ~~was thinking~~ *thought* of you. The last time I saw you, you walked down the aisle to marry Dave. That was more than two years ago. How are you? How is married life?

A lot has happened to me since then. While I worked at Lenox Hospital, I decided to pursue a career in writing. In 2014, I was publishing a book on women's health issues. It was quite successful here in Australia. I even had several interviews on TV. When I was receiving a contract to write a second book, I decided to quit my hospital job to write full-time. That's what I'm doing now. Paul, too, has had a career change. While I was writing, he was attending law school. He was getting his degree last summer. Then Paul and his father established their own law firm.

Oh, the reason I thought of you while I wrote was because the chapter was about rashes. Remember the time you were getting that terrible rash? We rode our bikes when you were falling into a patch of poison ivy. And that's how you met Dave! When you were falling off the bike, he offered to give us a ride home. Life's funny, isn't it?

Well, please write soon, and send my love to Dave. I miss you!

Monique

## EXERCISE 6  LISTENING

02|04  **A** Look at the pictures. Then listen to a woman explain how she met her husband. Listen again and circle the number of the set of pictures that illustrates the story.

**1.**

**2.**

**3.**

🔘02|04 **B** Listen to the interview again. Then work with a partner. Discuss your answer in A. Why did you choose that set of pictures? Why didn't you choose one of the other two sets of pictures?

EXAMPLE: **A:** How did you decide which set of pictures to choose?
**B:** Well, it was because . . .

## EXERCISE 7 WHAT ABOUT YOU?

CONVERSATION Work in a group. Think about the first time you met someone who became influential in your life: a best friend, teacher, husband, or wife. Tell your group about the meeting. Answer the questions below.

EXAMPLE: **A:** I met my best friend in 2013.
**B:** What were you doing?
**A:** I was walking to class when this guy came over. . . .
**C:** What happened then?
**A:** He started . . .

1. What were you doing?
2. What happened then?
3. How did that person influence your life?

## EXERCISE 8 THE TIMES OF MY LIFE

**A** CONVERSATION Before you talk with a partner, complete this timeline with some important events in your life. Include things that you have accomplished and your first meeting with someone who is significant to you.

Events: _____ _____ _____ _____ _____

_____ _____ _____ _____ _____

Years:

**B** Work with a partner. Exchange your timelines and ask and answer questions about events on these timelines.

EXAMPLE: **A:** How did you get your first job?
**B:** I was studying at the university when I saw an ad for a job in a bookstore.

# EXERCISE 9 "IT WAS A DARK AND STORMY NIGHT..."[1]

**A** GAME Work in a group and form a circle. Create your own story. The first person begins with "It was a dark and stormy night." The second person adds one sentence to the story. Continue around the circle until the story is complete. Use your imagination. Choose one student in the group to write each line of the story.

EXAMPLE:

**B** Share your story. Choose one member of your group to read the group's story to the class.

EXAMPLE: It was a dark and stormy night. The wind was blowing. Samantha was sitting at home alone when suddenly, . . .

---

1 *"It was a dark and stormy night":* the opening line of a novel by British author Edward Bulwer-Lytton

# FROM GRAMMAR TO WRITING

**A** BEFORE YOU WRITE  Think about a relationship that is important to you. Complete the outline.

**My First Meeting with** _____

Where we met: _____

What we were doing when we met: _____

**Important Events in the Relationship**

_____    _____   _____

**B** WRITE  Use your outline to write two paragraphs about your important relationship. In the first paragraph, write about your first meeting. In the second paragraph, write about important events in the relationship. Use the simple past and the past progressive. Try to avoid the common mistakes in the chart.

EXAMPLE:  I met my friend Andrea while I was living in Germany. . . .

### Common Mistakes in Using the Simple Past and Past Progressive

| | |
|---|---|
| Use the **simple past** for **completed** actions. Do not use the past progressive. | I **met** Andrea in 2014.<br>NOT  I ~~was meeting~~ Andrea in 2014. |
| Use the **past progressive** for **interrupted** actions. Do not use the simple past. | I **was leaving** the airport when I first saw her.<br>NOT  I ~~left~~ the airport when I first saw her. |
| Use a **comma after a time clause when it comes first**. Do not use a comma after the main clause when the main clause comes first. | *While* **I was getting into a taxi,** I fell.<br>NOT  I fell‚ while I was getting into a taxi. |

**C** CHECK YOUR WORK  Read your paragraphs. Underline once the verbs in the simple past. Underline twice the verbs in the past progressive. Circle *when* or *while*. Use the Editing Checklist to check your work.

### Editing Checklist

**Did you use . . . ?**

- [ ] the simple past to show the completion of a past action
- [ ] the past progressive to show the duration of a past action
- [ ] the simple past with non-action verbs such as *be, like, seem,* and *want*
- [ ] *when* with a simple past action or a past progressive action
- [ ] *while* with a past progressive action
- [ ] commas after time clauses at the beginning of a sentence

**D** REVISE YOUR WORK  Read your paragraphs again. Can you improve your writing? Make changes if necessary. Give your paragraphs a title.

# UNIT 2 REVIEW

**Test yourself on the grammar of the unit.**

**(A)** Circle the correct words to complete the sentences.

1. I first (met) / was meeting my wife in 2007.

2. She worked / was working at the museum the day I went to see a Picasso exhibit.

3. I saw / was seeing her as soon as I walked into the room.

4. She had / was having long dark hair and a beautiful smile.

5. While / When I had a question about a painting, I went over to speak to her.

6. The whole time she was talking, I thought / was thinking about asking her on a date.

7. When I left the museum, she gave / was giving me her phone number.

**(B)** Complete the conversation with the simple past or past progressive form of the verbs in parentheses.

A: What _____ you _____ when you first _____ Ed?
                                    **1.** (do)                              **2.** (meet)

B: We _____ for a bus. We started to talk, and, as they say, "The rest is history."
            **3.** (wait)

   What about you? How did you meet Karl?

A: Oh, Karl and I _____ in school while we _____ English.
                              **4.** (meet)                        **5.** (study)

   I _____ him as soon as I _____ the room on the first day
            **6.** (notice)                      **7.** (enter)

   of class.

B: It sounds like it was love at first sight!

**(C)** Find and correct six mistakes.

was studing.     when.

    It was 2005. I ~~studied~~ French ~~in~~ Paris ~~while~~ I met Paul. Like me, Paul was from California.

                                                       went

We were both taking the same 9:00 a.m. conversation class. After class, we always were ~~going~~

                                                     were.

to a café with some of our classmates. One day, while we ~~was~~ drinking café au lait, Paul was

   asked.

~~asking~~ me to go to a movie with him. After that, we started to spend most of our free time

together. We really got to know each other well, and we discovered that we had a lot of

                                                      went.

similar interests. When the course was over, we left Paris and were ~~going~~ back to California

together. The next year, we got married!

**Now check your answers on page 475.**

# Simple Past, Present Perfect, and Present Perfect Progressive

## HOBBIES AND INTERESTS

**OUTCOMES**
- Recognize when to use the simple past, the present perfect, or the present perfect progressive
- Show that something was not completed, using *for* or *since* and time expressions
- Identify key details in a reading or a recording
- Discuss hobbies and interests
- Research an interesting hobby and present findings to the class
- Write about a recent trend

---

**STEP 1**    **GRAMMAR IN CONTEXT**

## BEFORE YOU READ

Look at the photo. Discuss the questions.

1. What is the student doing?
2. Can cooking be a hobby?
3. What do *you* like to do in your free time?

## READ

 03|01   Read this article from an online student blog about hobbies.

## STUDENT VOICES

# Adventures in Student Living

BY HANK WASHINGTON

I moved into my first apartment about three months ago. That explains a lot about my new hobby—cooking. My main motivation is eating, but I've also found out that I actually like to cook. And I've been reading food blogs recently. One of the best is *Nutmegs, seven,* by student blogger Elly McCausland.

McCausland is part of a trend among young people in the United Kingdom. They've been learning about delicious, healthy alternatives to fast food. Since April 2010, McCausland has been writing about her passion for cooking on her blog. She often describes new kinds of food that she has discovered. Since she started her blog, she has taken trips to places like Costa Rica and Thailand and has described the connection between her interests in food and

travel. Recently, McCausland's blog has become even more interesting because she has started to grow fruits and vegetables in her garden. I can't wait to read more about how she uses the fresh produce from her garden for breakfast, lunch, and dinner.

Elly McCausland hasn't been experimenting with food all her life. In fact, she survived on cheese sandwiches as a child. McCausland is now 25 years old. She has been studying for a Ph.D. in literature for a couple of years. And of course, she has continued to write about her culinary adventures.

Have you ever wanted to try your hand at[1] cooking? What hobbies have you been enjoying lately? Add a comment to keep the discussion going.

---

1 *try your hand at:* do something for the first time to see if you like it or are good at it

## AFTER YOU READ

**A** VOCABULARY **Choose the word or phrase that best completes each sentence.**

1. An activity that is part of a **trend** is _____.
   a. necessary      b. expensive      (c.) popular

2. **Motivation** makes you _____ to do something.
   a. hate      (b.) want      c. forget

3. An **alternative** gives you _____.
   a. an explanation      (b.) a choice      c. energy

4. A student with a **passion** for learning probably spends time _____.
   (a.) at the library      b. in stores      c. at parties

5. A person who **survives** a car accident _____.
   a. dies      (b.) lives      c. disappears

6. People who **experiment** with food _____ try recipes from different cultures.
   a. never      b. seldom      (c.) often

**B** COMPREHENSION **Read the list of activities in Elly's life. Which activities are finished? Which are unfinished? Check (✓) Finished or Unfinished.**

| | Finished | Unfinished |
|---|---|---|
| 1. writing the *Nutmegs, seven* blog | ☐ | ✓ |
| 2. trying new kinds of food | ✓ | ☐ |
| 3. taking a vacation in Costa Rica | ✓ | ☐ |
| 4. growing fruits and vegetables | ✓ | ☐ |
| 5. eating only cheese sandwiches | ✓ | ☐ |
| 6. getting a Ph.D. | ☐ | ✓ |

**C** DISCUSSION **Work with a partner. Compare your answers in B. Why did you check *Finished* or *Unfinished*?**

## SIMPLE PAST

### Affirmative Statements

I **moved** three months ago.

### Negative Statements

She **didn't write** a blog post last night.

### Yes/No Questions

**Did** he **cook** dinner?

### Short Answers

**Yes**, he **did**.
**No**, he **didn't**.

### Wh- Questions

Where **did** he **eat**?

Who **read** the food blog?

## PRESENT PERFECT
## PRESENT PERFECT PROGRESSIVE

### Affirmative Statements

I**'ve lived** here for three months.
I**'ve been living** here for three months.

*[handwritten: have/has + pp    have/has + Been + ing]*

### Negative Statements

She **hasn't written** a new blog post.
She **hasn't been writing** lately.

### Yes/No Questions

**Has** he **cooked** dinner?
**Has** he **been cooking**?

### Short Answers

**Yes**, he **has**.
**No**, he **hasn't**.

### Wh- Questions

Where **has** he **eaten**?
Where **has** he **been eating**?

Who**'s read** the food blog?
Who**'s been reading** the food blog?

## GRAMMAR NOTES

### 1 Simple Past

Use the simple past to show that something happened and was **completed in the past**.

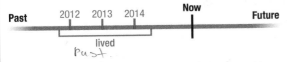

I **lived** in the dorm for two years.   *[handwritten: finish]*
   *(I don't live in the dorm now.)*

We often use **specific past time expressions** such as *in 2014, last year, last summer, last month,* and *yesterday* with the simple past.

She **traveled** to Thailand *in 2014*.   *[handwritten: finish]*
She **went** to Costa Rica *last summer*.

We often use *ago* with the simple past to show when something started.

They **joined** a cooking club *a year ago*.

Use the present perfect or the present perfect progressive **with *for* or *since*** to show that something **started in the past** but was **not completed**. This action or situation **continues** up to the present and may continue into the future.

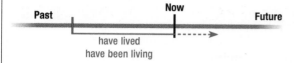

I**'ve lived** in my apartment ***for*** three months.
I**'ve been living** in my apartment ***for*** three months.
 *(I moved to my apartment three months ago, and I'm still living there today.)*

We often use **verbs of duration** such as *live, teach, wear, work,* and *study* in this way.

She**'s worked** hard ***for*** weeks.
She**'s been working** hard ***for*** weeks.

Use *for* or *since* and a time expression:

- *for* + **a length of time** to show *how long* a present condition has been true

She**'s studied** in York ***for two years***.

- *since* + **a point of time** to show *when* a present condition *started*

She**'s been studying** there ***since she graduated*** from high school.

**BE CAREFUL!** **Time expressions** such as *for the past week, for the last two months,* and *for the past ten years* show that something started in the past but was **not completed**. Use the **present perfect** or the **present perfect progressive**. Do not use the simple past.

I**'ve taken** classes here ***for the past three years***.
NOT I took classes here for the past three years.
I**'ve been cooking** dinner ***for the last hour***.
NOT I cooked dinner for the last hour.

**BE CAREFUL!** The **present perfect** with *for* has a very **different meaning** from the **simple past** with *for*.

He **has taught** a cooking class ***for*** six months.
 *(He is still teaching the class.)*
He **taught** a cooking class ***for*** six months.
 *(He no longer teaches the class.)*

**BE CAREFUL!** Use the **simple past** with expressions that refer to a **specific time in the past**. Do not use the present perfect with a specific time (except after *since*).

He **moved** to London ***in 2014***.
NOT He has moved to London in 2014.
He**'s lived** there ***since 2014***.

**USAGE NOTE** It is more common to put the **expression with *for* or *since*** at the **end of the sentence**.

He's been writing ***since 2010***. *(more common)*
***Since 2010***, he's been writing. *(less common)*

**IN WRITING** Use a **comma** when the expression with *for* or *since* comes at the **beginning** of the sentence. Do not use a comma when the expression with *for* or *since* comes at the end of the sentence.

***For several months,*** I have been reading the blog.
***Since I started cooking,*** my health has improved.
NOT I've been reading the blog, for several months.
NOT My health has improved, since I started cooking.

Remember that we usually do not use **non-action verbs** in the progressive.

I**'ve known** Elly for a short time.
NOT I've been knowing Elly for a short time.

**USAGE NOTE** In **informal conversation**, some people use the **progressive** with **verbs of emotion** (*feel, like, love, want*).

She**'s been feeling** a little worried for a while.
I**'ve been wanting** to learn how to cook for ages.

## 3 Present Perfect for an Indefinite Time in the Past

Use the present perfect **without *for* or *since*** to show that something happened at an **indefinite time in the past** and was **completed**.

She**'s written** a new blog post.
*(We don't know when she wrote the blog post, or the time is not important.)*

We sometimes use the **present perfect** with **adverbs of time** such as *already, yet, ever, never, just, lately,* and *recently* to show that something happened at an **indefinite time in the past**.

I've *already* **gone** to the supermarket.
I **haven't had** lunch *yet*.
**Have** you **seen** Lea *lately*?
He**'s started** to watch food shows *recently*.

USAGE NOTE In American English, we sometimes use the **simple past** with *already, yet, just,* and *recently*.

I**'ve** *already* **eaten**. or I *already* **ate**.

BE CAREFUL! Use the **present perfect or the present perfect progressive** with *lately*. Do not use the simple past.

I **have baked** a lot of pies *lately*.
I **have been baking** a lot of pies *lately*.
NOT I ~~baked~~ a lot of pies lately.

We use the **present perfect** (not the simple past) to show that the result of the action or situation is important in the present. The present perfect always has some **connection to the present**.

She**'s completed** her master's degree, and she's studying for a Ph.D.
*(Because she has her master's degree, she can now study for her Ph.D.)*

USAGE NOTE We often use the **present perfect** without *for* or *since* to show **how many things** or **how many times** someone has done something.

She**'s read** *three books* about healthy food choices.
She**'s read** that book *three times*.

BE CAREFUL! *She's read that book* and *She's been reading that book* have very different meanings.

She**'s read** that book.
*(She finished the book.)*
She**'s been reading** that book.
*(She's still reading the book.)*

## 4 Present Perfect or Simple Past

Use the present perfect or the simple past **with time expressions for unfinished time periods** (*today, this week,* etc.) to show **if things might happen again**.

Use the **present perfect** for things that **might happen again** in that time period.

She**'s written** three blog posts *this week*.
*(The week isn't over. She might write another post.)*

Use the **simple past** for things that **probably won't happen again** in that period.

She **wrote** three blog posts *this week*.
*(The week isn't over, but she won't write another post.)*

BE CAREFUL! *This morning, this afternoon,* and *this evening* can refer to either unfinished or finished time. Use the **simple past** if the time period is **finished**.

I**'ve had** three cups of coffee *this morning*.
*(It's still morning.)*
I **had** three cups of coffee *this morning*.
*(It's now afternoon.)*

## REFERENCE NOTES

For a list of **irregular past verbs**, see Appendix 1 on page 453.

For a list of **irregular past participles** used in forming the **present perfect**, see Appendix 1 on page 453.

---

**STEP 3**     **FOCUSED PRACTICE**

### EXERCISE 1   DISCOVER THE GRAMMAR

**A** GRAMMAR NOTES 1–4   Read this article about a famous chef. Circle the simple past verbs. Underline once the verbs in the present perfect. Underline twice the verbs in the present perfect progressive.

# One Amazing Chef, One Amazing Hobby

ETHAN STOWELL has been working in the restaurant business for many years. Stowell has received numerous awards as a top chef in the United States. Although he grew up in a family of dancers, Stowell didn't want to join the family business. He quickly realized that his true passion is food. In recent years, Stowell has opened several popular restaurants in Seattle. In addition, he has been collecting cookbooks for years. He has about 2,000 of them!

Ethan Stowell

Since he started his collection in 1995, Chef Stowell has become obsessed with cookbooks. He's been buying new and used books in stores, on websites, at yard sales, and just about anywhere else he can find them. What's more, the books haven't been sitting on shelves all these years. The chef has actually used them to experiment with new kinds of food.

Chef Stowell didn't attend culinary school. Instead, he learned about food by working in restaurants. He got his first cookbooks in order to add to his knowledge. Since then, he has discovered the importance of combining the history of food with his own experiences in life. With this winning combination, he has developed his own style of simply prepared food and has attracted loyal fans.

**Read the statements about Ethan Stowell. Check (✓) _True_ or _False_.**

| | True | False |
|---|:---:|:---:|
| 1. There have always been many chefs in Ethan Stowell's family. | ☐ | ✓ |
| 2. Stowell has become passionate about food recently. | ☐ | ☐ |
| 3. Stowell bought his first cookbook in 1995. | ☐ | ☐ |
| 4. He has stopped buying cookbooks. | ☐ | ☐ |
| 5. As an alternative to cooking school, he worked in restaurants. | ☐ | ☐ |
| 6. Stowell hasn't read any of his cookbooks yet. | ☐ | ☐ |
| 7. It is possible that Ethan Stowell will win more awards. | ☐ | ☐ |

## EXERCISE 2 SIMPLE PAST, PRESENT PERFECT, OR PRESENT PERFECT PROGRESSIVE

GRAMMAR NOTES 1–3 **Complete this article about another hobby—collecting rocks. Circle the correct words.**

# A Hobby That Helps

High school student Sydney Martin (has always loved)/ has always been loving rocks, and
**1.**
several years ago, she has found /(found) the perfect way to use her rock collection.
**2.**
Sydney's rocks come from the Lake Michigan beaches near

Sydney Martin

her home. She (has been using)/ used them to make necklaces
**3.**
since she has been /(was) eight years old. In 2005, Sydney
**4.**
has sold /(sold) her first necklaces to family and friends and
**5.**
put the money in the bank. Two years later, when doctors
have told /(told) Sydney that she had LCH,[1] she immediately
**6.**
has known /(knew) what to do with the profits from her
**7.**
jewelry. She has decided /(decided) to give the money to doctors trying to find a cure for
**8.**
LCH, and she (hasn't stopped)/ didn't stop since. Sydney (has started)/ has been starting a
**9.** **10.**
business, Syd Rocks, to sell her rock jewelry. So far,(she has donated)/ donated more than
**11.**
$420,000. Sydney's motivation is simple. She wants to help in the fight against LCH.

---

1 _LCH:_ Langerhans Cell Histiocytosis, a rare blood disease

# EXERCISE 3 SIMPLE PAST, PRESENT PERFECT, OR PRESENT PERFECT PROGRESSIVE

GRAMMAR NOTES 1–4 Complete these paragraphs about three people and their hobbies. Use the correct form of the verbs in parentheses—simple past, present perfect, or present perfect progressive. Sometimes more than one answer is correct.

## Paragraph 1

May ___*has been taking*___ photos ever since her parents ___*bought*___
    **1.** (take)                       **2.** (buy)

her a camera when she ___*was*___ only ten years old. At first, she only
    **3.** (be)

___*took*___ color snapshots of friends and family, but then she suddenly
    **4.** (take)

___*changed*___ to black and white. Lately, she ___*has shot*___ a lot of
    **5.** (change)                       **6.** (shoot)

nature photographs. This year, she ___*has been competing*___ in three amateur photography
    **7.** (compete)

contests—and it's only April! She hopes to win several awards before the end of this year.

Last month, she ___*won*___ second prize for her nighttime photo of a
    **8.** (win)

lightning storm.

## Paragraph 2

Carlos _____ playing music when he _____ an
    **1.** (begin)                       **2.** (get)

electric guitar for his twelfth birthday. He _____ a day without his guitar
    **3.** (not spend)

since. In fact, the guitar _____ more than just a way of having some fun
    **4.** (become)

with his friends. Last year, he _____ a local band. Since then, they
    **5.** (join)

_____ all over town, in cafés, at parties, and in concerts. So far this year,
    **6.** (perform)

the band _____ six concerts, and they have plans for many more.
    **7.** (give)

## Paragraph 3

Kate _____ a beautiful old stamp last month. It is now part of the
    **1.** (find)

fantastic collection she _____ on for the past two years. At first, she just
    **2.** (work)

_____ stamps from letters that she _____ from friends.
    **3.** (save)                       **4.** (get)

After some time, however, she _____ to look more actively for stamps.
    **5.** (begin)

Lately, she _____ them from special stores and _____
    **6.** (buy)                       **7.** (trade)

stamps with other collectors on philatelic websites. So far, she _____ over
    **8.** (find)

200 stamps from all over the world.

# EXERCISE 4
## SIMPLE PAST, PRESENT PERFECT, OR PRESENT PERFECT PROGRESSIVE

GRAMMAR NOTES 1–4  A student is interviewing adventure traveler Rafeh Abad for a research project. Use the words in parentheses to write the student's questions. Use her notes to complete Abad's answers. Choose between the simple past, the present perfect, and the present perfect progressive. Use the present perfect progressive and contractions when possible.

first adventure trip (Lake Louise in Canada) – ten years ago

second adventure (scuba diving trip in Mexico)

    cost – $1,200

from hobby to business – started in 2015

    adventure travel tours along with two employees

    recent trips to Costa Rica, Peru, and Alaska

adventure travel blog – started last year

    1,000 readers in the first two weeks of this month

travel to Africa – not yet

1. (how long / you / do / adventure travel)

    STUDENT: _How long have you been doing adventure travel?_

    ABAD: _I've been doing adventure travel for ten years._

2. (where / you / go / on your first adventure trip)

    STUDENT: _Where did you go on your first adventure trip_

    ABAD: _I went to Lake Louise in Canada._

3. (how much / your diving trip in Mexico / cost)

    STUDENT: _How much did your diving trip in Mexico cost?_

    ABAD: _It cost $1,200_

4. (how long / you and your team / lead / adventure tours)

    STUDENT: _How long have you and your team been leading adventure tours._

    ABAD: _We've been leading adventure tours since 2015._

5. (what trips / you / take / recently)

    STUDENT: _What trip have you taken recently._

    ABAD: _I've taken trips to Costa Rica, Peru and Alaska._

6. (how long / you / write / a travel blog)

    STUDENT: _How long have you been writing a travel blog._

    ABAD: _I've been writing for one year._

**7.** (how many people / read / your blog / this month)

STUDENT: _How many people have read your blog this month_

ABAD: _1000 people have read the blog this mounth_

**8.** (how many times / you / visit / Africa)

STUDENT: _How many times have you visted Africa_

ABAD: _I haven't yet._

## EXERCISE 5 EDITING

GRAMMAR NOTES 1–4 Read these comments to the online article about hobbies on page 33. There are nine mistakes in the use of the simple past, the present perfect, and the present perfect progressive. The first mistake is already corrected. Find and correct eight more.

○ ○ ○

**COMMENTS**

*I've been cooking*
~~I'm cooking~~ since I was in elementary school. When I was ten years old, my mother has taught

me how to make simple things such as fried eggs and chicken salad. Then we moved on to more

*Loved.*
complicated meals. I've always ~~been loving~~ to cook as a way to relax and be creative. Lately, I've

been trying my hand at baking, too. Last month, I made my first strawberry cheesecake. BTW,[1] I've

*read.*
~~been reading~~ the *Nutmegs, seven* blog several times. You're right. It's incredible. —**jg20133**

*for*
I've been passionate about Do It Yourself ~~since~~ several years. DIY gives me an alternative to

*took* *have made*
spending lots of money in stores. I have ~~taken~~ a knitting class last year, and since then, I ~~made a~~

hat, a scarf, and gloves for my boyfriend. My current DIY project is all about upcycling.[2] Last week,

my roommate gave me all of her old magazines, and I've been creating a sculpture from them. I

haven't finished the sculpture yet, but it's going to be beautiful. —**Claudia**

No one has mentioned video games yet. My friends and I have been playing Mortal Kombat vs DC

Universe since this semester has started. We enjoy the challenge. And here's something interesting.

*have been*
I ~~was~~ a fan of Pokémon all my life. In my opinion, there's nothing better than Pikachu! —**Fanboy**

1 *BTW:* a common online and texting abbreviation for "by the way"
2 *upcycling:* using an old product for a new, more valuable purpose

## EXERCISE 6 LISTENING

▶03|02 **A** Lara and Pablo are discussing hobbies. Listen to their conversation. Read the statements. Then listen again to the conversation and check (✓) *True* or *False*. If there isn't enough information to decide, check (✓) *Don't Know*.

|  | True | False | Don't Know |
|---|:---:|:---:|:---:|
| 1. Pablo's hobby has had a negative effect on his life. | ☐ | ✓ | ☐ |
| 2. One of Pablo's friends explained the importance of hobbies to him. | ☐ | ✓ | ☐ |
| 3. According to Lara, she has had no free time for two weeks. | ✓ | ☐ | ☐ |
| 4. Hobbies can help people do well at school and at work. | ✓ | ☐ | ☐ |
| 5. Pablo has started taking photos of buildings. | ✓ | ☐ | ☐ |
| 6. Pablo is a good photographer because he has become more creative. | ☐ | ☐ | ✓ |
| 7. Lara has still not changed her mind about getting a hobby. | ✓ | ☐ | ☐ |

▶03|02 **B** Work with a partner. Listen again to the conversation. Discuss your answers in A. Give reasons for your answers.

EXAMPLE: A: So, why is the answer for number 1 false?
B: Well, Pablo's hobby hasn't had a negative effect on his life. On the contrary, Lara says he looks happy and relaxed.
A: OK. What about number 2?

▶03|02 **C** Work in a group. Listen again to the conversation. Discuss answers to the following questions.

1. What are the advantages of having photography as a hobby? Give examples from your personal knowledge and experience.

   EXAMPLE: A: I started taking photos as a way to reduce stress.
   B: How can photography lower your stress level?
   A: Well, for one thing, I've been spending more time outdoors. That means . . .
   C: There are other advantages, too. For example, I've been . . .

2. How can Lara find time for a hobby? Give examples.

3. According to Pablo, everyone needs a hobby to survive. Do you agree with Pablo? Give reasons to support your answer. Include examples.

Simple Past, Present Perfect, and Present Perfect Progressive   **43**

## EXERCISE 7 WHAT ABOUT YOU?

CONVERSATION Work in a group. Talk about your hobbies and interests. What did you do in the past with your hobby? What have you been doing lately? Find out about other people's hobbies.

EXAMPLE: A: Do you have any hobbies, Ben?

B: Yes. Since I was in high school, my hobby has been running. . . . Recently, I've been training for a marathon. What about you? Do you have a hobby?

C: I collect sneakers. I got my first pair of Nikes when I was ten, and I've been collecting different kinds of sneakers ever since. . . .

## EXERCISE 8 DONE, DONE, NOT DONE

**A** INTERVIEW What did you plan to do last month to develop your hobbies and personal interests? Make a list. Include things you did and things that you still haven't done. Do not check (✓) any of the items. Exchange lists with a partner.

*Buy a new pair of running shoes.*
*Research healthy snacks for marathon runners.*

**B** Now ask questions about your partner's list. Check (✓) the things that your partner has already done. Answer your partner's questions about your list. When you finish, find out if the information that you recorded on your partner's list is correct.

EXAMPLE: A: Have you bought your new running shoes yet?

B: Yes, I have. I bought them last week.

A: And what about the research on healthy snacks?

B: I haven't done it yet.

A: OK. I think we've talked about everything on our lists. Let's make sure our answers are correct.

# EXERCISE 9 NOT YOUR EVERYDAY HOBBY

**A** GROUP PROJECT  Work in a group. Choose one of the hobbies from the list to research. Answer some of the questions below.

EXAMPLE:  A: Apiculture is beekeeping.
B: In the past, this was an activity for farmers.
C: But it has recently become . . .
D: Right. Since . . .

**Hobbies to research:**

- apiculture
- cosplay
- couch surfing
- egg carving
- genealogy
- geocaching
- spelunking
- ultimate Frisbee

**Possible questions:**

- What is the activity?
- When did people start doing the activity?
- Where did the activity start?
- How long has the hobby been popular?
- Why has the hobby become popular?
- What is the most interesting fact that you've learned about the hobby?

**B** Report back to your class. If your group chose the same hobby as another group, do you have the same information about that hobby? Compare answers.

EXAMPLE:  A: Beekeeping has been going on for about nine thousand years.
B: But in the past, it was usually an activity for farmers.
A: In the twenty-first century, beekeeping has become . . .
B: Surprisingly, the popularity of beekeeping has been increasing in . . .

## FROM GRAMMAR TO WRITING

**A** BEFORE YOU WRITE  Think about trends at your school or among your friends. What is new or different? Think about hobbies, fashion, classroom activities, etc. Complete the outline.

An Interesting Trend: _Skate board._

When the Trend Started: _In the 80's_

Advantages of the Trend: _Improve skills such as balance, strength, flexibility._

Disadvantages of the Trend: _Many falls and blows to the body, broken bones_

**B** WRITE  Use your outline to write a paragraph about an interesting trend. Use the simple past, the present perfect, and the present perfect progressive. Try to avoid the common mistakes in the chart.

EXAMPLE:  Zumba is an exercise program that uses dance styles like salsa and hip hop. People have been doing Zumba for many years. However, it suddenly became . . .

### Common Mistakes in Using the Simple Past, Present Perfect, or Present Perfect Progressive

| | |
|---|---|
| Use the **simple past** with **specific past time expressions**. Do not use the present prefect (except after *since*). | I **started** a Zumba class *two weeks ago*. NOT I've started a Zumba class two weeks ago. |
| Use the **present perfect** or the **present perfect progressive** to show that something **started in the past** but was **not completed**. Do not use the simple past. | People **have been doing** Zumba *since 1986*. NOT People did Zumba since 1986. |
| Use the **present perfect** to show that something happened at an **indefinite time in the past** and was **completed**. Do not use the present perfect progressive. | We**'ve finished** today's Zumba class. NOT We've been finishing today's Zumba class. |

**C** CHECK YOUR WORK  Read your paragraph. Circle the verbs in the simple past. Underline once the verbs in the present perfect. Underline twice the verbs in the present perfect progressive. Use the Editing Checklist to check your work.

### Editing Checklist

Did you use . . . ?

☐ the simple past for things that happened and were completed in the past

☐ the present perfect and present perfect progressive with *for* or *since* for things that started in the past but were not completed

☐ the present perfect for things that were completed at an indefinite time in the past

**D** REVISE YOUR WORK  Read your paragraph again. Can you improve your writing? Make changes if necessary. Give your paragraph a title.

# UNIT 3 REVIEW

**Test yourself on the grammar of the unit.**

**A** Circle the correct words to complete the sentences.

1. Isabel was / **has been** interested in yoga since high school.

2. She finally **took** / has taken her first yoga class last week.

3. She has read / **has been reading** a book about yoga. She'll probably finish it tomorrow.

4. She has felt much healthier since she **started** / has started the yoga class.

5. She went / **has gone** to three yoga classes this week, and it's only Tuesday.

6. Isabel's roommate has been doing yoga since / **for** eight months.

7. More and more students became / **have become** fans of yoga in the past several years.

**B** Complete the sentences with the simple past, present perfect, or present perfect progressive form of the verbs in parentheses.

Lisa _has been working / has worked_ on her stamp collection for five years, and she still enjoys
    **1.** (work)

it. Last year, she _discovered_ a very valuable stamp on an old letter in her attic.
                    **2.** (discover)

At first, she _didn't know_ it was valuable. She _found it out_ after
               **3.** (not know)                        **4.** (find out)

she did some research on the Internet. Of course, she _got_ really
                                                     **5.** (get)

excited. Since then, she _has been going / has gone_ to garage sales and flea markets every
                        **6.** (go)

weekend. Unfortunately for Lisa, she _hasn't found_ another valuable stamp, but
                                      **7.** (not find)

she _has had / has been having_ a great time searching.
       **8.** (have)

**C** Find and correct five mistakes.

A: How long ~~did~~ have you been doing adventure sports?

B: I've ~~gotten~~ got interested five years ago, and I haven't stopped since then.

A: You're lucky to live here in Colorado. It's a great place for adventure sports. Did you live

   here long? _How long have you been living here_

B: No, not long. I've ~~moved~~ I moved here last year. I used to live in Alaska.

A: I haven't ~~go~~ gone there yet, but I've heard it's great.

B: It *is* great. When you go, be sure to visit Denali National Park.

**Now check your answers on page 475.**

# Past Perfect and Past Perfect Progressive

## MUSICIANS

**OUTCOMES**
- Describe events that happened, or were in progress, before a specific time in the past
- Show the order of two past events, using adverbs and expressions with *by*
- Identify the order of events in a biographical article and in a radio interview
- Discuss talents and past achievements
- Discuss one's schedule for the previous day
- Write about a famous person's life and career

## STEP 1 GRAMMAR IN CONTEXT

### BEFORE YOU READ

Look at the photo, the title, and the first paragraph of the article. Discuss the questions.

1. What is the man doing? Describe him.
2. What type of music do you like? Do you enjoy classical music? Which composers?
3. Why do you think the article is called "The People's Conductor"?

### READ

04|01 Read this article about Gustavo Dudamel.

Gustavo
Dudamel

# The People's Conductor

He's exciting. He's great-looking. He's "The
Dude,"[1] and he's changing the way people
around the world feel about classical music.

Gustavo Dudamel grew up in Barquisimeto,
Venezuela. A child prodigy,[2] he had already
started taking music lessons by the early age of
four. His father played the trombone in a salsa
band, and young Dudamel had been hoping to
take up the same instrument. But his arms were
too short, and so he studied the violin instead.

It wasn't too long before Dudamel became
part of El Sistema—a program created to teach
young Venezuelans, mostly from poor families,
how to play musical instruments. Many of
these kids had been getting into trouble before
participating in the program. "The music
saved me. I'm sure of this," said Dudamel in a
TV interview.

---

1 *dude:* a man (an informal word, used to express positive
   feelings about the person)
2 *child prodigy:* a very young person who has a great natural
   ability in a subject or skill

In El Sistema, Dudamel's amazing talent was obvious, and by the time he was fifteen, he had become the conductor of the Simón Bolívar National Youth Orchestra. But that wasn't the first time he had led an orchestra. According to Dudamel, he had been conducting in his imagination since he was six.

On October 3, 2009, Dudamel lifted his baton for the first time as music director of the famed Los Angeles Philharmonic. He was only twenty-eight, and he had just signed a five-year contract as conductor. Tickets for this free concert at the 18,000-seat Hollywood Bowl had become available two months earlier. By the time the Bowl's ticket office opened on August 1, hundreds of people had already arrived. They had been lining up for hours in the hot Californian sun. The tickets were gone in minutes. On October 3, that lucky audience, a mix of all ages and ethnic backgrounds, had come for one thing—to see "Gustavo the Great" conduct. They were not disappointed. By the end of the concert, they had all risen to their feet and had been applauding enthusiastically for ten minutes.

After his successful debut, Dudamel continued to attract new fans to his concerts. To help young people, he worked with the Los Angeles Philharmonic to set up a program modeled on El Sistema, the program that had transformed his life. Today, Dudamel is an award-winning conductor who wants to inspire others and share his love of classical music.

## AFTER YOU READ

**A** VOCABULARY  **Complete the sentences with the words from the box.**

| conducted | contract | ethnic | inspired | participated | transformed |

1. The experience ___transformed___ her life. It really changed everything for her.
2. The pianist's performance ___inspired___ me to study piano.
3. How many times has Dudamel ___conducted___ the orchestra this season?
4. The audience was a real ___ethnic___ mix of African Americans, Asians, Hispanics, and whites.
5. Many musicians and singers ___participated___ in the event.
6. One violinist signed a(n) ___contract___ with the orchestra for two years.

**B** COMPREHENSION  **Read the statements. Put the events in Dudamel's life in the correct time order (1 = first, 6 = last).**

___5___ He became conductor of the Simón Bolívar National Youth Orchestra.

___1___ He turned four.

___3___ He started a program based on El Sistema.

___6___ He became music director of the Los Angeles Philharmonic.

___2___ He started taking music lessons.

___4___ He became part of El Sistema.

**C** DISCUSSION  **Work with a partner. Compare your answers in B. Why did you choose each answer?**

## PAST PERFECT

*Had + Past Participle*

### Statements

| Subject | Had (not) | Past Participle | | |
|---------|-----------|-----------------|---|---|
| I<br>You<br>He<br>She<br>It<br>We<br>You<br>They | **had** (not) | **arrived** | in the U.S. | by then. |
| | | **become** | famous | |

### Contractions

| I had | = | **I'd** |
|-------|---|---------|
| you had | = | **you'd** |
| he had | = | **he'd** |
| she had | = | **she'd** |
| it had | = | **it'd** |
| we had | = | **we'd** |
| they had | = | **they'd** |
| had not | = | **hadn't** |

### Yes/No Questions

| Had | Subject | Past Participle | | |
|-----|---------|-----------------|---|---|
| **Had** | you<br>he<br>they | **arrived** | in the U.S. | by then? |
| | | **become** | famous | |

### Short Answers

| Affirmative | | | Negative | | |
|-------------|---|---|----------|---|---|
| **Yes,** | I<br>he<br>they | **had.** | **No,** | I<br>he<br>they | **hadn't.** |

### Wh- Questions

| Wh- Word | | Had | Subject | Past Participle | |
|----------|---|-----|---------|-----------------|---|
| How many | concerts | **had** | he | **given** | by then? |

## PAST PERFECT PROGRESSIVE

*Had + Been + ing*

### Statements

| Subject | Had (not) been | Base Form + -ing | |
|---------|----------------|------------------|---|
| I<br>You<br>He<br>She<br>It<br>We<br>You<br>They | **had (not) been** | **playing** | all over the world by then. |

## Yes/No Questions

| Had | Subject | Been + Base Form + -ing | |
|---|---|---|---|
| Had | you he they | **been playing** | the violin by then? |

## Short Answers

| Affirmative | | | Negative | | |
|---|---|---|---|---|---|
| Yes, | I he they | **had**. | No, | I he they | **hadn't**. |

## Wh- Questions

| Wh- Word | Had | Subject | Been + Base Form + -ing | |
|---|---|---|---|---|
| How long | **had** | he | **been playing** | classical music by then? |

# GRAMMAR NOTES

## 1 Past Perfect

Use the past perfect to show that something **happened before a specific time in the past.**

By 1986, Dudamel **had begun** violin lessons.
*(Dudamel began taking violin lessons before 1986.)*

With the past perfect, the focus is often on the **completion** of the action or situation.

**By 2010**, Kato **had conducted** Beethoven's Ninth Symphony for the first time.
*(The performance took place and ended before 2010.)*

## 2 Past Perfect Progressive

Use the past perfect progressive to show that something was **in progress before a specific time in the past.** The action or situation **may have continued** after that time. The focus is on the **continuation** of the action or situation, not the end result.

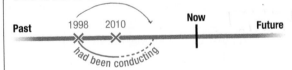

**By 2010**, Kato **had been conducting** an orchestra **for 12 years**.
*(She was still conducting in 2010, and possibly continued to conduct.)*

**USAGE NOTE** We also use the past perfect progressive for actions that had **just ended**. You can often still see the results of the action.

She was out of breath. It was clear that she **had been running**.
*(She was no longer running when I saw her.)*

**BE CAREFUL!** Do not use the past perfect progressive with most **non-action verbs**.

It was 2008. He **had been** a conductor for two years.
NOT He ~~had been being~~ a conductor for two years.

## 3 Past Perfect or Past Perfect Progressive + Simple Past

Use the past perfect or the past perfect progressive with the simple past to show the **time order between two past events.**

Use the **past perfect** or the **past perfect progressive** for the **earlier event**. Use the **simple past** for the **later time or event**.

He **had conducted** once when he **left** for Germany.
  *(He had conducted once before he left for Germany.)*

He **had been conducting** for years when he **left** for Germany.
  *(He was conducting before he left for Germany.)*

| | |
|---|---|
| **USAGE NOTE** We often mention **a period of time with the past perfect progressive** to show how long an event was in progress when another event occurred. We often use the **past progressive** when we **do not mention the length of time.** | He **had been studying** in El Sistema *for five years* when he received his first job as a conductor.<br><br>He **was studying** in El Sistema when he received his first job as a conductor. |
| **USAGE NOTE** When the **time relationship between two past events is clear** (for example, with *before, after, as soon as, until,* and *because*), we often use the **simple past for both events.** | *After* Dudamel **had joined** El Sistema, he **studied** the violin.<br>or<br>*After* Dudamel **joined** El Sistema, he **studied** the violin. |
| **BE CAREFUL!** In sentences with a time clause starting with *when*, notice t he difference in meaning between the **simple past** and the **past perfect** in the main clause. | *When* the concert ended, she **left**.<br>  *(First the concert ended. Then she left.)*<br>*When* the concert ended, she **had left**.<br>  *(First she left. Then the concert ended.)* |

## 4 Adverbs or Expressions with *By* to Show the Order of Events

| | |
|---|---|
| Use **adverbs** such as *already, yet, ever, never,* or *just* with the **past perfect** or **past perfect progressive** to emphasize the **first event.** | A: Jason and I watched Dudamel on YouTube last night. Jason **had *already*** seen him conduct.<br>B: **Had** you *ever* seen him before?<br>A: No, I hadn't. I **had *never*** heard of him. |
| **BE CAREFUL!** Do not put an adverb between the **main verb** and a **direct object.** | I hadn't **seen him *yet*.** or I hadn't ***yet* seen him.**<br>NOT I hadn't ~~seen yet him.~~ |

CONTINUED ▶

| | |
|---|---|
| Use **expressions with** *by* to refer to the **second event**. | |
| • *by* + time or event | ***By 2006***, Dudamel **had gotten** married.<br>***By the end of the concert***, they **had been applauding** enthusiastically for ten minutes. |
| • *by the time* (to introduce a **clause** in the **simple past**) | ***By the time he was fifteen***, he **had started** to conduct.<br>***By the time we got tickets***, we **had been waiting** in line for an hour. |
| IN WRITING   Use a **comma after the time clause or phrase** when it comes at the **beginning** of the sentence. Do not use a comma after the main clause when the main clause comes first. | ***By the time I sat down***, the concert had started.<br>NOT  The concert had started<sub>x</sub> by the time I sat down. |

## REFERENCE NOTES

For a list of **irregular past participles**, see Appendix 1 on page 453.
For **spelling rules for progressive forms**, see Appendix 23 on page 463.

## STEP 3   FOCUSED PRACTICE

## EXERCISE 1  DISCOVER THE GRAMMAR

GRAMMAR NOTES 1–4  Read each numbered situation. Decide if the description that follows is *True* (*T*) or *False* (*F*). If there is not enough information to know, write a question mark (*?*).

1. The talk-show host invited the musician on her show because he had won a competition.

   _F_  The musician won the competition after his appearance on the show.

2. When I arrived, the musician had been explaining why he had chosen to play the violin.

   _?_  The musician's explanation was finished.

3. It was 4:00 p.m. They had been selling tickets for an hour.

   _?_  They were still selling tickets at 4:05.

4. When I found my seat, the concert started.

   _F_  First the concert started. Then I found my seat.

5. When I found my seat, the concert had started.

   _T_  First the concert started. Then I found my seat.

6. When I saw Mei Ling, she was very enthusiastic. She had been rehearsing with Dudamel.

   _T_  She wasn't rehearsing when I saw her.

7. By the end of the concert, the audience had fallen in love with Dudamel.

   _F_  The audience fell in love with Dudamel after the concert.

# EXERCISE 2  PAST PERFECT STATEMENTS WITH *ALREADY* AND *YET*

GRAMMAR NOTES 1–4  Look at some important events in Gustavo Dudamel's career. Then complete the sentences. Use the past perfect with *already* or *not yet*.

| born in Venezuela | began violin lessons | started to study conducting | became conductor of youth orchestra | won prize; met Eloisa Maturen in Germany | got married in Caracas, Venezuela | moved to L.A. as musical director of L.A. Symphony |
|---|---|---|---|---|---|---|
| 1981 | 1985 | 1992 | 1999 | 2004 | 2006 | 2009 |

1. It was 1984. Dudamel *hadn't yet begun* _____ violin lessons.
2. By age six, he __had already begun__ violin lessons.
3. In 1991, he __hadn't yet started__ to study conducting.
4. By 2000, he __had already become__ the conductor of an orchestra.
5. Before age twenty-five, he __had already won__ a conducting prize.
6. It was 2003. He and Maturen __hadn't yet got (gotten)__ married.
7. It was 2010. He and Maturen __had already moved__ to L.A.

# EXERCISE 3  PAST PERFECT QUESTIONS AND SHORT ANSWERS

GRAMMAR NOTE 1  Carly plays cello in an orchestra. Read her diary notes. Then complete the questions about her day and give short answers. Use the past perfect.

DATE: Thursday, December 15, 2016

8:30    took yoga class at the gym

10:00   started rehearsing at the concert hall for Saturday's concert

12:30   ate lunch

2:30    had cello lesson with Sofia Gregor

4:00    gave cello demonstration at Performing Arts High School

6:00    shopped for dress for Saturday night's concert

7:30    did relaxation exercises

8:30    ordered takeout from favorite ethnic restaurant

11:00   fell asleep—forgot to eat!

1. It was 9:30 a.m. Carly was at the gym.

   A: _Had she taken_ _____ her yoga class yet?

   B: _Yes, she had._ _____

2. At 10:15, Carly was at the concert hall.

   A: _____ for Saturday's concert yet?

   B: _____

3. It was 1:30. Carly was in the practice room of the concert hall.

   A: _____ her lunch by that time?

   B: _____

4. At 2:15, Carly was talking to Sofia Gregor.

   A: _____ cello lesson yet?

   B: _____

5. It was 3:30.

   A: _____ her cello demonstration yet?

   B: _____

6. At 4:45, Carly was still at the high school.

   A: _____ for her dress by then?

   B: _____

7. It was 8:00 p.m. Carly was changing her clothes.

   A: _____ her relaxation exercises that day?

   B: _____

8. At 10:00 p.m., Carly was listening to a CD of her last performance.

   A: _____ takeout yet?

   B: _____

9. It was 11:00 p.m. Carly was sleeping.

   A: _____ her dinner yet?

   B: _____

# EXERCISE 4  PAST PERFECT PROGRESSIVE STATEMENTS

GRAMMAR NOTE 2  Gustavo Dudamel was a musical child prodigy. Complete the information about two other prodigies. Use the past perfect progressive form of the verbs in parentheses.

Judit Polgár

**JUDIT POLGÁR** is known as the strongest female chess player who has ever lived. In 1991, she became the youngest Grandmaster ever at age fifteen, which was not really very surprising because Polgar ___*had been playing*___ the
1. (play)
game since she was only five years old. For five years, she ___had been winning___ games
2. (win)
against older chess masters. By age twenty, Polgár was ranked the tenth best player in the world—the first woman to achieve a rating in the top 10. In 2002, she defeated Garry Kasparov, the highest rated player in the world. It was a great personal victory. She had lost to Kasparov in 1994, and she ___had been waiting___ to try again.
3. (wait)
In 2000, Polgár married Gusztav Font. Font, a veterinarian, ___had been treating___
4. (treat)
Polgár's dog when the two met. Between 2004 and 2007, the couple had two children, and Polgár competed less often. Because she ___hadn't been competing___ as much, her rank
5. (not compete)
dropped to twentieth, but by 2008, Polgár was playing for Hungary in the Chess Olympiad, her career back on track. Although she is now retired, Polgár is still the best of the best.

   **AKRIT JASWAL** has been called "the world's smartest boy" and "the Mozart of modern medicine." By the age of six, he ___had___ already ___been reading___.
6. (read)
Shakespeare in his native village in northern India. Even more amazing, young Jaswal ___had been studing___ medical textbooks on his own. He ___had___ even
7. (study)
___been observing___ surgeries at local hospitals. Then at age seven, he operated on
8. (observe)
a young girl whose hand had been severely injured in a fire. The operation, which he performed for free in his home, was a success, and Jaswal became famous. His family ___had been hoping___ that their son could start medical school when he was eight,
9. (hope)
but he had to wait three years before he enrolled at Punjab University—the youngest student ever admitted. Jaswal's dream is to someday find a cure for cancer.

# EXERCISE 5 PAST PERFECT PROGRESSIVE QUESTIONS

GRAMMAR NOTES 2–4  A talk-show host is making a list of questions for her research
about violinist Midori Goto. Use the words in parentheses to write questions with the past
perfect progressive. Use *when* to introduce the time clause with the simple past.

1. Midori Goto gave her first public performance in Osaka, Japan, at the age of six.

   *How long had she been playing violin when she gave her first public performance in Osaka, Japan, at the age of six?*
   (how long / she / play violin)

2. Ten-year-old Midori began classes at the Juilliard School in New York City.

   Where had been taking music lesson when she was ten years old
   (where / she / take music lessons)

3. Midori performed with the New York Philharmonic for the first time.

   _____
   (how long / she / study at Juilliard)

4. She made her first recording.

   _____
   (her fans / wait a long time)

5. She started the Midori & Friends program.

   _____
   (what / she / notice about children and music)

6. She became a United Nations Messenger of Peace.

   _____
   (how / she / help children around the world)

7. Young musicians were on stage with her for a concert in Tokyo.

   _____
   (how many hours a day / they / practice)

8. The concert started at 7:00 p.m.

   _____
   (reporters / take photos)

# EXERCISE 6 PAST PERFECT OR PAST PERFECT PROGRESSIVE

GRAMMAR NOTES 1–4 Complete this report on El Sistema. Use the past perfect or past perfect progressive form of the verbs in the boxes. Use the past perfect progressive when possible.

| come up | help | observe | ~~receive~~ | show up | teach | win |
|---------|------|---------|-------------|---------|-------|-----|

It was 1975. José Antonio Abreu _____*had received*_____ his degree in economics

1.

and _____ economics at Simón Bolívar University for years. As an

2.

economist, he _____ the poverty he saw around him. As a trained

3.

musician, he _____ with a creative solution—a music program for

4.

children. El Sistema began in a parking garage in 1975. Abreu remembers the first night of the

program. Only eleven children _____, but, Abreu says, he still felt it

5.

was the start of something very big. It was. By 2009, Abreu _____

6.

many prizes for his work, and he _____ hundreds of thousands of

7.

Venezuela's kids turn their lives around with music.

| arrest | be | go | hope | live | work |
|--------|-----|-----|------|------|------|

Gustavo Dudamel, a world-famous conductor, _____ one of

8.

those kids. He, in turn, established similar programs, such as Youth Orchestra Los Angeles.

Canadian singer Measha Brueggergosman participated in the program, and in October 2009

the kids attended Dudamel's concert at the Hollywood Bowl. They were wildly enthusiastic.

"A lot of the people . . . _____ never _____ to a classical music

9.

concert before. They were crying and screaming," she recalls. But Dudamel is only one of El

Sistema's success stories. Here are just two more out of thousands: At age nine, Edicson Ruiz

_____ at a Caracas supermarket to help support his family. El Sistema

10.

helped him put down the supermarket packages and pick up the bow.[1] He is now a successful

double bass player with the Berlin Philarmonie. And then there's Lennar Acosta. Before he got

his clarinet, Acosta _____ a life of crime. Police _____ already

11.

_____ the troubled youth nine times for robbery and drug use. But

12.

thanks to El Sistema, he traded in his gun for a musical instrument and became a clarinetist at

the Caracas Youth Orchestra. As Abreu said, "Music is a weapon against poverty." It is also a

way to change lives.

---

1 *bow*: a long thin piece of wood used for playing instruments such as the violin, cello, and double bass

# EXERCISE 7 TIME ORDER IN SENTENCES

GRAMMAR NOTES 1–4 Combine the pairs of sentences about Edson Natareno, a student in Youth Orchestra Los Angeles. Decide on the correct time order of the sentences. Use the past perfect or the past perfect progressive to express the event that occurred first. Use the past perfect progressive when possible.

1. A teacher heard Edson Natareno singing in her class. She talked to his mother about his musical talent.

   After *a teacher had heard Edson Natareno singing in her class*_____,
   *she talked to his mother about his musical talent*_____.

2. Edson joined Youth Orchestra Los Angeles in 2007. His mother encouraged him to join.

   _____

   because _____.

3. Edson listened to the sounds of other instruments. He finally decided to play the clarinet.

   _____

   before _____.

4. Edson played music for a year. His story appeared in a newspaper article.

   When _____,

   _____.

5. Edson performed with Youth Orchestra Los Angeles for six years. He traveled to London with the orchestra in 2013.

   By the time _____,

   _____.

6. Edson was able to begin classes at Colburn School. He won a scholarship to the world-famous performing arts school.

   _____

   after _____.

7. Edson graduated from high school. He already played in orchestras with Gustavo Dudamel three times.

   By the time _____,

   _____.

## EXERCISE 8 EDITING

GRAMMAR NOTES 1–4  Read this article about Canadian singer Measha Brueggergosman.
There are eight mistakes in the use of the past perfect and the past perfect progressive.
The first mistake is already corrected. Find and correct seven more.

# A Diva¹ with a Difference

MEASHA BRUEGGERGOSMAN'S first-grade teacher urged her parents to give her music

lessons. They did, and by age fifteen, she ~~had been deciding~~ *had decided* on a singing career. Not growing

up in a large cultural center, she didn't have the chance to attend concerts or the opera.

However, by the time she enrolled at the University of Toronto, she listening to classical music

on the radio for years, and she participated in her church's music program since childhood.

After she received her degree in Toronto, Brueggergosman had moved to Düsseldorf,

Germany, to study. By age twenty-five, she had been performing internationally for several

years and had won a number of important prizes. One enthusiastic judge said she had

never been meeting a singer with such perfect vocal control. By her

thirtieth birthday, Brueggergosman has become both a classical music

sensation² and a popular celebrity.

A diva with a Facebook fan club who had develop her own unique

fashion style, Brueggergosman's fame continued to grow. However,

when she experienced a serious health problem in June 2009,

Brueggergosman stopped performing. Amazingly, she

recovered in time to sing at the *¡Bienvenido Dudamel!*

concert four months later. When she stepped

onto the stage at the Hollywood Bowl and began

singing, the audience had fallen in love with her

again for her beautiful voice, her style, and her

bravery. Brava Brueggergosman!

---

1 *diva:* a very successful female opera singer
2 *sensation:* something or someone that causes a lot of excitement or interest

## EXERCISE 9 LISTENING

04|02 **A** A radio host is interviewing several musicians. Listen to the interview. Read the statements. Then listen again and check (✓) *True* or *False*.

|  | True | False |
|---|---|---|
| 1. Before Julio started music lessons, he'd wanted to play the trombone. | ☐ | ☑ |
| 2. By the time Marta and Julio got to Berlin, they had become friends. | ☐ | ☐ |
| 3. Marta and Julio got married six months after they joined the orchestra. | ☐ | ☐ |
| 4. Klaus had seen Dudamel conduct many times before the concert in Caracas. | ☐ | ☐ |
| 5. The Dudamel concert inspired Klaus to make a change in his life. | ☐ | ☐ |
| 6. Ling decided she wanted a violin before she turned ten. | ☐ | ☐ |
| 7. Ling and her sister started taking violin lessons in the same year. | ☐ | ☐ |
| 8. After Antonio started making music, he got into a lot of trouble. | ☐ | ☐ |

04|02 **B** Listen to the interview again. Then work with a partner. Discuss your answers in A. Why did you choose *True* or *False*?

EXAMPLE: A: So, the first statement is false.
 B: Right. Julio had been planning to study the flute, but his school gave him a trombone because there was no flute available.
 A: What did you choose for the second statement?

## EXERCISE 10 WHAT ABOUT YOU?

CONVERSATION **Work in a group. Think about a talent or skill that you have such as playing a musical instrument, drawing, playing basketball, dancing, or taking photos. Tell your group what your talent is and how you developed it. Answer questions from the group.**

EXAMPLE: A: I'm good at playing the piano. In fact, I won a piano competition when I was nine years old.
 B: How long had you been playing the piano by then?
 A: Five years.
 C: So you had started piano lessons when you were only four?

# EXERCISE 11 THINKING BACK

**A** CONVERSATION  Before you talk with a partner, think about what you did yesterday. Indicate whether it was or wasn't a busy day. Complete the sentences.

Yesterday was / wasn't a busy day for me.

**1.** By 9:00 a.m., _____.

**2.** By the time I got to work/school, _____.

**3.** By the time I had lunch, _____.

**4.** By the time I left work/school, _____.

**5.** By the time I had dinner, _____.

**6.** By 9:00 p.m., I _____.

**7.** By the time I went to bed, I had done so much/little that I felt _____.

**B**  Work with a partner. Compare your day with your partner's day.

EXAMPLE:  A:  By 9:00 a.m., I'd already been practicing the piano for two hours. What about you?

   B:  By 9:00 a.m., I hadn't even gotten up!

# EXERCISE 12 AMAZING CHILD PRODIGIES STORIES

**A**  GROUP PROJECT  Work in a group. Choose one of the people listed below, who were child prodigies. Do research about the person and answer some of the questions below.

- Nadia Comaneci, gymnast
- Amadeus Mozart, composer
- Clara Schumann, musician
- Stevie Wonder, musician
- Tiger Woods, golfer
- Sho Yano, physician

Sho Yano

**Possible questions:**
- When was the person born?
- What special skill(s) did the person have as a child?
- What had the person accomplished by the age of five? Ten? Fifteen?
- What is the most surprising fact that you learned about the person?

EXAMPLE:  A:  Sho Yano was a child prodigy.

   B:  He had already started composing music by the age of five.

   C:  And by the time he was ten, . . .

   D:  Here's something even more amazing. By his tenth birthday, . . .

**B**  Report back to your class. If your group chose the same person as another group, do you have the same information about that person? Compare answers.

EXAMPLE:  A:  Sho Yano is a physician and he was a child prodigy.

   B:  He's also a musician. By the age of five, he had learned how to play the piano.

   A:  And he had started composing music by the time he was five.

   B:  By his tenth birthday, . . .

# EXERCISE 13 NOW YOU SEE IT, NOW YOU DON'T

PICTURE COMPARISON  Work with a partner. Look at the two pictures. There are eleven differences in the pictures. Find and discuss them. Use *by* + past perfect in your discussion.

EXAMPLE:  A: At 4:00 p.m., the woman wasn't wearing a sweater. By 6:00 p.m., she had put her sweater on.

B: And the boy had fallen asleep.

# FROM GRAMMAR TO WRITING

**A** BEFORE YOU WRITE  Find information in the library or on the Internet about the life and career of a musician or singer that you like. Make a timeline using five events in the artist's life and career. Give details.

Events: _____  _____  _____  _____  _____

Years:  [ ]  [ ]  [ ]  [ ]  [ ]

**B** WRITE  Use your timeline to write two paragraphs about the artist you researched. In the first paragraph, include information about the person's career. In the second paragraph, write about the artist's personal life. Use the past perfect and the past perfect progressive. Try to avoid the common mistakes in the chart.

EXAMPLE:    Vanessa-Mae only uses her first name professionally. She was born in Singapore on October 27, 1978. By age five, she had been playing the piano for two years. By the time she was a teenager, she had already made three classical recordings. . . .

## Common Mistakes in Using the Past Perfect and Past Perfect Progressive

| | |
|---|---|
| Use **the past perfect or the past perfect progressive** to show that an event came **first**. Do not use the simple past. | I was late. By the time I arrived, the concert **had started**.<br>NOT By the time I arrived, the concert ~~started~~. |
| Use **the past perfect** with most **non-action verbs**. Do not use the past perfect progressive. | Before he left, he **had seemed** tired.<br>NOT Before he left, ~~had been seeming~~ tired. |
| Use a **comma after the time clause or phrase** when it comes at the **beginning** of the sentence. Do not use a comma after the main clause when the main clause comes first. | *By the end of the evening*, I had decided to attend another concert.<br>NOT I had decided to attend another concert, by the end of the evening. |

**C** CHECK YOUR WORK  Read your paragraphs. Underline once the verbs in the past perfect. Underline twice the verbs in the past perfect progressive. Circle the verbs in the simple past. Use the Editing Checklist to check your work.

## Editing Checklist

**Did you use . . . ?**

☐ the past perfect for things that happened before a specific time in the past

☐ the past perfect progressive for things that were in progress before a specific time in the past

☐ time clauses to show the time order between two past events

☐ adverbs or expressions with *by* to show the order of events

☐ commas after time clauses or phrases at the beginning of a sentence

**D** REVISE YOUR WORK  Read your paragraphs again. Can you improve your writing? Make changes if necessary. Give your paragraphs a title.

# UNIT 4 REVIEW

**Test yourself on the grammar of the unit.**

**A** Circle the correct words to complete the sentences.

1. By the time I was ten, I got / had gotten my first violin.

2. It was 2007. I have been studying / had been studying the violin for two years by then.

3. By 2010, I had graduated / had been graduating from Juilliard School of Music.

4. After I finished school, I moved / had been moving to Los Angeles.

5. I had given / hadn't given a concert yet.

**B** Complete the interview with the simple past, past perfect, or past perfect progressive form of the verbs in parentheses. Use the past perfect progressive when possible.

A: You're only twenty-five. How long _____ you _____ the
  **1.** (play)

  violin when you _____ the Philharmonic Orchestra?
              **2.** (join)

B: Ten years. By the time I was thirteen, I _____ to become a
                                **3.** (decide)

  professional, and I _____ for three hours a day. My father was a
                  **4.** (practice)

  musician, and he _____ me to play the piano, too.
                **5.** (teach)

A: _____ you _____ to this country yet?
              **6.** (come)

B: Yes. We _____ already _____ here. We
                          **7.** (move)

  _____ here for a year.
        **8.** (live)

A: Well, congratulations on winning the grand prize. Were you surprised?

B: Very! I _____ it, so I was very excited.
        **9.** (not expect)

**C** Find and correct six mistakes.

When five-year-old Sarah Chang enrolled in the Juilliard School, she has already been

playing the violin for more than a year. Her parents, both musicians, had been moving from

Korea to further their careers. They had gave their daughter a violin as a fourth birthday

present, and Sarah had been practiced hard since then. By seven, she already performed

with several local orchestras. A child prodigy, Sarah became the youngest person to receive

the Hollywood Bowl's Hall of Fame Award. She had already been receiving several awards

including the Nan Pa Award—South Korea's highest prize for musical talent.

**Now check your answers on page 475.**

# Future: Review and Expansion

## PART 2

**OUTCOMES**

- Discuss future facts, predictions, plans, and scheduled events
- Describe events that will be in progress at a specific time in the future
- Identify key details in a reading or recording
- Discuss schedules and make plans
- Discuss life in the future
- Write about how one's school will be in the future

**OUTCOMES**

- Describe events that will happen, or will be in progress, before a specific time in the future
- Show the order of two future events, using adverbs and expressions with *by*
- Identify specific information in a business article and a conversation
- Discuss future goals and aspirations
- Write about a classmate's future goals

MY GOALS

# Future and Future Progressive

## LIFE IN THE FUTURE

**OUTCOMES**
- Discuss future facts, predictions, plans, and scheduled events
- Describe events that will be in progress at a specific time in the future
- Identify key details in a reading or recording
- Discuss schedules and make plans
- Discuss life in the future
- Write about how one's school will be in the future

---

| STEP 1 | **GRAMMAR IN CONTEXT** |

## BEFORE YOU READ

Look at the picture and at the section titles in the article. Discuss the questions.

1. How will the cities of the future look?

2. What kinds of problems do you think people will face in the future?

3. How do you think they can solve them?

## READ

▶ 05|01  Read this article about the future.

# Cities of the Future

The world's population is exploding. By 2050, futurists[1] predict that 10 billion people will be living on the planet, up to 70 percent of them in cities. At the same time, the oceans are rising as global warming melts the ice at the North and South Poles. This means that while the population is growing, land will be shrinking. In addition, there is not going to be enough fresh water or oil and other types of fuel. Where will people live when room on dry land gets too crowded? How will 10 billion people feed themselves and travel from place to place? We're going to need a lot of innovative solutions. Fortunately, some very creative individuals are already thinking about them. Here's what they are predicting:

## Homes: Water World

Some futurists believe that as rising oceans cover the land, the oceans themselves are going to become valuable real estate.[2] Architects and engineers will be building floating cities that will use

---

1 *futurists:* people who predict future events and developments
2 *real estate:* land and houses that people buy and sell

solar, wind, and wave power.[3] Some cities will even be traveling long distances and using their large gardens to supply food. Science fiction? Maybe not. Some of the technology is already being used in underwater hotels and laboratories.

## Food: The Sky's the Limit

According to the United Nations Food and Agriculture Organization, the world is going to need 70 percent more food by 2050. This will require additional farmland equal to the size of Brazil. Where will we find it? Dr. Dickson Despommier, of Columbia University, says urban farmers will be growing food on vertical farms, and that "sky farms" in New York will produce enough chicken, vegetables, and fruit to feed the entire city. Instead of fuel-guzzling[4] farm machines, farmers will be using robots for difficult and dangerous work. The farms will also save energy because food won't be traveling into the city by truck from distant farms.

## Travel: Back to the Future?

More than eighty years ago, luxurious airships—large "balloons" filled with helium[5]—carried passengers around Europe and across the Atlantic. However, after one terrible accident, travelers stopped using them. Now, with fuel becoming more expensive, airships are coming back. A Spanish company is developing a solar-powered airship that will fly on sunshine during the day and use fuel only at night. Commuters will be taking airships to work, and the company predicts many other uses for the vehicles. For example, disaster relief organizations, such as the Red Cross and Red Crescent Societies, will be using them as flying hospitals to help earthquake and storm victims.

The future is coming, with all its opportunities and challenges. Will we be ready? With enough imagination and hard work, we will be!

3 *solar, wind, and wave power:* energy from the sun, wind, and ocean waves
4 *fuel-guzzling:* using too much fuel. *Guzzle* means "to drink large amounts of something."
5 *helium:* a gas that is lighter than air, often used to make balloons and airships float in the air

# AFTER YOU READ

**A** VOCABULARY  **Choose the word or phrase that best completes each sentence.**

1. An **innovative** plan is _____.
   a. new               b. old                     c. easy

2. Creative **individuals** are _____ that find solutions to problems.
   a. methods           b. people                  c. machines

3. **Technology** is the _____ we use to do things.
   a. money and skills  b. machines and knowledge  c. people and animals

4. A _____ is not usually **vertical**.
   a. tall building     b. tree                    c. table

5. A(n) _____ is an example of a **vehicle**.
   a. accident          b. car                     c. hospital

6. A **challenge** is a task that is _____.
   a. new and difficult b. easy and safe           c. in the distant future

**B** COMPREHENSION  **Read the statements. Check (✓) *True* or *False*.**

| | True | False |
|---|---|---|
| 1. The world's population is already growing fast. | ☐ | ☐ |
| 2. People are already living on floating cities. | ☐ | ☐ |
| 3. Tourists are already staying in underwater hotels. | ☐ | ☐ |
| 4. Sky farms are already using robots as workers. | ☐ | ☐ |
| 5. A company is already building a solar-powered airship. | ☐ | ☐ |
| 6. Commuters are already riding to work in airships. | ☐ | ☐ |

**C** DISCUSSION  **Work with a partner. Compare your answers in B. Why did you check** *True* or *False*?

## FUTURE

### Affirmative Statements

| | |
|---|---|
| We **are going to take** | |
| We **will take** | the airship at 9:00. |
| We **are taking** | |
| We **take** | |

### Negative Statements

| | |
|---|---|
| We **are not going to take** | |
| We **will not take** | the airship at 10:00. |
| We **are not taking** | |
| We **don't take** | |

### Yes/No Questions

| | |
|---|---|
| **Is** she **going to take** | |
| **Will** she **take** | the airship at 9:00? |
| **Is** she **taking** | |
| **Does** she **take** | |

### Short Answers

| Affirmative | | | Negative | | |
|---|---|---|---|---|---|
| Yes, | she **is**. | | No, | she **isn't**. | |
| | she **will**. | | | she **won't**. | |
| | she **is**. | | | she **isn't**. | |
| | she **does**. | | | she **doesn't**. | |

### Wh- Questions

| | |
|---|---|
| When **is** she **going to take** | |
| When **will** she **take** | the airship? |
| When **is** she **taking** | |
| When **does** she **take** | |

## FUTURE PROGRESSIVE

### Statements

| Subject | Be (not) going to / Will (not) | Be + Base Form + -ing | |
|---|---|---|---|
| People | **are (not) going to** **will (not)** | **be traveling** | to Mars by 2050. |

### Yes/No Questions

| Be/Will | Subject | Going to | Be + Base Form + -ing | |
|---|---|---|---|---|
| **Are** | they | **going to** | **be traveling** | to Mars? |
| **Will** | | | | |

### Short Answers

| Affirmative | | Negative | |
|---|---|---|---|
| Yes, | they **are**. | No, | they**'re not**. |
| | they **will**. | | they **won't**. |

### Wh- Questions

| Wh- Word | Be/Will | Subject | Going to | Be + Base Form + -ing | |
|---|---|---|---|---|---|
| When | **are** | they | **going to** | **be traveling** | to Mars? |
| | **will** | | | | |

# GRAMMAR NOTES

## 1 Referring to Future Events

There are **several ways to refer to future events**. Sometimes only one form of the future is appropriate, but in many cases more than one form is possible.

| | |
|---|---|
| • *be going to* | I'**m going to take** the airship tomorrow. |
| • *will* | It'**ll be** a nice trip. |
| • present progressive | It'**s leaving** from Barcelona. |
| • simple present | It **takes off** at 9:00 a.m. |

Past     **Now**     take     **Future**

tomorrow

## 2 Future Facts

For facts or events that you are **certain will happen in the future**, you can use *be going to* or *will*.

| | |
|---|---|
| • *be going to* | The sun **is going to rise** at 6:43 tomorrow. |
| • *will* | The sun **will rise** at 6:43 tomorrow. |

## 3 Predictions

For predictions about things you are **quite sure will happen in the future**, you can also use *be going to* or *will*.

| | |
|---|---|
| • *be going to* | I think people **are going to use** robots for a lot of tasks. |
| • *will* | I think people **will use** robots for a lot of tasks. |

| | |
|---|---|
| USAGE NOTE   We often use *I think* before a prediction. | *I think* almost everyone **is going to have** a robot. |
| IN WRITING   We use *will* more in **formal writing** and *be going to* more in **conversation**. | Prices **will increase** next month. *(formal writing)* <br> Prices **are going to increase** next month. *(conversation)* |
| BE CAREFUL!   Use *be going to* when something that you **notice right now** makes you almost certain an event is going to happen. Do not use *will*. | Look! That robot **is going to serve** our coffee! <br> NOT Look! That robot ~~will serve~~ . . . |

## 4 Future Plans

For plans or things that are **already decided**, use *be going to* or the **present progressive**.

| | |
|---|---|
| • *be going to* | **I'm going to fly** to Tokyo next week. |
| • **present progressive** | **I'm flying** to Tokyo next week. |

| | |
|---|---|
| **USAGE NOTE** We often use the **present progressive** for plans that are **already arranged**. | **I'm flying** to Tokyo next week. I already have a ticket. |

| | |
|---|---|
| **USAGE NOTE** When the main verb is *go*, it is much more common to use the **present progressive** (*be going*) than *be going to go*. | He**'s going** home at 2:30. *(more common)* <br> He**'s going to go** home at 2:30. *(less common)* |

## 5 Quick Decisions, Offers, and Promises

For decisions that you make quickly while you are speaking, or to make offers or promises, use *will*.

| | |
|---|---|
| • **quick decision** <br><br> • **offer** <br> • **promise** | A: The Robot Show opens next week. <br> B: Sounds interesting. I think I**'ll go**. <br> A: I'd like to go, too, but I don't have a ride. <br> B: I**'ll drive** you, but I'd like to leave by 7:00. <br> A: No problem. I**'ll be** ready. |

| | |
|---|---|
| **USAGE NOTE** *Shall* is not common in American English except for **offers** and **suggestions**. | **Shall** I pick you up at 8:00? *(offer)* <br> **Shall** we take the bus? *(suggestion)* |

## 6 Future Scheduled Events

For scheduled events such as **timetables**, **programs**, and **schedules**, you can use the **simple present**.

| | |
|---|---|
| • **simple present** | The airship **leaves** at 9:00 a.m. |

| | |
|---|---|
| **USAGE NOTE** We often use the simple present with verbs such as *begin*, *start*, *leave*, *arrive*, *last*, and *end* to show scheduled events. | The conference **starts** tomorrow morning. <br> It **lasts** three days. <br> My final meeting of the day **ends** at 5:00 p.m. |

| | |
|---|---|
| **USAGE NOTE** We can also use *be going to* and *will* for scheduled future events. | My final meeting **is going to end** at 5:00 p.m. <br> My final meeting **will end** at 5:00 p.m. |

## 7 Future Progressive

Use the **future progressive** with *be going to* or *will* to show that an action will be in progress at a specific time in the future.

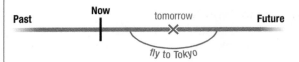

At this time tomorrow, I**'m going to be flying** to Tokyo.
At this time tomorrow, I**'ll be flying** to Tokyo.

**USAGE NOTE** We often use the **future progressive** instead of the future to make a question about someone's plans **more polite**.

When **are** you **going to hand in** your paper, Ana?
When **will** you **be grading** our tests, Professor Lee?
  *(more polite)*

**USAGE NOTE** We also use the **future progressive** to ask about future plans in order to request a favor. This makes the request **more polite**.

**Will** you **be going** by the post office tomorrow? I need some stamps.

## 8 Future Time Clauses

Use **the simple present** or **the present progressive** in **future time clauses**.

In sentences with a **future time clause**, use:

- **future** or **future progressive** in **main clause**

MAIN CLAUSE        TIME CLAUSE
I**'ll call** you when the robot finishes the laundry.
I**'ll be enjoying** dinner while he is dusting.

- **present** or **present progressive** in **time clause**

MAIN CLAUSE        TIME CLAUSE
I'll call you when the robot **finishes** the laundry.
I'll be enjoying dinner while he **is dusting**.

**BE CAREFUL!** Do not use the future or the future progressive in the time clause.

NOT I'll call you when the robot ~~will finish~~ the laundry.
NOT I'll be enjoying dinner while he ~~is going to be~~ dusting.

**IN WRITING** Use a **comma after the time clause or phrase** when it comes at the **beginning** of the sentence. Do not use a comma after the main clause when the main clause comes first.

***When the price drops***, more people will buy robots.
NOT More people will buy robots，when the price drops.

## EXERCISE 1   DISCOVER THE GRAMMAR

**A** GRAMMAR NOTES 1–7   Reporter Will Hapin just met his friend Dr. Nouvella Eon at a technology conference. Read their conversation and underline all the verbs that refer to the future.

HAPIN:   Nouvella! It's nice to see you. <u>Are you presenting</u> a paper today?

EON:   Hi, Will! Yes. In fact, <u>my talk starts</u> at two o'clock.

HAPIN:   Oh, I think <u>I'll go</u>. What do you plan to talk about? <u>Will you be discussing robots</u>?

EON:   Yes. <u>I'm focusing</u> on personal robots for household work. My talk is called "Creative Uses of Home Robots."

HAPIN:   *I want one of those! But seriously, you promised me an interview on personal robots.* <u>Will you be getting</u> some free time in the next few weeks?

EON:   I'm not sure. <u>I'll call</u> you after the conference, OK?

HAPIN:   Great! Where's your son, by the way? Is he with you?

EON:   No. Rocky stays in Denver with his grandparents in the summer. <u>I'm going to visit</u> him right after the conference. <u>He'll be ten years</u> old in a few days. I can't believe it!

HAPIN:   It's his birthday, huh? Here, take this little model of the flying car for him.

EON:   Oh, <u>he's going to love</u> this! Thanks, Will. So what are you working on these days?

HAPIN:   Well, *Futurist Magazine* just published my article on cities of the future. And next month at their convention, <u>I'm interviewing</u> members of the World Future Association about flying cars.

EON   <u>That'll be</u> exciting! Good luck!

**B** Read the conversation again. Complete the chart. List the twelve future verb forms in Part A. Then check (✓) the correct column for each form.

| | Facts | Predictions | Plans | Quick Decisions | Promises | Schedules |
|---|---|---|---|---|---|---|
| 1. Are you presenting | | | ✓ | | | |
| 2. My talk starts. | | | | | | ✓ |
| 3. Will you be discussing | | | ✓ | | | |
| 4. I'm focusing | | | ✓ | | | |
| 5. Will you be getting | | | ✓ | | | |
| 6. I'll call. | | | | | ✓ | |
| 7. I'm going to visit. | | | ✓ | | | |
| 8. He'll be | ✓ | | | | | |
| 9. He's going to love. | | ✓ | | | | |
| 10. I'll go | | | | ✓ | | |
| 11. I'm interviewing. | | | ✓ | | | |
| 12. That'll be exciting. | | ✗ | | | | |

## EXERCISE 2 FORMS OF THE FUTURE

**A** GRAMMAR NOTES 1–6 Circle the correct words to complete these conversations.

1. EON: Which projects do you report / (are you going to report) on?

   HAPIN: I haven't decided for sure. Probably flying cars.

2. HAPIN: Look at those dark clouds!

   EON: Yes. It looks like it's raining / it's going to rain any minute.

3. EON: I'd better get back to my hotel room before it starts to rain. Call me, OK?

   HAPIN: OK. I'm talking / I'll talk to you later.

4. DESK: Dr. Eon, your son just called.

   EON: Oh, good. I think I'll call / I'm calling him back right away.

5. EON: Hi, honey. How's it going?

   ROCKY: Great. And guess what? I go / I'm going fishing with Grandpa tomorrow.

6. EON: Have fun, but don't forget you still have to finish that paper.

   ROCKY: I know, Mom. I send / I'm sending it to my teacher tomorrow. I already discussed it with her.

7. ROCKY: How's the conference?

   EON: Good. I'm giving / I'll give my talk this afternoon.

**8.** ROCKY: Good luck. When <u>are you / will you</u> be here?

     EON:     Tomorrow. The airship <u>lands / will land</u> at 7:00, so <u>I see / I'll see you</u> about 8:00.

**9.** ROCKY: Great! <u>Are we going / Do we go</u> to the car show on my birthday?

     EON:     Sure! Oh, I saw Will Hapin, and he gave me something for you. I think

                <u>you like / you're going to like</u> it.

05|02 **B** LISTEN AND CHECK **Listen to the conversations and check your answers in A.**

## EXERCISE 3 FUTURE PROGRESSIVE

**A** GRAMMAR NOTE 7 **Will Hapin is interviewing Nouvella Eon. Complete the interview. Use the future progressive form of the words in parentheses and short answers.**

HAPIN: I noticed that you've been presenting a lot of papers recently. _____*Will*_____ you

        _____*be going*_____ to the robotics conference in Tokyo next month?
          **1.** (will / go)

EON:   _____*Yes, I will*_____. But I _____. The Japanese are doing very
        **2.**                **3.** (won't present)

     innovative things with personal robotics, and I _____ every
                                **4.** (be going to / attend)

     lecture possible.

HAPIN: What _____ their new robots _____ for us?
                          **5.** (be going to / do)

EON:   A lot! Oh, personal robots _____ still _____ the elderly
                           **6.** (be going to / help)

     and individuals with disabilities. But the new 'bots _____ our
                            **7.** (will / improve)

     lives in a lot of other ways, too. They _____ complicated
                     **8.** (will / cook)

     recipes. They _____ music and many other creative tasks. So
             **9.** (will / perform)

     _____ you _____ one for your family, Will?
             **10.** (be going to / buy)

HAPIN: _____. They look too much like machines to me. _____ their appearance
      **11.**

     _____?
     **12.** (be going to / change)

EON:   _____—and very soon. Companies are starting to meet that challenge now. In
      **13.**

     just a couple of years, they _____ 'bots that look exactly like
                      **14.** (will / sell)

     humans—and show human emotions.

HAPIN: Amazing! Well, thanks for the interview, Nouvella. Oh! Look at the time. This afternoon, I

     _____ a test drive in the new flying car. You should see it. The
         **15.** (be going to / take)

     technology is really amazing. Why don't you come with me?

05|03 **B** LISTEN AND CHECK **Listen to the interview and check your answers in A.**

Future and Future Progressive    **77**

## EXERCISE 4 FUTURE PROGRESSIVE AFFIRMATIVE AND NEGATIVE STATEMENTS

GRAMMAR NOTE 7 Dr. Eon's family uses a robot for household chores. Look at Botley the Robot's schedule for tomorrow. Write sentences using the words in parentheses and the future progressive.

| TOMORROW | |
|---|---|
| **8:00** | make breakfast |
| **9:00** | vacuum |
| **10:00** | dust |
| **11:00** | shop for food |
| **12:00** | do laundry |
| **12:30** | make lunch |
| **1:00** | recycle the garbage |
| **2:00** | pay bills |
| **3:00** | give Dr. Eon a massage |
| **5:00** | make dinner |
| **6:00** | play soccer with Rocky |

1. _At 8:05, Botley won't be vacuuming. He'll be making breakfast._
   (8:05 / vacuum)

2. _At 9:05, he'll be vacuuming._
   (9:05 / vacuum)

3. At 10:05, He'll be dusting.
   (10:05 / dust)

4. At 11:05. He won't be doing laundry. He'll be shopping for food.
   (11:05 / do laundry)

5. At 12:05 He won't be shopping for food. He'll be doing laundry
   (12:05 / shop for food)

6. At 1:05 He'll be recycling the garbage
   (1:05 / recycle the garbage)

7. At 2:05 He won't be giving Dr. Eon a message. He'll be paying bills
   (2:05 / give Dr. Eon a massage)

8. At 3:05 He'll be giving Dr Eon a Message.
   (3:05 / give Dr. Eon a massage)

9. At 5:05 He'll be making dinner.
   (5:05 / make dinner)

10. At 6:05 He wont be playin card with Rocky. He'll be playing soccer with Rocky
   (6:05 / play cards with Rocky)

## EXERCISE 5 FUTURE PROGRESSIVE STATEMENTS AND TIME CLAUSES

GRAMMAR NOTES 7–8 Complete the ad for a getaway[1] in space with the verbs in parentheses. In sentences with time clauses, use the future progressive in the main clause. Use the simple present or the present progressive in the time clause.

**Need a break?** Call today and in just a few days, you _____'ll be traveling_____

1. (travel)

skyward for a week at Starburst Suites Hotel. No rockets necessary—our comfortable

modern elevator _____ you quietly into space while

2. (lift)

everyone else _____ stuck in the crowds and noise back

3. (be)

on Earth. While you _____ a meal on this luxurious

4. (enjoy)

vehicle, a friendly flight robot _____ amazing views of

5. (point out)

our planet from space. And before you _____ it, you

6. (know)

_____ to check into your hotel for a week of "fun

7. (get ready)

near the Sun." After you _____ your spacesuit, you

8. (unpack)

_____ the other guests for a tour. Do you love sunsets?

9. (join)

You're in luck! You _____ sixteen of them every day from

10. (watch)

the hotel's huge windows. Do you prefer adventure? Picture this! While other guests

_____ in the spa, you _____

11. (relax)                                         12. (put on)

your spacesuit for a walk under the stars.

So call for a reservation. Once aboard, we guarantee it—

you _____ about anything

13. (not think)

except returning again and again and again. . . .

**STARBURST SUITES HOTEL**

---

1 *getaway:* a short vacation trip

## EXERCISE 6 EDITING

GRAMMAR NOTES 1–8 **Read this article about cars of the future. There are ten mistakes in the use of the future and the future progressive. The first mistake is already corrected. Find and correct nine more.**

# Flying Cars

YOUR CLASS starts in ten minutes, but you're stuck in traffic. Don't panic. With just a press of a button, your car will ~~lifts~~ *lift* off the ground, and you'll be on your way to school. No bad roads, no stop signs, no worries! It seems like science fiction, but it isn't. Experts predict that we'll all be use these amazing vehicles one day.

According to *Car Trends Magazine*, one model, part car and part plane, is going be on the market in the not-so-distant future. It will look like a regular car when it's on the road, but its wings will unfold when the driver will decide to take to the skies. It will runs on the same fuel for both land and air travel, and you'll be able to keep it in your garage. (But you're still going need an airport to take off and land.)

A better model will be a vertical takeoff and landing vehicle (VTOL). You won't need to go to the airport anymore, and all controls will being automatic. Imagine this: You'll be doing your homework while your car will be getting you to school safely and on time.

And what does this future dream car cost? Well, fasten your seatbelts—the price will going to be sky-high. At first, it will be about a million dollars, but after a few years, you'll be able to buy one for "only" $60,000. Don't sell your old vehicle just yet!

## EXERCISE 7
## LISTENING

▶ 05|04  **A** Four members of the Mars Association are trying to organize a conference on Venus. Listen to their conversation. Then listen again and mark the chart with an *X* for the times each member cannot meet. Then figure out when everyone will be available.

When they're all available:

_____

| WEEKS | JULY |  |  |  | AUGUST |  |  |  |
|---|---|---|---|---|---|---|---|---|
|  | 1 | 2 | 3 | 4 | 1 | 2 | 3 | 4 |
| Skyler |  |  |  |  |  |  | X | X |
| Jarek |  |  |  |  |  |  |  |  |
| Lorna |  |  |  |  |  |  |  |  |
| Zindra |  |  |  |  |  |  |  |  |

X = not available

▶ 05|04  **B** Listen to the conversation again. Then work with a partner. Discuss your answers in A. Explain how you decided when everyone is available.

EXAMPLE:  **A:** When do you think they'll all be available?
          **B:** Well, Skyler is going to be taking a vacation the last two weeks . . .
          **A:** That's right. And Jarek won't . . .

## EXERCISE 8  LET ME CHECK MY CALENDAR

**A** REACHING AGREEMENT  You're going to try to make plans with a partner to do an activity together next week. First, complete your schedule for next week. If you have no plans, write *free*.

|  | Monday | Tuesday | Wednesday | Thursday | Friday |
|---|---|---|---|---|---|
| 9:00 |  |  |  |  |  |
| 11:00 |  |  |  |  |  |
| 1:00 |  |  |  |  |  |
| 3:00 |  |  |  |  |  |
| 5:00 |  |  |  |  |  |
| 7:00 |  |  |  |  |  |

**B** Work with a partner. Without showing each other your schedules, find a time to get together. Then make plans.

EXAMPLE: A: What are you doing on Tuesday morning?
B: I'm going to see the Robot Show at the Science Museum.
A: I'll go with you. I'll be free at 11:00.
B: Great. The coffee shop opens at 10:00. Shall we meet for coffee first?

## EXERCISE 9 HOW MUCH IS TOO MUCH?

**A** DISCUSSION  Before you discuss the work of robots, look at the list of activities. Check (✓) the ones you think robots *Will Be Doing* or *Won't Be Doing* for humans in the near future.

| Robots | Will Be Doing | Won't Be Doing |
|---|:---:|:---:|
| • answer the phone | ☐ | ☐ |
| • drive cars | ☐ | ☐ |
| • find information on the Internet | ☐ | ☐ |
| • go shopping | ☐ | ☐ |
| • guide vacation tours | ☐ | ☐ |
| • have a conversation | ☐ | ☐ |
| • invent new technology | ☐ | ☐ |
| • make dinner | ☐ | ☐ |
| • paint pictures | ☐ | ☐ |
| • plant gardens | ☐ | ☐ |
| • play musical instruments | ☐ | ☐ |
| • report the news | ☐ | ☐ |
| • take a vacation | ☐ | ☐ |
| • take care of children | ☐ | ☐ |
| • teach English | ☐ | ☐ |
| • teach themselves new skills | ☐ | ☐ |
| • write letters | ☐ | ☐ |
| • write laws | ☐ | ☐ |

**B** Work in a group. Share and explain your opinions about what robots will be doing for humans. Do you think robots will be doing too much for humans? Why?

EXAMPLE: A: I don't think robots will be teaching English, but they'll be taking care of children. Children will think they're fun—like big toys.
B: I think it's a bad idea to have robots take care of children. Children need human contact to help them develop emotional security.
C: Do you think robots will be driving cars?

# EXERCISE 10  DR. EON'S CALENDAR

**A** INFORMATION GAP  Work with a partner. Student A will follow the instructions below. Student B will follow the instructions on page 485.

---

**STUDENT A**

- Complete Dr. Eon's calendar. Get information from Student B. Ask questions and fill in the calendar. Answer Student B's questions.

    EXAMPLE:  **A:** What will Dr. Eon be doing on Sunday the first?
    **B:** She'll be flying to Tokyo. What about on the second? Will she be taking the day off?
    **A:** No, she'll be meeting with Dr. Kato.

## FEBRUARY 2077

| SUNDAY | MONDAY | TUESDAY | WEDNESDAY | THURSDAY | FRIDAY | SATURDAY |
|---|---|---|---|---|---|---|
| 1<br>fly to Tokyo | 2<br>meet with Dr. Kato | 3 | 4 ⟶ | 5 | 6 | 7 → |
| 8<br>take Bullet Train to Osaka | 9<br>sightseeing | 10 ⟶ | 11 → | 12 | 13 | 14 ⟶→ |
| 15<br>fly home | 16 | 17 | 18<br>attend energy seminar ⟶ | 19 | 20 → | 21<br>shop with Rocky and Botley |
| 22 | 23 | 24 ⟶ | 25 | 26 | 27 → | 28<br>take shuttle to Mars |

**B** Now compare calendars with your partner. Are they the same?

**A** BEFORE YOU WRITE  Think about changes that will happen at your school in the future. Make a list of ways that your school will be different twenty-five years from now. Complete the outline.

**Changes in the Classrooms, Library, etc.**          **Changes in the Teachers and Students**

_____          _____

_____          _____

_____          _____

**B** WRITE  Use your outline to write two paragraphs about your school twenty-five years from now. Describe what the school will look like and what both teachers and students will be doing. Use different forms of the future. Try to avoid the common mistakes in the chart.

EXAMPLE:  Twenty-five years from now, our school will be very different. First, the classrooms are going to be . . .

### Common Mistakes in Using the Future and Future Progressive

| | |
|---|---|
| Use the **present** or the **present progressive** in **future time clauses**. Do not use the future or the future progressive. | You'll be surprised when you **enter** a classroom of the future.<br>NOT You'll be surprised when you ~~will enter~~ a classroom of the future. |
| Use a **comma after the time clause or phrase** when it comes at the **beginning of the sentence**. Do not use a comma after the main clause when the main clause comes first. | **_When I return for a visit_**, I'll see many changes.<br>NOT I'll see many changes<sub>x</sub> when I return for a visit. |

**C** CHECK YOUR WORK  Read your paragraphs. Underline once the verbs in the future. Underline twice the verbs in the future progressive. Circle the verbs in the future time clauses. Use the Editing Checklist to check your work.

### Editing Checklist

**Did you use . . . ?**

☐ *be going to* or *will* for facts and predictions

☐ the future progressive for actions that will be in progress at a specific time in the future

☐ the simple present or the present progressive in future time clauses

☐ commas after time clauses at the beginning of a sentence

**D** REVISE YOUR WORK  Read your paragraphs again. Can you improve your writing? Make changes if necessary. Give your paragraphs a title.

# UNIT 5 REVIEW

**Test yourself on the grammar of the unit.**

**A** Circle the correct words to complete the sentences.

1. Our daughter will <u>turns / turn</u> fifteen next week.

2. <u>Are / Do</u> you going to school today?

3. What will you be <u>doing / do</u> at 3:00 this afternoon?

4. The sun <u>will / is</u> going to rise at 6:22 tomorrow morning.

5. Be careful! Your coffee <u>will / is</u> going to spill!

6. While <u>you're / you'll</u> be driving to work tomorrow, we'll be flying to Beijing.

7. Roboid will let us know when he <u>will finish / finishes</u> cooking dinner.

**B** Complete the conversation with the future or future progressive form of the verbs in parentheses or with a short answer. Use the future progressive when possible.

A: What _____ you _____ at 10:00 tomorrow morning?
<br>**1.** (do)

B: Ten o'clock? Well, let's see. I _____ for the airport at 8:30, so at
<br>**2.** (leave)

   10:00, I _____ probably _____ through airport security.
<br>**3.** (go)

A: So I guess you _____ to the office at all tomorrow.
<br>**4.** (not come)

B: Doesn't look like it. Why? _____ that _____ a problem?
<br>**5.** (cause)

A: _____, it _____. It _____ fine. Have a
<br>**6.**            **7.** (be)

   good trip.

B: Thanks. I _____ you in a couple of weeks.
<br>**8.** (see)

**C** Find and correct five mistakes.

A: How long are you going to staying in Beijing?

B: I'm not sure. I'll let you know as soon as I'll find out. OK?

A: OK. It's going to be a long flight. What will you doing to pass the time?

B: I'll be work a lot of the time. And I'm going to try to sleep.

A: Good idea. Have fun, and I'm emailing you all the office news. I promise.

**Now check your answers on page 476.**

# Future Perfect and Future Perfect Progressive
## GOALS

**OUTCOMES**
- Describe events that will happen, or will be in progress, before a specific time in the future
- Show the order of two future events, using adverbs and expressions with *by*
- Identify specific information in a business article and a conversation
- Discuss future goals and aspirations
- Write about a classmate's future goals

## STEP 1    GRAMMAR IN CONTEXT

### BEFORE YOU READ

Read the definition of *entrepreneur* and look at the photo. Discuss the questions.

1. How are entrepreneurs different from other business people?

2. Who are some famous entrepreneurs?

> **en•tre•pre•neur** /ˌɑntrəprəˈnɚ, -ˈnʊr/ *n.*
> someone who starts a company, arranges business deals, and takes risks in order to make a profit

### READ

06|01  Read this article about teen entrepreneur Shubham Banerjee.

## Young Entrepreneur Looks Toward the Future

Who is fourteen-year-old entrepreneur Shubham Banerjee, and will he have become a millionaire by his thirtieth birthday? Like other entrepreneurs, Shubham shows great initiative and is willing to take risks in order to succeed. However, money is not his only goal. Shubham wants to use his problem-solving talent to create devices that will help others and make the world a better place.

At the age of twelve, Shubham invented Braigo 1.0, a printer that converts traditional text to braille.[1] He created his printer for a school science project because he wanted to make a better, less expensive braille printer. With money from his father and corporate sponsors,[2] Shubham started his own company,

---

1  *braille:*  a system of writing that uses raised dots that blind people can read by touching
2  *sponsors:*  people or organizations that pay for the cost of an activity

Braigo Labs, and began developing Braigo 2.0. By the time his printer is available for purchase, he will have been working on the device for several years, and the cost of a braille printer will have dropped from $2,000 to $500 or less. It is important to Shubham that he will have produced an affordable way for the blind and others with limited vision—285 million of them worldwide—to print and read digital documents.

In keeping with his entrepreneurial spirit, Shubham is already finding ways to make his dreams come true. Meanwhile, he is still a teenager who is just beginning high school. By the time he graduates, he will have improved his skills in science and technology. Like most teenagers, he will have played sports and joined clubs. And because education is important to him, Shubham says that he will have applied to several universities to study medical engineering. Clearly, the teen won't have been wasting time, but what about future inventions?

Shubham reports that he already has plans for his next projects. That means by the age of thirty, he will probably have become a well-known engineer working to make the world a better place. As for his millionaire status, there is no doubt that he will have achieved that goal as well.

## AFTER YOU READ

**A** VOCABULARY **Complete the sentences with the words from the box.**

| affordable | convert | corporate | initiative | meanwhile | status |
|---|---|---|---|---|---|

1. Entrepreneurs _____convert_____ ideas into money-making products.
2. Getting a good education can help you improve your economic _____status_____.
3. You should show _____initiative_____ instead of waiting to be told what to do.
4. Creative people often have problems following _____corporate_____ rules.
5. Shoppers are always looking for _____affordable_____ prices.
6. Price is important, but _____meanwhile_____, they want the latest fashion and high quality.

**B** COMPREHENSION **Read the statements. Check (✓) True or False.**

|  | True | False |
|---|---|---|
| 1. Shubham Banerjee's printer will be in stores. Then he will work on Braigo 2.0 for several years. | ☐ | ✓ |
| 2. Because of Shubham's invention, braille printers will be more affordable. | ✓ | ☐ |
| 3. Shubham will improve his science and technology skills in high school. | ✓ | ☐ |
| 4. Shubham will not have time for sports in high school. | ☐ | ✓ |
| 5. After he graduates from high school, he will apply to a university. | ☐ | ✓ |
| 6. Before his thirtieth birthday, he will probably invent more devices to help people. | ✓ | ☐ |
| 7. Shubham will be a millionaire when he is thirty. | ✓ | ☐ |

**C** DISCUSSION **Work with a partner. Compare your answers in B. Why did you check** *True* **or** *False***?**

## FUTURE PERFECT

### Statements

| Subject | Will (not) | Have + Past Participle | |
|---|---|---|---|
| I<br>You<br>He<br>She<br>It<br>We<br>They | **will (not)** | **have finished** | by next week. |

### Yes/No Questions

| Will | Subject | Have + Past Participle | |
|---|---|---|---|
| **Will** | you<br>she<br>they | **have finished** | by next week? |

### Short Answers

| Affirmative | | | | Negative | | |
|---|---|---|---|---|---|---|
| **Yes,** | I<br>she<br>they | **will (have).** | | **No,** | I<br>she<br>they | **won't (have).** |

### Wh- Questions

| Wh- Word | Will | Subject | Have + Past Participle | |
|---|---|---|---|---|
| How much | **will** | you<br>she<br>they | **have finished** | by next week? |

# FUTURE PERFECT PROGRESSIVE

**Statements**

| Subject | *Will (not)* | *Have been* + Base Form + *-ing* | |
|---|---|---|---|
| I<br>You<br>He<br>She<br>It<br>We<br>They | **will (not)** | **have been working** | for a month. |

**Yes/No Questions**

| *Will* | Subject | *Have been* + Base Form + *-ing* | |
|---|---|---|---|
| **Will** | you<br>she<br>they | **have been working** | for a month? |

**Short Answers**

| Affirmative | | | | Negative | | |
|---|---|---|---|---|---|---|
| **Yes,** | I<br>she<br>they | **will (have).** | | **No,** | I<br>she<br>they | **won't (have).** |

**Wh- Questions**

| *Wh-* Word | *Will* | Subject | *Have been* + Base Form + *-ing* | |
|---|---|---|---|---|
| How long | **will** | you<br>she<br>they | **have been working** | by then? |

# GRAMMAR NOTES

## 1 Future Perfect

Use the future perfect to show that something **will happen before a specific time in the future.** The focus is often on the **completion** of an action or situation.

*By next week*, he **will have achieved** his goal.
**She'll have started** to sell her new product *by May*.
**I'll have been** in college for a year *by then*.
We**'ll have learned** a lot *by the end of this class*.

## 2 Future Perfect Progressive

Use the future perfect progressive to show that something **will be in progress until a specific time in the future**. The action or situation **may continue** after that time. The focus is on the **continuation** of the action or situation, not the end result.

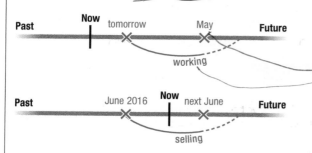

A: I start my job at the computer store tomorrow.
B: But what about our trip in May?
A: *By May*, **I'll have been working** for six months. I'm sure my boss will give me a week off.

He opened his business in 2016. *By next June*, he**'ll have been selling** computer software for several years.

Notice that the action may start sometime in the future or it may have already started.

**BE CAREFUL!** Do not use the future perfect progressive with most **non-action verbs**.

By June, we**'ll have owned** our business for five years.
**NOT** By June, we'll have ~~been owning~~ our business for five years.

## 3 Future Perfect or Future Perfect Progressive + Simple Present in Time Clause

Use the future perfect or the future perfect progressive with the simple present in the time clause to show the **time order between two future events**.

Use the **future perfect** or the **future perfect progressive** in the main clause for the **earlier event**. Use the **simple present** in the time clause for the **later time or event**.

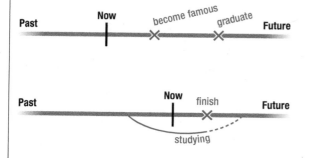

TIME CLAUSE ②  MAIN CLAUSE ①
By the time we **graduate**, you **will have become** a famous inventor.

> (First you'll become a famous inventor. Then we'll graduate.)

TIME CLAUSE  MAIN CLAUSE
When I **finish** my degree, **I'll have been studying** here for four years.

> (First I'll be studying here for four years. Then I will finish my degree.)

**CONTINUED ▶**

| **BE CAREFUL!** Use the **simple present** in the **future time clause**. Do not use *will* or *be going to*. | By the time I'**m** twenty, I'll have started my company.<br>**NOT** By the time I'll be twenty, I'll have started my company.<br><br>When he **retires**, he'll have been working here for thirty-five years<br>**NOT** When he's going to retire, he'll have been working here for thirty-five years. |
| --- | --- |

## 4 Adverbs or Expressions with *By* to Show the Order of Events

| Use **adverbs** such as *already* and *yet* with the **future perfect** or the **future perfect progressive** to emphasize the **first event**. | **A:** I can help you clean the apartment tomorrow.<br>**B:** I'll *already* **have finished** by then. But I **won't have gone** to the supermarket *yet.* Can you do the shopping? |
| --- | --- |
| **BE CAREFUL!** Do not put an adverb between the **main verb** and a **direct object**. | We **will** *already* **have completed** our research by Monday.<br>**NOT** We will have completed already our research by Monday.<br><br>We **will not have taken** the final exam *yet.*<br>**or**<br>We **will not** *yet* **have taken** the final exam.<br>**NOT** We will not have taken yet the final exam. |
| Use **expressions with** *by* to refer to the **second event**.<br>• *by* + time or event | *By the age of thirty*, he **will** probably **have become** a millionaire.<br>*By graduation*, he'**ll have been working** on other creative ideas. |
| • *by the time* (to introduce a **clause** in the **simple present**) | *By the time he is thirty*, he **will** probably **have become** a millionaire.<br>*By the time he graduates*, he'**ll have been working** on other creative ideas. |
| **IN WRITING** Use a **comma after the time clause or phrase** when it comes at the **beginning** of the sentence. Do not use a comma after the main clause when the main clause comes first. | *When he celebrates his thirtieth birthday,* he **will** probably **have become** a millionaire.<br>**NOT** He will probably have become a millionaire, when he celebrates his thirtieth birthday. |

## REFERENCE NOTES

For a list of **irregular past participles**, see Appendix 1 on page 453.
For **spelling rules for progressive forms**, see Appendix 23 on page 463.

## EXERCISE 1  DISCOVER THE GRAMMAR

GRAMMAR NOTES 1–4  **Read each numbered statement from members of a high school club for young entrepreneurs. Choose the sentence (*a* or *b*) that is similar in meaning.**

1. By the end of this month, our company will have been doing computer repairs for two years.
   **a.** The team of students started their business almost two years ago.
   **b.** The team will continue offering computer services for two more years.

2. Meanwhile, our computer classes for senior citizens will have started.
   **a.** The students haven't started teaching the classes yet.
   **b.** The students are already teaching computer skills to senior citizens.

3. Our company is WeRTees. By the next meeting, we'll have finished designing a new t-shirt.
   **a.** The students will work on the t-shirt design while they are at the next meeting.
   **b.** The students will work on the design before the next meeting.

4. By the time we graduate, we'll have been selling our t-shirts for the same price for three years.
   **a.** The t-shirts will be the same price when the students graduate.
   **b.** The price of the t-shirts will be higher when the students graduate.

5. We have a new company. By 12:00 noon tomorrow, we'll have selected our company's name.
   **a.** The students know what the name of their company will be.
   **b.** The students still don't have a name for their company.

6. I won't have completed our team's business plan by noon.
   **a.** The student will finish at noon.
   **b.** The student will still be working at noon.

## EXERCISE 2  FUTURE PERFECT

GRAMMAR NOTES 1, 4  **Debbie Hart has a lot of goals. Look at the timeline. Write sentences describing what Debbie *will have done* or *won't have done* by the year 2022. Use the words in parentheses and the future perfect.**

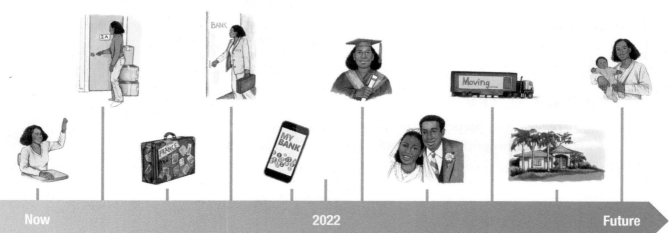

| Now | 2022 | Future |

1. By 2022, _Debbie will have started college_ .
   (start college)
2. By 2022, _Debbie won't have gotten married_ .
   (get married)
3. By 2022, _Debbie will have found an affordable apartment_ .
   (find an affordable apartment)
4. By 2022, _Debbie won't have moved to Miami_ .
   (move to Miami)
5. By 2022, _Debbie will have spent a summer in France_ .
   (spend a summer in France)
6. By 2022, _Debbie will have started working at a bank_ .
   (start working at a bank)
7. By 2022, _Debbie will have created a new app for online banking_ .
   (create a new app for online banking)
8. By 2022, _Debbie won't have bought a house_ .
   (buy a house)
9. By 2022, _Debbie won't have graduated from college_ .
   (graduate from college)
10. By 2022, _Debbie won't have become a parent_ .
    (become a parent)

## EXERCISE 3  SIMPLE PRESENT + FUTURE PERFECT WITH *ALREADY* AND *YET*

GRAMMAR NOTES 1, 3–4  Read Debbie's goals in parentheses. What will or won't she have achieved by the time the second event occurs? Use the information in the timeline from Exercise 2. Write sentences using the words in parentheses and *already* and *yet*.

1. By the time _Debbie finds an affordable apartment, she'll already have started college_ .
   (find an affordable apartment / start college)
2. By the time _Debbie finds an affordable apartment, she won't have gotten married yet_ .
   (find an affordable apartment / get married)
3. By the time _Debbie stars college, she won't have spended a summer in france yet_ .
   (start college / spend a summer in France)
4. By the time _Debbie graduates from college, she'll already have found an .._ .
   (graduate from college / find an affordable apartment)
5. By the time _Debbie spends a summer in france, she won't have found a job at a bank yet_ .
   (spend a summer in France / find a job at a bank)
6. By the time _Debbie graduates from college, she'll already have created a_ .
   (graduate from college / create a new banking app)
7. By the time _Debbie gets married she'll already have graduated from_ .
   (get married / graduate from college)
8. By the time _Debbie moves to Miami, she won't have bought a house yet_ .
   (move to Miami / buy a house)
9. By the time _Debbie becomes a parent, she'll already have graduate from_ .
   (become a parent / graduate from college)
10. By the time _Debbie buys a house, she'll won't have become a parent_ .
    (buy a house / become a parent)

## EXERCISE 4
## FUTURE PERFECT OR FUTURE PERFECT PROGRESSIVE

GRAMMAR NOTES 1–4 Ask and answer questions about these people's accomplishments. Use the words in parentheses and choose between the future perfect and the future perfect progressive. Use the calendar to answer the questions.

| January | | | | | | |
|---|---|---|---|---|---|---|
| S | M | T | W | T | F | S |
| | | | | | 1 | 2 |
| 3 | 4 | 5 | 6 | 7 | 8 | 9 |
| 10 | 11 | 12 | 13 | 14 | 15 | 16 |
| 17 | 18 | 19 | 20 | 21 | 22 | 23 |
| 24 31 | 25 | 26 | 27 | 28 | 29 | 30 |

| February | | | | | | |
|---|---|---|---|---|---|---|
| S | M | T | W | T | F | S |
| | 1 | 2 | 3 | 4 | 5 | 6 |
| 7 | 8 | 9 | 10 | 11 | 12 | 13 |
| 14 | 15 | 16 | 17 | 18 | 19 | 20 |
| 21 | 22 | 23 | 24 | 25 | 26 | 27 |
| 28 | | | | | | |

| March | | | | | | |
|---|---|---|---|---|---|---|
| S | M | T | W | T | F | S |
| | 1 | 2 | 3 | 4 | 5 | 6 |
| 7 | 8 | 9 | 10 | 11 | 12 | 13 |
| 14 | 15 | 16 | 17 | 18 | 19 | 20 |
| 21 | 22 | 23 | 24 | 25 | 26 | 27 |
| 28 | 29 | 30 | 31 | | | |

| April | | | | | | |
|---|---|---|---|---|---|---|
| S | M | T | W | T | F | S |
| | | | | 1 | 2 | 3 |
| 4 | 5 | 6 | 7 | 8 | 9 | 10 |
| 11 | 12 | 13 | 14 | 15 | 16 | 17 |
| 18 | 19 | 20 | 21 | 22 | 23 | 24 |
| 25 | 26 | 27 | 28 | 29 | 30 | |

| May | | | | | | |
|---|---|---|---|---|---|---|
| S | M | T | W | T | F | S |
| | | | | | | 1 |
| 2 | 3 | 4 | 5 | 6 | 7 | 8 |
| 9 | 10 | 11 | 12 | 13 | 14 | 15 |
| 16 | 17 | 18 | 19 | 20 | 21 | 22 |
| 23 30 | 24 31 | 25 | 26 | 27 | 28 | 29 |

| June | | | | | | |
|---|---|---|---|---|---|---|
| S | M | T | W | T | F | S |
| | | 1 | 2 | 3 | 4 | 5 |
| 6 | 7 | 8 | 9 | 10 | 11 | 12 |
| 13 | 14 | 15 | 16 | 17 | 18 | 19 |
| 20 | 21 | 22 | 23 | 24 | 25 | 26 |
| 27 | 28 | 29 | 30 | | | |

**1.** On January 1, Debbie Hart started saving $15 a week.

QUESTION: *By February 19, how long will Debbie have been saving?*
(by February 19 / how long / save)

ANSWER: *By February 19, she'll have been saving for seven weeks.*

**2.** On March 1, Matt Rodriguez began working eight hours a day on his latest invention.

QUESTION: _____
(by April 16 / how many days / work)

ANSWER: _____

**3.** On March 3, Janet Haddad began reading a book a week.

QUESTION: _____
(by June 16 / how many books / read)

ANSWER: _____

**4.** On April 24, Don Caputo began running one mile (1.6 km) a day.

QUESTION: _____
(how long / run / by May 29)

ANSWER: _____

**5.** On April 24, Tania Zakov began running two miles (3.2 km) a day.

QUESTION: _____
(how many miles / run / by May 29)

ANSWER: _____

**6.** On February 6, Mary Gregory began saving $10 a week.

QUESTION: _____
(save $100 / by March 27)

ANSWER: _____

**7.** On May 8, Tim Rigg began painting two apartments a week in his building.

QUESTION: _____
(how many apartments / paint / by May 29)

ANSWER: _____

**8.** Tim's building has twelve apartments.

QUESTION: _____
(finish / by June 19)

ANSWER: _____

## EXERCISE·5 EDITING

**GRAMMAR NOTES 1–4  Read this blog entry. There are eight mistakes in the use of the future perfect and the future perfect progressive. The first mistake is already corrected. Find and correct seven more.**

# In Praise of the Business Leaders of Tomorrow

**ALEXA IOANNIDIS**

*will have reached*

By 2025, today's young entrepreneurs ~~have reached~~ adulthood. Almost certainly, they'll have converted

*they'll have shown*

their creative ideas into cash. And if we're lucky, they'll ~~had~~ shown the corporate world that making

money by solving problems and helping others is a good business model to follow.

*will have designed*

■ The Inventioneers designed the SMARTwheel to address the problem of drivers, especially teen

drivers, who take their hands off the steering wheel when distracted by activities such as texting,

talking on the phone, or eating. By the end of next year, more than 3,000 people in the United States

*died*

will have ~~die~~, and there will have been more than 400,000 injuries as a result of distracted driving.

*received*

With the SMARTwheel, drivers will have ~~been receiving~~ a warning to put both hands on the wheel and

pay attention before an accident can occur. And it's possible that they'll have changed their driving

*are*

habits by the time they will ~~be~~ on the road again.

■ Zollipops are Alina Morse's way of helping kids who will eat candy, lots of it, before their next visit

to the dentist. "Zollis" are sugar-free, so they won't cause tooth decay. Meanwhile, by the end of this

*have*

year, Alina will ~~has~~ donated ten percent of the profits from her candy business to health education

programs for children.

■ Moziah Bridges has earned status and respect as the teen owner of Mo's Bows. By the time he's

*selling*

twenty-one, Moziah will have been ~~sold~~ his bow ties for nine years. If all goes according to plan, he'll

have added already a collection of jackets and pants by then. Moziah's product line currently includes

the Go Mo! bow tie, which earns money to send children to summer camp.

How about a round of applause for the business leaders of tomorrow?

## EXERCISE 6   LISTENING

🔊 06|02   **A**   Listen to the conversation between Iza and her father, Don. They are discussing Iza's daughter Beth, a young entrepreneur. Read the statements. Then listen again and check (✓) *True* or *False*.

|  |  | True | False |
|---|---|:---:|:---:|
| 1. | Iza believes that the bicycle business is good for her daughter. | ✓ | ☐ |
| 2. | When she graduates from high school, Beth will have owned her business for four years. | ☐ | ✓ |
| 3. | Beth uses math skills to operate her business. | ✓ | ☐ |
| 4. | Beth will probably stop "thinking outside the box" when she graduates. | ☐ | ✓ |
| 5. | Don finally changed his mind about Beth's bicycle business. | ✓ | ☐ |
| 6. | Beth has already started filling out her college applications. | ☐ | ✓ |
| 7. | Beth is still working on Don's bicycle. | ✓ | ☐ |

🔊 06|02   **B**   Work with a partner. Listen again to the conversation. Discuss your answers in A. Give reasons for your answers.

EXAMPLE:   **A:** The answer for number 1 is *True*. Do you know why?
      **B:** According to Iza, her daughter Beth is doing something that she loves. And Beth will have gotten valuable skills from her bicycle business by the time she graduates from high school.
      **A:** OK, I understand. Now, let's talk about number 2.

*She will have owned her business*
*created ways to solve some*
*- Important innovation*
*responsibly*

🔊 06|02   **C**   Work in a group. Listen again to the conversation. What will Beth have achieved by the time she graduates from high school? Make a list of her top five achievements.

EXAMPLE:   **A:** Beth will have done a lot by the time she graduates. Let's write everything that her mother mentions. Then we can choose her top five achievements.
      **B:** OK. She'll have improved her math skills. What else do you want to put on the list?
      **C:** I think this is important. She will have . . .

# EXERCISE 7 BY THE END OF . . .

CONVERSATION Work with a partner. What will some of the people in your life (including you!) have achieved by the end of this year, this month, or this week? Talk about some of these accomplishments. (Remember, even small accomplishments are important!) Use some of the ideas in the list below and ideas of your own.

EXAMPLE: A: I'm really proud of my roommate. She's always had a problem oversleeping, but by the end of this month, she won't have missed any of her morning classes!

B: That's great. How did she solve her problem? *By the end of the month, I'll have visited Chicago.*

- making a budget
- managing time
- exercising
- learning new things
- overcoming a bad habit

- starting a good habit *By the end of the day, I'll have*
- spending time with friends and family *finished my classes for today.*
- _____
- _____
- _____

# EXERCISE 8 LONG-TERM GOALS

**A** CONVERSATION Work in a group. Think of three goals you would like to achieve in the next five to ten years and talk about them. They can be big goals, such as buying a house, or smaller goals, such as learning a new skill.

EXAMPLE: A: I'd like to get fit and then run in a 10 km race. What about you?

B: I want to learn how to use photo editing software like a pro.

C: I'd like to learn to skateboard.

**B** Arrange your goals on the timeline. Write the goals and the years you want to achieve them.

Goals: *(will)* _____  _____  _____

_____  _____  _____

Years: [ ]          [ ]          [ ]

**C** Discuss your goals in detail. Talk about things you'll need to do before you achieve each goal.

EXAMPLE: A: Before I run my first 10 km race, I'll have been training for three months.

B: By the holidays this year, I'll have taken an online photo-editing class.

C: By then, I'll have bought a skateboard!

# FROM GRAMMAR TO WRITING

**A** BEFORE YOU WRITE  Ask a classmate about his or her goals and what he or she is doing to achieve these goals by the end of the year. Complete the outline.

| Classmate's Name | Classmate's Goal(s) | Activities This Year to Achieve Goals | Time Doing Activities by End of Year | Achievements by End of Year |
|---|---|---|---|---|
| Daniele. | Vert + noun. Travel to California go to disney | gerund + noun (she is) saving money. she is scheduling. she is saving money. | 6 months. 1 mounth. | She'll have visited California She'll have saved money for her trip. She'll have vised Disney |

**B** WRITE  Use your outline to write a paragraph about your classmate. Use the future perfect and the future perfect progressive. Try to avoid the common mistakes in the chart.

EXAMPLE:   Danny Munca wants to buy a new phone. He got a part-time job in the library to help him save money. By the end of the year, he'll have been working there for two months. He'll have saved about $200 by then, and he'll be able to get his new electronic toy.

## Common Mistakes in Using the Future Perfect and Future Perfect Progressive

| | |
|---|---|
| Use *will have* + **past participle** to form the future perfect. Do not use the base form of the verb. | He **will have saved** $200 by then. <br> NOT He will have ~~save~~ $200 by then. |
| Use *will have been* + **base form** + *-ing* to form the future perfect progressive. Do not use *will have been* + past participle. | By the end of the year, he**'ll have been working** there for two months. <br> NOT By the end of the year, he'll have been ~~worked~~ there for two months. |
| Use the **simple present** in a **future time clause**. Do not use *will* or *be going to*. | By the time the year is over, he will have learned a lot. <br> NOT By the time the year ~~will be~~ over, he will . . . |

**C** CHECK YOUR WORK  Read your paragraph. Underline once the verbs in the future perfect. Underline twice the verbs in the future perfect progressive. Use the Editing Checklist to check your work.

## Editing Checklist

**Did you use . . . ?**

☐ the future perfect for actions that will already be completed by a specific time in the future

☐ the future perfect progressive for actions that will still be in progress at a specific time in the future

☐ time clauses to show the time order between two future events

☐ the simple present in a future time clause

☐ adverbs or expressions with *by* to show the order of events

**D** REVISE YOUR WORK  Read your paragraph again. Can you improve your writing? Make changes if necessary. Give your paragraph a title.

# UNIT 6 REVIEW

**Test yourself on the grammar of the unit.**

**A** Circle the correct words to complete the sentences.

1. Kareem will has been selling / have been selling his new phone app for six months by January 1.
2. When we get / we'll get to my parents' house, they'll already have eaten dinner.
3. By the end of this week, Mia will exercise / have been exercising for six months.
4. When I finish this story by Sue Grafton, I'll have read / I'll have been reading all of her mysteries.
5. By / Since 2025, he'll have been living here for ten years.

**B** Complete the conversation with the simple present, future perfect, or future perfect progressive form of the verbs in parentheses. Use the future perfect progressive if possible.

A: Do you realize that in September we _____ here for two years?
            **1.** (live)

B: Amazing! And you _____ here for four years.
          **2.** (study)

A: I know. By next year at this time, I _____.
          **3.** (graduate)

B: Well, I certainly hope that by the time you _____,
          **4.** (graduate)

    I _____ a good job.
      **5.** (find)

A: Well, one thing is certain. By that time, we _____ a lot of
             **6.** (make)
    friends here.

B: Yes. And we _____ almost $2,000 selling our school t-shirts.
       **7.** (earn)

**C** Find and correct eight mistakes.

I'm so excited about your news! By the time you read this, you'll already have moving into your new house! And I have some good news, too. By the end of this month, I'll have save $5,000. That's enough for me to buy a used car! And that means that by this time next year, I drive to California to visit you! I have more news, too. By the time I will graduate, I will have been started my new part-time job. I hope that by this time next year, I'll also had finished working on my latest invention—a solar-powered flashlight.

It's hard to believe that in June, we will have been being friends for ten years. Time sure flies! And we'll have been stayed in touch even though we are 3,000 miles apart. Isn't technology a great thing?

**Now check your answers on page 476.**

# Negative and Tag Questions, Additions and Responses

## PART 3

**OUTCOMES**
- Check information or comment on a situation, using negative *yes/no* questions or tag questions
- Identify key details in interview transcripts and recorded interviews
- Interview a classmate, asking questions and checking information
- Discuss details about cities around the world
- Write an interview transcript about a classmate's home city, including questions and answers

**OUTCOMES**
- Show similarity, using *so*, *too*, *neither*, or *not either*, and show difference, using *but*
- Identify key details in an article on a scientific topic and in a conversation between two people
- Discuss similarities and differences between two people
- Research a pair of twins and report findings
- Write about the similarities and differences between two people

# Negative *Yes/No* Questions and Tag Questions

## PLACES TO LIVE

**OUTCOMES**
- Check information or comment on a situation, using negative *yes/no* questions or tag questions
- Identify key details in interview transcripts and recorded interviews
- Interview a classmate, asking questions and checking information
- Discuss details about cities around the world
- Write an interview transcript about a classmate's home city, including questions and answers

---

## STEP 1  GRAMMAR IN CONTEXT

### BEFORE YOU READ

Look at the photos. Discuss the questions.

1. How do these places look to you?
2. Which one of these places would you like to visit or live in? Why?
3. What do you like about the town or city where you live? What don't you like?

### READ

07|01  Read these transcripts of on-the-street interviews from cities around the world.

# It's a Great Place to Live, Isn't It?

## Rio de Janeiro, Brazil

**REPORTER:** Excuse me. Do you speak English?

**LYDIA:** Yes, I do. Hey! I've seen you on TV. . . . Aren't you Paul Logan?

**REPORTER:** That's right. I'm conducting a survey for *Life Abroad Magazine*. You're not from Rio, are you?

**LYDIA:** No, I'm not. I'm originally from Portugal. You could tell by my accent, couldn't you?

**REPORTER:** Uh-huh. You don't speak English like a Brazilian. So how do you like living here?

**LYDIA:** I love it. Just look around you—the beach, the bay, the mountains, the sky. Aren't they gorgeous? I walk along this beach every day on the way to my office.

**REPORTER:** It's not a bad way to get to work, is it?

**LYDIA:** It's not a bad place to play, either! There's constant excitement. Besides the beach, there are so many restaurants and clubs. It's a great place to live, isn't it?

## Cairo, Egypt

REPORTER: This is one of the oldest markets in Cairo, isn't it?

KINORO: Yes, and it's one of the most interesting. Hey, didn't you buy anything?

REPORTER: Not today. So what brought you from Nairobi to Cairo?

KINORO: My job. I work for a company that supplies Internet services for a lot of businesses here.

REPORTER: It gets extremely hot here in the summer, doesn't it?

KINORO: Yes, but the winters are mild. And it almost never rains. You can't beat that,[1] can you?

## Seoul, South Korea

*I'm pretty sure you are a student, am I right?*

REPORTER: You're a student, aren't you?

ANTON: No, actually, I'm a teacher. I'm teaching a course in architecture at the Kaywon School of Art and Design this semester.

REPORTER: So how do you like living here? Doesn't the cold weather bother you?

ANTON: Not really. I'm from Berlin, so I'm used to it. I love this city. You can see skyscrapers right next to ancient structures.

REPORTER: That's true. That's the old city gate over there, isn't it?

ANTON: Yes. And there are several beautiful palaces nearby.

## Vancouver, Canada

REPORTER: You're from England, aren't you?

TESSA: Yes. I moved here ten years ago.

REPORTER: Was it a difficult adjustment?

TESSA: No, not really. First of all, having the same language makes things easy, doesn't it? And people here are very friendly.

REPORTER: Why Canada?

TESSA: England's a very small country. I was attracted by Canada's wide-open spaces. It seems to offer endless possibilities.

---

1 *You can't beat that.*: Nothing is better than that.

# AFTER YOU READ

**A** VOCABULARY  Choose the word or phrase that best completes each sentence.

1. A _____ is not an example of a **structure**.
   a. bridge
   b. building
   c. beach

2. If you're **originally** from South Korea, you _____.
   a. were born there
   b. still live there
   c. have relatives there

3. A place with **constant** noise is _____ quiet.
   a. always
   b. sometimes
   c. never

4. If you are **attracted** to something, you want to _____ it.
   a. avoid
   b. get to know
   c. change

5. A _____ with thirty customers is **extremely** crowded.
   a. small café
   b. movie theater
   c. department store

6. If someone **supplies** you with information, he or she _____ the information.
   a. wants
   b. gives you
   c. corrects

**B** COMPREHENSION  Read the statements. Check (✓) *True* or *False*.

|  | True | False |
|---|---|---|
| 1. Lydia doesn't know the reporter. | ☐ | ☐ |
| 2. The reporter thinks Lydia is from Rio. | ☐ | ☐ |
| 3. The reporter bought a lot of things at the Cairo market. | ☐ | ☐ |
| 4. The reporter thinks the cold weather bothers Anton. | ☐ | ☐ |
| 5. The reporter thinks Tessa comes from Canada. | ☐ | ☐ |
| 6. The move was not a difficult adjustment for Tessa. | ☐ | ☐ |

**C** DISCUSSION  Work with a partner. Compare your answers in B. Why did you check *True* or *False*?

## NEGATIVE *YES*/*NO* QUESTIONS

*Av + Not + S + V* (handwritten)

### With *Be* as the Main Verb

| Questions |
| --- |
| *Be* + *Not* + Subject |
| **Aren't you** from Rio de Janeiro? |

| Short Answers | |
| --- | --- |
| Affirmative | Negative |
| **Yes**, I **am**. | No, **I'm not**. |

### With All Auxiliary Verbs Except *Do*

| Questions |
| --- |
| Auxiliary + *Not* + Subject + Verb |
| **Aren't you** moving? |
| **Hasn't he** been here before? |
| **Can't they** move tomorrow? |

| Short Answers | | | |
| --- | --- | --- | --- |
| Affirmative | | Negative | |
| **Yes,** | I **am**. | **No,** | **I'm not**. |
| | he **has**. | | he **hasn't**. |
| | they **can**. | | they **can't**. |

### With *Do* as the Auxiliary Verb

| Questions |
| --- |
| *Do* + *Not* + Subject + Verb |
| **Doesn't he** live here? |
| **Didn't they** move last year? |

| Short Answers | | | |
| --- | --- | --- | --- |
| Affirmative | | Negative | |
| **Yes,** | he **does**. | **No,** | he **doesn't**. |
| | they **did**. | | they **didn't**. |

## TAG QUESTIONS

### With *Be* as the Main Verb

| Affirmative Statement | Negative Tag |
|---|---|
| Subject + *Be* | *Be* + *Not* + Subject |
| You're from Rio, | aren't you? |

| Negative Statement | Affirmative Tag |
|---|---|
| Subject + *Be* + *Not* | *Be* + Subject |
| You're not from Rio, | are you? |

*(handwritten:)* No, I'm not. (I'm

Yes, I'm.

### With All Auxiliary Verbs Except *Do*

| Affirmative Statement | Negative Tag |
|---|---|
| Subject + Auxiliary | Auxiliary + *Not* + Subject |
| You're moving, | aren't you? |
| He's been here before, | hasn't he? |
| They can move tomorrow, | can't they? |

| Negative Statement | Affirmative Tag |
|---|---|
| Subject + Auxiliary + *Not* | Auxiliary + Subject |
| You're not moving, | are you? |
| He hasn't been here before, | has he? |
| They can't move tomorrow, | can they? |

### With *Do* as an Auxiliary Verb

| Affirmative Statement | Negative Tag |
|---|---|
| Subject + Verb | *Do* + *Not* + Subject |
| He lives here, | doesn't he? |
| They moved last year, | didn't they? |

| Negative Statement | Affirmative Tag |
|---|---|
| Subject + *Do* + *Not* + Verb | *Do* + Subject |
| He doesn't live here, | does he? |
| They didn't move, | did they? |

# GRAMMAR NOTES

## 1 Negative *Yes/No* Questions and Tag Questions

Use negative *yes/no* questions and tag questions to **check information** you believe is true or to **comment on a situation**.

| | |
|---|---|
| • **checking information** you believe is true | **Doesn't Anton** live in Seoul? |
| | Anton lives in Seoul, **doesn't he?** |
| | *(The speaker believes that Anton lives in Seoul.)* |
| • **commenting on a situation** | **Isn't it** a nice day? |
| | It's a nice day, **isn't it?** |
| | *(The speaker is commenting on the weather.)* |

Negative *yes/no* questions and tag questions are **different from affirmative *yes/no* questions**:

In **affirmative *yes/no* questions**, you have **no idea of the answer**.

**Do you work** here?
*(I don't know if you work here.)*

In **negative *yes/no* questions and tag questions**, you have **information** that you want to **check**, or you have an **opinion** and are **looking for agreement**.

**Don't you work** here?
*(I think you work here, but I'm not sure.)*
This is hard work, **isn't it?**
*(I think this is hard work, and I think you agree.)*

**USAGE NOTE** We use negative *yes/no* questions and tag questions mostly in **conversation** and **informal writing** (notes, emails, text messages, etc.).

**Isn't it** beautiful? *(conversation)*
You're moving next week, **aren't you?** *(email)*

## 2 Forming Negative *Yes/No* Questions

Like affirmative *yes/no* questions, negative *yes/no* questions **begin with a form of *be* or an auxiliary verb**, such as *have, do, will, can,* or *should.*

**Aren't you** Paul Logan?
**Haven't I** seen you on TV?
**Don't you** like the weather here?
**Won't you** be sorry to leave?
**Can't you** stay longer?

**USAGE NOTE** We almost always use **contractions** in negative questions. Full forms are very formal and not very common.

**Shouldn't we** go? *(informal)*
**Should we not** go? *(very formal)*

**BE CAREFUL!** Use *are* in negative questions with *I* and a contraction. Do not use *am.*

**Aren't I** right?
NOT ~~Amn't~~ I right?

## 3 Forming Tag Questions

| | |
|---|---|
| Form tag questions with **statement + tag**. The statement expresses an **assumption**. The tag means *Isn't that right?* or *Isn't that true?* | STATEMENT      TAG<br>You're Paul Logan, **aren't you?**<br>*(You're Paul Logan. Isn't that right?)*<br>You're not from Cairo, **are you?**<br>*(You're not from Cairo. Isn't that true?)* |
| If the statement verb is **affirmative**, the tag verb is **negative**. | AFFIRMATIVE      NEGATIVE<br>You **work** on Thursdays, **don't** you? |
| If the statement verb is **negative**, the tag verb is **affirmative**. | NEGATIVE      AFFIRMATIVE<br>You **don't work** on Thursdays, **do** you? |
| **BE CAREFUL!** Adverbs of frequency such as *never*, *rarely*, and *seldom* have a negative meaning. If they are in the statement, the tag verb is affirmative. | You've *never* **been** to Istanbul, **have** you?<br>NOT You've never been to Istanbul, ~~haven't~~ you? |
| Begin the **tag** with a **form of *be* or an auxiliary verb**, such as *have, do, will, can,* or *should.* Use the **same auxiliary** that is in the statement. | It**'s** a nice day, **isn't** it?<br>There **are** good schools here, **aren't** there?<br>You**'ve** lived here a long time, **haven't you?** |
| If the statement does not use *be* or an auxiliary verb, use an appropriate **form of *do*** in the tag. | You **come** from London, **don't** you?<br>You **came** from London, **didn't** you? |
| **USAGE NOTE** We almost always use **contractions** in the **tag**. Full forms are very formal and not very common. | You can drive, **can't** you? *(informal)*<br>You can drive, **can** you **not**? *(very formal)* |
| **BE CAREFUL!** Use *are* in tag questions with *I* and a contraction. Do not use *am.* | I**'m** right, **aren't I**?<br>NOT I'm right, ~~amn't~~ I? |
| **BE CAREFUL!** When the subject of the statement is a **noun**, the subject of the tag is the matching **pronoun**. When the subject of the statement is *this* or *that*, the subject of the tag is *it*. | *Tom* works here, doesn't **he**?<br>NOT Tom works here, doesn't ~~Tom~~?<br>*That's* a good idea, isn't **it**?<br>NOT That's a good idea, isn't ~~that~~? |

## 4 Answering Negative *Yes/No* Questions and Tag Questions

Answer negative *yes/no* questions and tag questions the **same way you answer affirmative *yes/no* questions**.

| | |
|---|---|
| • *yes* if the information is **correct** | A: **Don't you** work in Vancouver?<br>B: **Yes, I do.** I've worked there for years. |
| • *no* if the information is **not correct** | A: You work in Vancouver, **don't you?**<br>B: **No, I don't.** I work in Montreal. |

# PRONUNCIATION NOTE

**Intonation of Tag Questions**

In tag questions, our **voice rises** at the end when we expect another person to give us **information**.

A: You're not moving, **are you?**
B: Yes. I'm returning to Berlin.

Our **voice falls** at the end when we are making a comment and expect the other person to **agree**.

A: Seoul is interesting, **isn't it?**
B: Yes, it is.

## STEP 3 FOCUSED PRACTICE

## EXERCISE 1 DISCOVER THE GRAMMAR

**GRAMMAR NOTES 1–4** **Read this conversation between Anton Kada's mother, Petra, and a Canadian neighbor, Ken. Underline all the negative *yes/no* questions and circle all the tags.**

PETRA: Hi, Ken. Nice day, isn't it?

KEN: Sure is. What are you doing home today? Don't you usually work on Thursdays?

PETRA: I took the day off to help my son. He just got back to Berlin, and he's looking for an apartment. You don't know of any vacant apartments, do you?

KEN: Isn't he going to stay with you?

PETRA: Well, he just got a new job at an architecture firm downtown. He wants a place of his own in a quiet area, not one of those neighborhoods with constant noise. Do you know of anything?

KEN: As a matter of fact, I do. The Edwards family lives in a quiet residential neighborhood near the river. You know them, don't you?

PETRA: Yes, I think Anton went to school with their son. But they're not moving, are they?

KEN: Yes, they're moving back to Vancouver next month.

PETRA: Are they? What kind of apartment do they have?

KEN: A one-bedroom. It's very nice.

PETRA: It's not furnished, is it? Anton really doesn't have any furniture.

KEN: Can't he rent some? I did that in my first apartment.

PETRA: I don't know. Isn't it less expensive to buy?

**A quiet residential neighborhood in Berlin**

# EXERCISE 2 AFFIRMATIVE AND NEGATIVE TAG QUESTIONS

GRAMMAR NOTE 3  Mr. and Mrs. Edwards are talking about their move to Vancouver.
Match the statements with the tags.

**Statements**

*f*  1. You've called the movers,

*h*  2. They're coming tomorrow,

*e*  3. This is going to be expensive,

*d*  4. You haven't finished packing,

*a*  5. We don't need any more boxes,

*g*  6. We need to disconnect the phone,

*c*  7. The movers supply boxes for us,

*b*  8. Moving is never easy,

**Tags**

a. do we?

b. is it?

c. don't they?

d. have you?

e. isn't it?

f. haven't you?

g. don't we?

h. aren't they?

# EXERCISE 3  TAG QUESTIONS AND SHORT ANSWERS

**A** GRAMMAR NOTES 3–4  Complete this interview with Tessa Bradley. Use appropriate tags and short answers.

HOST:  You're originally from England, ___aren't you___ ?
1.

TESSA:  ___Yes, I am___ . I'm from London.
2.

HOST:  You've lived in Vancouver for many years, ___haven't you___ ?
3.

TESSA:  ___Yes, I have___ . Since I came here to teach video arts. Seems like ages ago.
4.

HOST:  You didn't know anyone here, ___did you___ ?
5.

TESSA:  ___No, I didn't___ . I was here all alone. And I didn't have a cent to my name. Just
6.

some ideas and a lot of hope. It sounds crazy, ___doesn't it___ ?
7.

HOST:  ___No, it doesn't___ Not when you look at all the TV shows you've done. Things
8.

have sure worked out for you, ___haven't they___ ? You've already worked on two
9.

big TV series, and you've done some work for the movies as well. You're working on

another film now, ___aren't you___ ?
10.

TESSA:  ___Yes, I am___ . It's a comedy about some kids who become invisible.
11.

HOST:  Speaking of kids, you and your husband have some of your own, ___Don't you___ ?
12.

TESSA:  ___Yes, we do___ . Two boys and a girl—all very visible!
13.

HOST:  I know what you mean. Do you ever wish they were invisible?

TESSA:  Hmm. That's an interesting thought, ___isn't it___ ?
14.

⏵07|03  **B** LISTEN AND CHECK  Listen to the conversation and check your answers in A.

# EXERCISE 4 NEGATIVE *YES/NO* QUESTIONS AND SHORT ANSWERS

Ⓐ GRAMMAR NOTES 2, 4 Anton Kada is looking at the apartment the Edwards family just left. Complete the negative *yes/no* questions. Write short answers. Use the verbs that are in the sentences following the short answers.

1. OWNER: Hi, you look familiar. *Isn't your name* _____ John Radcliffe?

   ANTON: *No, it isn't* _____. My name is Anton Kada.

2. OWNER: Oh. haven't you seen _____ this apartment before?

   ANTON: No, I haven't _____. I've never seen it before. This is the first time.

3. ANTON: The apartment feels hot. Doesn't it have _____ air conditioning?

   OWNER: No, It doesn't _____. It has ceiling fans but no air conditioners.

4. ANTON: I notice that there are marks on the walls. Aren't you going to paint them?

   OWNER: Yes I am. _____. I'm going to paint them next week.

5. OWNER: Isn't it _____ a nice apartment?

   ANTON: Yes, It is. _____. It's very nice. But I'm not sure I can take it.

6. OWNER: Isn't it _____ big enough?

   ANTON: Yes, it is. _____. It's big enough, but I can't afford it.

7. OWNER: Didn't you know _____ how much it was before you came here?

   ANTON: Yes, I did. _____. I knew the price, but I was hoping for a bargain.

▶07|04 Ⓑ LISTEN AND CHECK Listen to the conversations and check your answers in A.

# EXERCISE 5 NEGATIVE *YES/NO* QUESTIONS AND TAG QUESTIONS

GRAMMAR NOTES 1–3 Rewrite the sentences. Change the sentence in parentheses into a negative *yes/no* question or a tag question.

ROLAND: Hi, Tessa. *Isn't it a nice day? or It's a nice day, isn't it?*
   **1.** (I think it's a nice day.)

TESSA: It sure is. Don't you have a class today? You have a class today, don't you?
   **2.** (I think you have a class today.)

ROLAND: I do. But not until 3:00. Isn't it 2:30 now? It's only 2:30 now, isn't it?
   **3.** (I think it's only 2:30 now.)

TESSA: You're right. You have plenty of time. Don't you have a bike? You have a bike, don't
   **4.** (I'm surprised you don't have a bike.)

ROLAND: I lost it. That's why I'm walking.

TESSA: Well, it's a nice day for a walk. Isn't Vancouver a beautiful city? Vancouver is a beautiful city, isn't it
   **5.** (I think Vancouver is a beautiful city.)

ROLAND: Yes. And a great city for video artists. Aren't you coming to see ....? See my film, Aren't you
   **6.** (I'm pretty sure you're coming to see my film tonight.)

TESSA: I wouldn't miss it. Hey! Isn't your class that way? your class is that way, isn't it? We took the wrong path.
   **7.** (I'm pretty sure your class is that way.)

# EXERCISE 6 NEGATIVE *YES/NO* QUESTIONS AND TAG QUESTIONS

GRAMMAR NOTES 1–3  Read this information about video artist Nam June Paik. Imagine you are going to interview a guide at the Nam June Paik Art Center in Yongin, South Korea. You are not sure of the information in parentheses. Write negative *yes/no* questions or tag questions to check that information.

**Nam June Paik**

1. born July 1932 in Korea (in Seoul?)
2. at age 14, studied music (took piano lessons?)
3. family left Korea in 1950 (moved to Tokyo?)
4. moved to Germany in 1956 (originally studied music composition there?)
5. attracted to electronic music (didn't write traditional music, too?)
6. during the 1960s created a new art form with TV screens and video (didn't paint on paper again?)
7. produced a huge art installation for 1988 Seoul Olympics (the structure used 1,003 TV monitors?)
8. after an illness in 1996 started painting on flat surfaces (didn't do any more installations after that?)
9. lived in New York (became a U.S. citizen?)
10. died in January 2006 in Florida (was 75 years old?)

1. <u>Wasn't he born in Seoul?</u> **or** <u>He was born in Seoul, wasn't he?</u>

2. _____

3. _____

4. _____

5. _____

6. _____

7. _____

8. _____

9. _____

10. _____

## EXERCISE 7 RISING AND FALLING TAG QUESTIONS

07|05 **PRONUNCIATION NOTE** Read the tag questions. Then listen to each question and decide if the voice rises (↗) or falls (↘) at the end of the tag. Draw the correct arrow over the tag.

1. You're originally from Vancouver, aren't you?

2. It's a beautiful city, isn't it?

3. You don't like the weather here, do you?

4. They'll be moving soon, won't they?

5. That building isn't new, is it?

6. There aren't any more vacancies, are there?

7. You've never met Ann, have you?

8. She works around here, doesn't she?

9. This can't be true, can it?

10. I'm really lucky, aren't I?

## EXERCISE 8 EDITING

**GRAMMAR NOTES 1–4** Tessa Bradley is working on a script for a movie that takes place in Vancouver. There are ten mistakes in the use of negative *yes/no* questions, tag questions, and short answers. The first mistake is already corrected. Find and correct nine more.

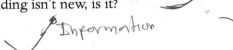

**BEN:** It's been a long time, Joe, ~~haven't~~ *hasn't* it?

**JOE:** That depends on what you mean by a long time, doesn't that?

**BEN:** Are not you afraid to show your face here in Vancouver?

**JOE:** I can take care of myself. I'm still alive, amn't I?

**BEN:** Until someone recognizes you. You're still wanted by the police, are you? But that has never bothered you, hasn't it?

**JOE:** I'll be gone by morning. Look, I need a place to stay. Just for one night.

**BEN:** I have to think about my wife and kid. Don't you have any place else to go?

**JOE:** Yes, I do. There's no one to turn to but you. You have to help me.

**BEN:** I've already helped you plenty. I went to jail for you, haven't I? And didn't I kept my mouth shut the whole time?

**JOE:** Yeah, OK, Ben. Don't you remember what happened in Vegas, do you?

**BEN:** You won't let me forget it, will you? OK, OK. I can make a call.

## EXERCISE 9  LISTENING

▶07|06  Ⓐ  Listen to the conversations. Read the statements. Then listen again and check (✓) *True* or *False*.

|  |  | True | False |
|---|---|---|---|
| 1. | The man wants to know if Rio is the capital of Brazil. | ✓ | ☐ |
| 2. | The man thinks Rio has an exciting nightlife. | ☐ | ☐ |
| 3. | The woman wants to know if Anton was teaching a course in Korea. | ☐ | ☐ |
| 4. | The woman wants to know if it is hard to find an apartment in Berlin. | ☐ | ☐ |
| 5. | The woman thinks the man has lived in Tokyo for a long time. | ☐ | ☐ |
| 6. | The man is sure that the weather is hot in Cairo. | ☐ | ☐ |
| 7. | The woman thinks Anne is from Vancouver. | ☐ | ☐ |
| 8. | The woman wants to know if the man is from Vancouver. | ☐ | ☐ |

▶07|06  Ⓑ  Listen to the conversations again. Then work with a partner. Discuss your answers in A. For each answer, repeat the part of the conversation that explains why you chose *True* or *False*.

EXAMPLE:  A: I see that the answer for number 1 is *True*. But isn't the answer actually *False*?
　　　　　 B: No, it isn't. It's *True* because the man is unsure about the capital of Brazil. His voice rises when he says, "Rio isn't the capital of Brazil, is it?" That means he wants to check the information.
　　　　　 A: OK. Now I understand. What's your answer for number 2?

## EXERCISE 10  HOW MUCH DO YOU REALLY KNOW?

Ⓐ  CONVERSATION  You are going to work with a partner. How well do you know him or her? Complete the questions with information about your partner that you think is correct.

EXAMPLE: *You're from Venezuela, aren't you?*

1. _____, aren't you?

2. Don't you _____?

3. _____, haven't you?

4. _____, did you?

5. _____, do you?

6. Aren't you _____?

Ⓑ  Now work with your partner. Ask the questions to check your information. Check (✓) each question that has the correct information. Which one of you knows the other one better?

EXAMPLE:  A: You're from Venezuela, aren't you?
　　　　　 B: Yes, I am.  **or**  No, I'm from Colombia.

# EXERCISE 11 LONDON AND VANCOUVER

INFORMATION GAP  Work with a partner. Student A will follow the instructions below.
Student B will follow the instructions on page 486.

---

**STUDENT A**

- What do you know about London? Complete the questions by circling the correct words and writing the tags.

  1. London (is) / isn't the largest city in the United Kingdom, *isn't it* _____?

  2. It is / isn't the capital of the United Kingdom, _____?

  3. London lies on a river / the ocean, _____?

  4. It consists of two / thirty-two "boroughs," or parts, _____?

  5. It has / doesn't have a lot of theaters, _____?

  6. Many / Not many tourists visit London, _____?

  7. It is / isn't a very safe city, _____?

- Ask Student B the questions. Student B will read a paragraph about London and tell you if your information is correct or not.

  EXAMPLE:  A: London is the largest city in the United Kingdom, isn't it?
  B: Yes, it is.

- Now read about Vancouver and answer Student B's questions.

  EXAMPLE:  B: Vancouver isn't the largest city in Canada, is it?
  A: No, it isn't. It's the third largest city.

## VANCOUVER

Vancouver is the third largest city in Canada. Lying on the Pacific coast, it is surrounded on three sides by water and has the largest and busiest seaport in the country. It is also home to Stanley Park, one of the largest city parks in North America. Because of its great natural and architectural beauty and its moderate climate, Vancouver is a very popular place to live. It also attracts millions of tourists each year. It is a very international city, and more than 50 percent of its residents do not speak English as their first language. Today, Vancouver is called the "Hollywood of the North" because of the number of films made in this exciting city.

# FROM GRAMMAR TO WRITING

**A** BEFORE YOU WRITE   Interview a classmate about his or her home city. Write eight questions. Use negative *yes/no* questions and tag questions. Ask your questions. Take notes of your classmate's answers.

EXAMPLE:   You're originally from Venezuela, aren't you? *Yes—Caracas.*
Isn't that the capital? *Yes.*

**B** WRITE   Use your notes to write up the interview. Include negative *yes/no* questions and tag questions. Try to avoid the common mistakes in the chart.

EXAMPLE:   INTERVIEWER:   You're originally from Venezuela, aren't you?
MIGUEL:        Yes, I am. I'm from Caracas.
INTERVIEWER:   Isn't that the capital?
MIGUEL:        Yes, it is.

## Common Mistakes in Using Negative *Yes/No* Questions and Tag Questions

| | |
|---|---|
| In **informal conversation**, use **contractions** in negative *yes/no* questions and tags. Do not use full forms. | **Isn't** Caracas the capital of Venezuela?<br>NOT ~~Is not~~ Caracas the capital of Venezuela?<br>Caracas is the capital of Venezuela, **isn't it**?<br>NOT Caracas is the capital of Venezuela, ~~is it not~~? |
| Use a **pronoun** in the **tag** that matches the noun in the statement. Do not use a noun in the tag. | **The city** is beautiful, isn't **it**?<br>NOT The city is beautiful, isn't ~~the city~~? |
| If there is an **auxiliary** in the statement, use the **same auxiliary in the tag**. Do not use a different auxiliary in the tag. | You **have** been here since 2016, **haven't** you?<br>NOT You have been here since 2016, ~~aren't~~ you? |

**C** CHECK YOUR WORK   Read your interview. Underline the negative *yes/no* questions. Circle the tags. Use the Editing Checklist to check your work.

## Editing Checklist

**Did you use . . . ?**

- [ ] contractions in negative *yes/no* questions
- [ ] contractions in tags
- [ ] negative tags with affirmative statements
- [ ] affirmative tags with negative statements
- [ ] the same auxiliary in the tag and in the statement
- [ ] pronouns (not nouns) in tags

**D** REVISE YOUR WORK   Read your interview again. Can you improve your writing? Make changes if necessary. Give your interview a title.

# UNIT 7 REVIEW

**Test yourself on the grammar of the unit.**

**A** Circle the correct words to complete the sentences.

1. It's a beautiful day, isn't / is it?

2. Didn't / Aren't you order coffee?

3. You've / You haven't heard from Raoul recently, haven't you?

4. That was a great movie, wasn't that / it?

5. Nick hasn't left San Francisco yet, did / has he?

6. Lara can't move out of her apartment yet, can Lara / she?

7. Shouldn't / Should not we leave soon? It's getting late.

**B** Complete the conversation with negative *yes/no* questions and tag questions. Use the correct verbs and short answers.

A: You haven't lived in Vancouver for very long, _____ you?
                                                        1.

B: _____. Only for a month. Why are you asking?
        2.

A: You're wearing so many clothes. _____ you hot?
                                              3.

B: _____. I think it's freezing today.
        4.

A: Oh, come on. You're not really *that* cold, _____ you?
                                                        5.

B: I'm originally from Rio de Janeiro. This is my first experience with cold weather. I'll get used

   to it someday, _____ I?
                          6.

A: _____. It won't take long, and winter here isn't very bad.
        7.

**C** Find and correct six mistakes.

A: Ken hasn't come back from Korea yet, has Ken?

B: No, he has. He got back last week. Didn't he call you when he got back?

A: No, he didn't. He's probably busy. There are a lot of things to do when you move, isn't there?

B: Definitely. And I guess his family wanted to spend a lot of time with him, won't they?

A: I'm sure they will. You know, I think I'll just call him. You have his phone number, have you?

B: Yes, I do. Could you wait while I get it from my phone? You're not in a hurry, aren't you?

**Now check your answers on page 476.**

# Additions and Responses: *So, Too, Neither, Not either,* and *But*

## SIMILARITIES AND DIFFERENCES

**OUTCOMES**
- Show similarity, using *so, too, neither,* or *not either,* and show difference, using *but*
- Identify key details in an article on a scientific topic and in a conversation between two people
- Discuss similarities and differences between two people
- Research a pair of twins and report findings
- Write about the similarities and differences between two people

| STEP 1 | GRAMMAR IN CONTEXT |
|---|---|

### BEFORE YOU READ

Look at the photos of twins. Discuss the questions.

1. What is different about each pair of twins? What is the same?

2. How are *you* similar to family members? How are *you* different?

### READ

08|01 Read this article about identical twins.

## The Twin Question: Nature or Nurture?

Mark and Gerald are identical twins. Mirror images of each other, they also share many similarities in lifestyle. Mark was a firefighter, and so was Gerald. Mark has never been married, and neither has Gerald. Mark likes hunting, fishing, and old movies. Gerald does too. These similarities might not be unusual in identical twins, except that Mark and Gerald were separated when they were five days old. They

**Mark and Gerald**

grew up in different states with different families. Neither one knew that he had a twin until they found each other at age thirty-one.

Average people are fascinated by twins, and so are scientists. Because identical twins share the same genes, they offer researchers the chance to study the effect of heredity[1] on health and personality. Identical twins with completely different childhoods allow researchers to investigate the influence of environment.[2]

Scientists have long wondered about the role of heredity and environment in our lives. In other words, which is the more important factor—nature or nurture? The example of Mark and Gerald seems to show the power of genetics. However, the lives of other identical twins separated at birth indicate that the question of nature or nurture is complicated.

Identical twins Anaïs Bordier and Samantha Futerman were adopted soon after their birth in Busan, South Korea. Twenty-five years later, a friend was sure he saw Anaïs in a YouTube video, that is, until he realized the woman on YouTube was American, while Anaïs was French. He told Anaïs immediately. When she saw the video, Anaïs was so shocked to see another person who looked exactly like her that she decided to find out who the American woman was.

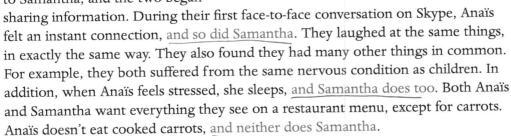
Anaïs and Samantha

Anaïs sent a Facebook message to Samantha, and the two began sharing information. During their first face-to-face conversation on Skype, Anaïs felt an instant connection, and so did Samantha. They laughed at the same things, in exactly the same way. They also found they had many other things in common. For example, they both suffered from the same nervous condition as children. In addition, when Anaïs feels stressed, she sleeps, and Samantha does too. Both Anaïs and Samantha want everything they see on a restaurant menu, except for carrots. Anaïs doesn't eat cooked carrots, and neither does Samantha.

However, Samantha and Anaïs are not totally alike. Of course, Samantha speaks American English, while Anaïs speaks British English and her native language, French. But there are other differences as well. Like her adoptive mother, Samantha is an outgoing person, but Anaïs isn't. She is more reserved like *her* adoptive mother. Samantha, an actor, has an excellent memory, but Anaïs doesn't. A fashion designer, she has stronger visual skills.

Clearly, our heredity doesn't completely control our lives. Our environment doesn't either. The lives of twins separated at birth suggest that we have a lot to learn about the complex role these two powerful forces play in shaping human lives.

---

1 *heredity:* the genes we receive from our parents
2 *environment:* everything around us, including family members, religion, education, financial situation, and location

# AFTER YOU READ

**A VOCABULARY** Complete the sentences with the words from the box.

| complex | factor | identical | image | investigate | reserved |
|---------|--------|-----------|-------|-------------|----------|

1. Some parents like to dress their twins in _____ clothes. Others prefer to focus on differences.

2. When Don saw the _____ of his twin in the photo, he thought at first that he was looking at himself.

3. Karyn's sister is friendly and talks a lot, but Karyn is _____.

4. The answer to the question about genetics was too _____ for me to understand.

5. Mia's education was an important _____ in her success.

6. I'm going to _____ twins and their emotional connection for my research project.

**B COMPREHENSION** Check (✓) the boxes to complete the sentences. Check all the true information from the article.

1. Mark and Gerald have had the same _____.
   ☑ marriage histories ☑ types of jobs ☑ hobbies

2. Scientists are fascinated by _____.
   ☐ average people ☑ twins ☑ nature and nurture

3. Samantha Futerman sleeps when she is _____.
   ☐ sick ☑ stressed ☐ with her sister

4. Anaïs and Samantha do not have the same _____.
   ☑ personality ☐ appearance ☑ adoptive mother

5. Anaïs does not _____.
   ☐ like to eat a lot ☐ have strong visual skills ☑ remember things perfectly

6. Environment _____ our lives.
   ☑ partly controls ☐ completely controls ☐ has a weak effect on

**C DISCUSSION** Work with a partner. Compare your answers in B. Why did you check the boxes you checked?

## SIMILARITY: *SO* AND *NEITHER*

*[handwritten: be / modal / Aux / Verb + Subject.]*

**Affirmative**

| Statement | Addition | |
|---|---|---|
| Subject + Verb | *And so* | Verb* + Subject |
| Amy *is* a twin, | and so | *am* I. |
| She *has* traveled, | | *have* we. |
| She *can* ski, | | *can* they. |
| She *likes* dogs, | | *does* Bill. |

*[handwritten: Y — tambien]*

*The verb in the addition is a form of *be*, an auxiliary, or a modal.

*[handwritten: be / Modal / Aux]*

**Negative**

| Statement | Addition | |
|---|---|---|
| Subject + Verb + *Not* | *And neither* | Verb + Subject |
| Amy *isn't* a twin, | and neither | *am* I. |
| She *hasn't* traveled, | | *have* we. |
| She *can't* ski, | | *can* they. |
| She *doesn't* like dogs, | | *does* Bill. |

*[handwritten: Y tampoco]*

## SIMILARITY: *TOO* AND *NOT EITHER*

**Affirmative**

*[handwritten: S + V + too. (object).]*

| Statement | Addition | |
|---|---|---|
| Subject + Verb | *And* | Subject + Verb + *Too* |
| Amy *is* a twin, | and | I *am* too. |
| She *has* traveled, | | we *have* too. |
| She *can* ski, | | they *can* too. |
| She *likes* dogs, | | Bill *does* too. |

*[handwritten: tambien.]*

**Negative**

*[handwritten: Sub + verb + Not either.]*

| Statement | Addition | |
|---|---|---|
| Subject + Verb + *Not* | *And* | Subject + Verb + *Not either* |
| Amy *isn't* a twin, | and | I'*m not* either. |
| She *hasn't* traveled, | | we *haven't* either. |
| She *can't* ski, | | they *can't* either. |
| She *doesn't* like dogs, | | Bill *doesn't* either. |

*[handwritten: tampoco]*

## DIFFERENCE: *BUT*

### Affirmative + Negative

| Statement | Addition | |
|---|---|---|
| **Subject + Verb** | *But* | **Subject + Verb + *Not*** |
| Amy *is* a twin, | | I'*m not*. |
| She *has* traveled, | but | we *haven't*. |
| She *can* ski, | | they *can't*. |
| She *likes* dogs, | | Bill *doesn't*. |

### Negative + Affirmative

| Statement | Addition | |
|---|---|---|
| **Subject + Verb + *Not*** | *But* | **Subject + Verb** |
| Amy *isn't* a twin, | | I *am*. |
| She *can't* ski, | but | we *can*. |
| She *hasn't* traveled, | | they *have*. |
| She *doesn't* like dogs, | | Bill *does*. |

# GRAMMAR NOTES

## 1 Additions to Show Similarity or Difference

**Additions** are clauses or short sentences that **follow a statement**. Use additions to **avoid repeating** the information in the statement.

Additions express **similarity** or **difference** with the information in the statement.

- **similarity**

  STATEMENT · ADDITION
  Anaïs sleeps a lot, **and so does Samantha**.
  *(Anaïs sleeps a lot. Samantha sleeps a lot.)*

- **difference**

  STATEMENT · ADDITION
  Anaïs grew up in France, **but Samantha didn't**.
  *(Anaïs grew up in France. Samantha didn't grow up in France.)*

## 2 Additions Showing Similarity with *So, Too, Neither,* or *Not Either*

Additions showing similarity can be **clauses or short sentences**. They use *so, too, neither,* or *not either* to express **similarity**.

Most additions of similarity are **clauses** starting with *and*.

CLAUSE
Mark is a firefighter, **and so is Gerald**.
Mark is a firefighter, **and Gerald is *too***.
Mark isn't married, **and *neither* is Gerald**.
Mark isn't married, **and Gerald *isn't either***.

**CONTINUED ▶**

| | SENTENCE |
|---|---|
| Additions of similarity can also be **short sentences**. | Mark is a firefighter. ***So is Gerald.***<br>Mark is a firefighter. **Gerald is *too*.**<br>Mark isn't married. ***Neither is Gerald.***<br>Mark isn't married. **Gerald *isn't either*.** |

| | AFFIRMATIVE STATEMENT |
|---|---|
| Use *so* or *too* if the addition follows an **affirmative statement**. *So* and *too* have the same meaning. | Mark **is** a firefighter, and ***so is*** Gerald.<br>Mark **is** a firefighter, and Gerald **is *too*.**<br>*(Mark is a firefighter. Gerald is a firefighter.)* |

| | NEGATIVE STATEMENT |
|---|---|
| Use *neither* or *not either* if the addition follows a **negative statement**. *Neither* and *not either* have the same meaning. | Mark **didn't** marry. ***Neither did*** Gerald.<br>Mark **didn't** marry. Gerald **did*n't either*.**<br>*(Mark isn't married. Gerald isn't married.)* |

| | |
|---|---|
| **BE CAREFUL!** Notice the **word order** after *so* and *neither*. The verb comes before the subject. | So **is** Gerald.   NOT   So ~~Gerald is~~.<br>Neither **did** Gerald.   NOT   Neither ~~Gerald did~~. |

| | |
|---|---|
| **USAGE NOTE** People sometimes use *as well* in additions that follow an affirmative statement. | Mark enjoys fishing, **and Gerald does *as well*.**<br>Mark is a fan of old movies, **and Gerald is *as well*.** |

## 3 Additions Showing Difference with *But*

Additions showing difference are **clauses** starting with *but*. They use *but* to express **difference**.

| | AFFIRMATIVE · · · NEGATIVE |
|---|---|
| If the statement is **affirmative**, the addition is **negative**. | Ana **has** short hair, ***but*** Eva **doesn't.**<br>Ana **lived** in Mexico, ***but*** Eva **didn't.** |

| | NEGATIVE · · · AFFIRMATIVE |
|---|---|
| If the statement is **negative**, the addition is **affirmative**. | Ana **doesn't like** to read, ***but*** Eva **does.**<br>Ana **didn't speak** English, ***but*** Eva **did.** |

## 4 Verbs in Additions

Additions always use a form of *be*, an **auxiliary verb**, or a **modal**.

| | |
|---|---|
| If the statement uses *be*, use *be* in the addition. | I**'m** a twin, and so **is** my cousin. |

| | |
|---|---|
| If the statement uses an auxiliary verb (*be*, *have*, *do*, or *will*) or a modal (*can*, *could*, *should*, *would*, or *must*), use the **same auxiliary verb or modal** in the addition. | My twin sister and I **have** always lived together, and so **have** my cousins.<br>I **can't** drive, and neither **can** my twin. |

| | |
|---|---|
| If the statement doesn't use *be* or an auxiliary verb, use an appropriate form of *do* in the addition. | Bill **owns** a dog, and so **does** Ed.<br>Bill **bought** a Chevrolet, and so **did** Ed. |

| | |
|---|---|
| **BE CAREFUL!** The verb in the addition **agrees with the subject of the addition**, not with the subject of the statement. | They**'ve** learned Spanish, and so **has she.**<br>NOT They've learned Spanish, and so ~~have she~~. |

## 5 Short Responses with *So, Too, Neither, Not Either,* or *But*

In **conversation**, you can use **short responses** with *so, too, neither, not either,* or *but.*

| | |
|---|---|
| Use *so, too, neither,* or *not either* to express **agreement** with another speaker. | A: I like sports. <br> B: *So do I.* or I do *too.* <br><br> A: I don't like sports. <br> B: *Neither do I.* or I *don't either.* |
| Use *but* to express **disagreement** with another speaker. You can often leave out *but.* | A: I wouldn't like to have a twin. <br> B: Oh, *(but)* I would. |
| **USAGE NOTE** In **informal speech**, we often say *Me too* to express agreement with an affirmative statement and *Me neither* to express agreement with a negative statement. | A: I think twin studies are fascinating. <br> B: *Me too.* <br><br> A: I don't know any mirror-image twins. <br> B: *Me neither.* |

## STEP 3  FOCUSED PRACTICE

## EXERCISE 1  DISCOVER THE GRAMMAR

GRAMMAR NOTES 1–5  Read these short conversations between Erica and several of her friends. Decide if the statement that follows each conversation is *True (T)* or *False (F)*.

1. **CAROL:** I went to Neil's party last night.
   **ERICA:** But I didn't.

   _T_ Erica wasn't at Neil's party.

2. **LISA:** Ed told me he saw you at Neil's party last night. I thought you weren't going.
   **ERICA:** I was in the library last night. So was my roommate. You can ask her.

   _F_ Erica's roommate was at Neil's party.

3. **DAVE:** Most people weren't taking pictures at Neil's party, but Pete was. Here they are.
   **ERICA:** And here's a photo of that girl who looks . . . just like me!

   _T_ Pete was taking pictures.

4. **JIM:** I met someone who looks just like you last night. Her name is María.
   **ERICA:** I know . . . I have long black hair and big blue eyes, and she does too.

   _T_ María has long black hair and big blue eyes.

5. **JIM:** One more thing. María doesn't like to dance. Neither do you.
   **ERICA:** Now this is getting interesting.

   _F_ Erica likes to dance.

6. **JIM:** I'd like to find out more about María.
   **ERICA:** Me too.

   _T_ Both Jim and Erica want to find out more about María.

7. **ERICA:** Everyone is talking about someone named María, but I haven't met her.
   **AMY:** I haven't either.

   _T_ Amy hasn't met María.

8. **ERICA:** Dave is having a party tonight. I can't go, but you can.
   **AMY:** Right, and if I'm lucky, I'll meet María, your long lost twin!

   _F_ Amy can't to go to Dave's party tonight.


## EXERCISE 2 ADDITIONS

GRAMMAR NOTES 1–4 **Circle the correct words to complete this paragraph about being a twin.**

Sometimes being a twin can cause trouble. In high school, I was in Mr. Jacobs's

history class. Neither / (So) was Joe. One day we took a test. The results were identical.
                    **1.**

I got questions 18 and 20 wrong. Joe did so / too.
                                          **2.**

   I didn't spell *Constantinople* correctly, and either / neither did Joe. The teacher
                                                        **3.**

was sure we had cheated. As a result, I got an *F* on the test, and so did / got Joe. We
                                                                        **4.**

tried to convince Mr. Jacobs that it was just a coincidence. After all, I had sat on the

left side of the room, but Joe didn't / hadn't. As always, he sat on the right. But Mr.
                                      **5.**

Jacobs just thought we had developed some complex way of sharing answers across

the room. Our parents believed we were honest, but Mr. Jacobs didn't / weren't. The
                                                                        **6.**

principal didn't either / too. They finally agreed to give us another test.
               **7.**

   Even though we were in separate rooms and cheating *couldn't* be a factor, I

got questions 3 and 10 wrong. Guess what? Neither / So did Joe. Our teacher was
                                                  **8.**

astounded, and / but we weren't.
          **9.**

# EXERCISE 3  SHORT RESPONSES

**Ⓐ GRAMMAR NOTE 5** Two twins are talking. They agree on everything. Complete their conversation with short responses.

MARTA: I love having someone who's my mirror image. I'm so happy we finally found each other.

CARLA: So _____*am I*_____. I always felt like something was missing from my life.
　　　　　　　　1.

MARTA: So _____. I always knew I had a double somewhere out there.
　　　　　　　2.

CARLA: I can't believe how alike we look!

MARTA: Neither _____.
　　　　　　　　　3.

CARLA: And we like and dislike all the same things.

MARTA: Right. I hate lettuce.

CARLA: I _____. And I detest liver.
　　　　　　4.

MARTA: So _____. I love pizza, though.
　　　　　5.

CARLA: So _____. Especially with mushrooms. But I can't stand pepperoni.
　　　　　6.

MARTA: Neither _____.
　　　　　　　　7.

CARLA: This is amazing! I'd like to find out if our husbands have a lot in common, too.

MARTA: So _____! That might be fun to investigate!
　　　　　8.

▶08|02 **Ⓑ LISTEN AND CHECK** Listen to the conversation and check your answers in A.

# EXERCISE 4 ADDITIONS FOR SIMILARITY OR DIFFERENCE

GRAMMAR NOTES 1–4 Look at this chart about the twins' husbands. Then complete the sentences about them. Add statements with *so, too, neither, not either,* and *but.*

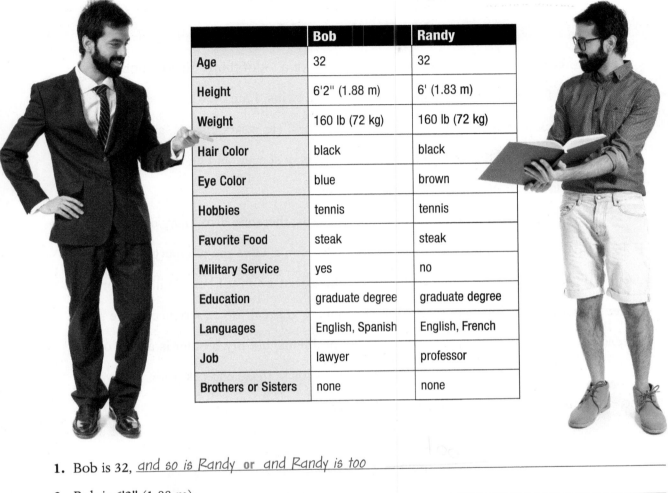

|  | Bob | Randy |
|---|---|---|
| Age | 32 | 32 |
| Height | 6'2" (1.88 m) | 6' (1.83 m) |
| Weight | 160 lb (72 kg) | 160 lb (72 kg) |
| Hair Color | black | black |
| Eye Color | blue | brown |
| Hobbies | tennis | tennis |
| Favorite Food | steak | steak |
| Military Service | yes | no |
| Education | graduate degree | graduate degree |
| Languages | English, Spanish | English, French |
| Job | lawyer | professor |
| Brothers or Sisters | none | none |

1. Bob is 32, _and so is Randy **or** and Randy is too_ _____.

2. Bob is 6'2" (1.88 m), _____.

3. Bob weighs 160 pounds (72 kg), _____.

4. Bob has black hair, _____.

5. Bob doesn't have green eyes, _____.

6. Bob plays tennis, _____.

7. Bob likes steak, _____.

8. Bob served in the military, _____.

9. Bob has attended graduate school, _____.

10. Bob doesn't speak French, _____.

11. Bob became a lawyer, _____.

12. Bob doesn't have any brothers or sisters, _____.

## EXERCISE 5 EDITING

GRAMMAR NOTES 1–5 **Read this composition about two brothers. There are six mistakes in the use of sentence additions. The first mistake is already corrected. Find and correct five more.**

# My Brother and I

My brother is just a year older than I am. We have a lot of things in common. We
look alike. In fact, sometimes people ask us if we're twins. I am 5'10", and so ~~he is~~ *is he*. I
have thick black hair and dark brown eyes. So he does. He wears glasses, and I do too.
We also share some of the same interests. I love to play soccer, and he too. Both of us
swim every day, but I can't dive, and either can he.

Although there are a lot of similarities between us, there are also many differences.
For example, he likes eating all kinds of food, but I don't. Give me hamburgers and fries
every day! My brother doesn't want to go to college, but I don't. I believe it's important
to get as much education as possible, but he wants to get real-life experience. I like
to read a lot and think carefully about complex problems, but my brother is a man of
action. I think our personalities are an important factor in these choices. I am reserved
and easygoing, but he doesn't. He talks a lot and
has strong opinions. When I think about it,
despite the many things we have in common,
we really are more different than similar.

## EXERCISE 6   LISTENING

▶08|03   **A**   A couple is on their first date. Listen to their conversation. Look at the information. Listen again to the couple's conversation. Check (✓) the correct box(es).

|  | Man | Woman |  |  | Man | Woman |
|---|---|---|---|---|---|---|
| **1.** loves Italian food | ✓ | ✓ | **6.** enjoys fiction | | ☐ | ☐ |
| **2.** cooks | ☐ | ☐ | **7.** plays sports | | ☐ | ☐ |
| **3.** eats out a lot | ☐ | ☐ | **8.** watches sports on TV | | ☐ | ☐ |
| **4.** enjoys old movies | ☐ | ☐ | **9.** loves documentaries | | ☐ | ☐ |
| **5.** reads biographies | ☐ | ☐ | **10.** wants to see the documentary | | ☐ | ☐ |

▶08|03   **B**   Listen to the conversation again. Then work with a partner. Discuss your answers in A. Explain your choices.

EXAMPLE:   **A:** So, the answer to number 1 is the man *and* the woman.
                **B:** Right. That's because the man says, "I really love Italian food." And then the woman says, "So do I."
                **A:** OK. Now, what about number 2? Who cooks?

## EXERCISE 7   FIND SOMEONE WHO . . .

**A**   GAME   Complete the statements. Then read your statements to a classmate. He or she will give you a short response. Check (✓) the items the two of you have in common. Then do the same with another classmate.

EXAMPLE:   **A:** I like to walk in the rain.
                **B:** So do I. **or** Oh, I don't. I like to stay home and watch TV.

**I have these things in common with:**

|  | (Classmate 1) | (Classmate 2) |
|---|---|---|
| **1.** I like to _____. | ☐ | ☐ |
| **2.** I never _____. | ☐ | ☐ |
| **3.** I love _____.<br>(name of food) | ☐ | ☐ |
| **4.** I can't _____. | ☐ | ☐ |
| **5.** I would like to _____. | ☐ | ☐ |
| **6.** I've never _____. | ☐ | ☐ |
| **7.** When I was younger, I didn't _____. | ☐ | ☐ |
| **8.** I'll never _____. | ☐ | ☐ |

**B**   Count the number of checkmarks for each of the two classmates. Which classmate do you have more in common with?

# EXERCISE 8 CAN YOU TELL THEM APART?

PICTURE COMPARISON   Work with a partner. Look at the pictures of twins Michael and Matthew. How many things do they have in common? How many differences can you find? Discuss their similarities and differences.

EXAMPLE:   A: Michael has a mustache, and so does Matthew.
           B: Michael doesn't . . .

# EXERCISE 9 TOGETHER AGAIN

**A** GROUP PROJECT   Work in a group. Choose one of the sets of twins listed below, all of whom were separated at birth and then later reunited. Do research about the twins and answer some of the questions.

- Paula Bernstein and Elyse Schein
- Adriana Scott and Tamara Rabi
- Jim Springer and Jim Lewis
- Debbie Mehlman and Sharon Poset

**Possible Questions:**
- When and where were the twins born?
- Where did each twin grow up?
- What kind of environment (family, school, education, etc.) did each twin grow up in?
- What similarities do the twins have?
- What differences do the twins have?
- What interesting facts did you learn about the twins?

**Paula Bernstein and Elyse Schein**

EXAMPLE:
A: Paula Bernstein and Elyse Schein were born in New York City in 1968.
B: Paula grew up there, and so did Elyse.
C: They have a lot in common. When they met for the first time, Paula was a writer, and so was Elyse.
A: But there were differences, too. Paula was married, but Elyse . . .

**B** Report back to your class. If your group chose the same pair of twins as another group, do you have the same information about those twins? Compare answers.

EXAMPLE:
A: Paula Bernstein and Elyse Schein were born in New York City.
B: That's right. Paula grew up in New York, and Elyse did too.
A: Then Paula stayed in New York, but Elyse didn't. She moved to Paris.
B: Here's something interesting. When they first met, they had the same job. Paula was a writer, and . . .

## EXERCISE 10 WHAT DO *YOU* THINK ABOUT NATURE VS. NURTURE?

DISCUSSION Work in a group. Which do you think is more important, nature or nurture? Give examples from your research in Exercise 9 and your own experience to support your views.

EXAMPLE:
A: I think that nature is more important. Look at Paula and Elyse. They . . .
B: Right. Paula . . . , and Elyse does too.
C: I disagree. I think . . .
D: So do I. For example, . . .

# FROM GRAMMAR TO WRITING

**A** BEFORE YOU WRITE  Think about two people you know who are close (twins, siblings, spouses, friends, etc.). List their similarities and differences (in appearance, personalities, daily activities, hobbies, etc.). Complete the outline.

Names: _____ and _____

| Similarities | Differences |
|---|---|
| _____ | _____ |
| _____ | _____ |
| _____ | _____ |

**B** WRITE  Use your outline to write two paragraphs about the people you are describing. In the first paragraph, focus on their similarities. In the second paragraph, focus on their differences. Use *so, too, neither, not either,* and *but.* Try to avoid the common mistakes in the chart.

EXAMPLE:  My friends Kim and Ann are identical twins, but they work very hard to be separate individuals. Kim is 5'3", and so is Ann. Kim . . .

## Common Mistakes in Using Additions and Responses

| | |
|---|---|
| Use the **correct word order** with *so* and *neither*: **verb + subject**. Do not use subject + verb. | Kim is 5'3", and **so is Ann**. <br> NOT Kim is 5'3", and so ~~Ann is~~. |
| Use the **same auxiliary verb or modal** in the addition as in the statement. | Kim **has** won several awards, but Ann **hasn't**. <br> NOT Kim has won several awards, but Ann ~~didn't~~. |
| Use **correct agreement**. The verb in the addition **agrees with the subject of the addition**, not with the subject of the statement. | **I wear** a lot of jewelry, but **my twin doesn't**. <br> NOT I wear a lot of jewelry, but my twin ~~do not~~. |

**C** CHECK YOUR WORK  Read your paragraphs. Underline once the additions of similarity. Underline twice the additions of difference. Circle *so, too, neither, not either,* and *but.* Use the Editing Checklist to check your work.

## Editing Checklist

**Did you use . . . ?**

☐ *so, too, neither,* or *not either* to express similarity

☐ *so* or *too* after an affirmative statement

☐ *neither* or *not either* after a negative statement

☐ *but* to express difference

☐ the correct form of *be, have, do, will,* or a modal in the additions

**D** REVISE YOUR WORK  Read your paragraphs again. Can you improve your writing? Make changes if necessary. Give your paragraphs a title.

# UNIT 8 REVIEW

**Test yourself on the grammar of the unit.**

**A** Circle the correct words to complete the sentences.

1. Mary lives in Houston, and so lives / (does) Jan.

2. Doug moved to Florida. (So) / Neither did his brother.

3. Mia hasn't gotten married. Her sister has too / (hasn't either.)

4. My friends play tennis, (but) / so I don't.

5. I often stay up late, but she does / (doesn't.)

6. Dan enjoys traveling, and I do so / (too.)

7. I don't like peanuts. My husband doesn't neither / (either.)

**B** Combine each pair of sentences. Use an addition with *so*, *too*, *neither*, *not either*, or *but*.

1. I speak Spanish. My brother speaks Spanish.
   _I speak spanish, and my brother does too._
   _and so does my brother._

2. I can't speak Russian. My brother can't speak Russian.
   _I can't speak Russian, and neither can my brother._

3. Jaime lives in Chicago. His brother lives in New York.
   _Jame lives in Chicago, but His brother don't._
   _but his brother lives in NY._

4. Chen doesn't play tennis. His sister plays tennis.
   _Chen doesn't play tennis, but His sister does too_
   _And so His sister does_

5. Diego doesn't eat meat. Lila doesn't eat meat.
   _Diego doesn't eat meat, and neither does Lila._
   _and Lila doesn't either._

**C** Find and correct eight mistakes.

My friend Alicia and I have a lot in common. She comes from Los Angeles, and so I do. She speaks Spanish. I speak too. Her parents are both teachers, and mine do too. She doesn't have any brothers or sisters. Either do I. There are some differences, too. Alicia is very reserved, but I am. I like to talk about my feelings and say what's on my mind. Alicia doesn't like sports, but I don't. I'm on several school teams, and she isn't. I think our differences make things more interesting, and so do Alicia!

**Now check your answers on page 477.**

# Gerunds, Infinitives, and Phrasal Verbs

## PART 4

**OUTCOMES**

- Discuss activities or make general statements, using gerunds or infinitives
- Explain the purpose of an action, using an infinitive
- Identify key details in a social science article and in a conversation
- Discuss food and fast-food restaurants
- Write about the food at one's school, expressing one's opinion

**OUTCOMES**

- Describe how someone forces, causes, persuades, or allows someone else to do things
- Describe how someone makes things easier for someone else
- Identify key information and ideas in an opinion article and in a conversation
- Describe how someone has influenced one's life
- Research and discuss animals in captivity
- Write about keeping animals in captivity

**OUTCOMES**

- Use phrasal verbs in everyday speech
- Recognize the difference between transitive / intransitive and separable / inseparable phrasal verbs
- Identify specific information in a magazine article and in a telemarketing phone call
- Discuss telemarketing and advertising
- Write about an experience you had on the phone

# Gerunds and Infinitives: Review and Expansion

## FAST FOOD

OUTCOMES
- Discuss activities or make general statements, using gerunds or infinitives
- Explain the purpose of an action, using an infinitive
- Identify key details in a social science article and in a conversation
- Discuss food and fast-food restaurants
- Write about the food at one's school, expressing one's opinion

## STEP 1   GRAMMAR IN CONTEXT

### BEFORE YOU READ

Look at the title of the article and at the photos. Discuss the questions.

1. What do you think of fast-food restaurants?
2. Do you eat in fast-food restaurants? Why or why not?

### READ

09|01   Read this article about fast-food restaurants.

# Fast Food in a Fast World

"I'll have a hamburger, fries, and a Coke." The language may change, but you can expect to hear this order in hundreds of countries all around the world. In fact, dining in fast-food restaurants has become a way of life for millions and millions of people from Buenos Aires, Argentina, to Ho Chi Minh City, Vietnam.

### The Pluses

What is it about eating on the run that so many of us find appealing? Of course, the most obvious answer is that, true to its name, fast food is fast. In today's hectic society, people don't want to waste time. But apart from the speed of ordering and getting served, satisfied customers mention other factors such as convenience, reliability, price, and, yes, good taste!

Many people choose to eat fast food because it's convenient. There are so many fast-food locations that they can stop to have a quick meal almost anywhere. People who don't like to cook are especially happy to find one of these restaurants on their way home from work or school. In addition, because fast-food restaurants usually belong to chains,[1] customers like their reliability. They say they can count on finding the same things every time, every place.

Price is also very important. In fast-food restaurants, people can eat large amounts of food without it costing an arm and a leg.[2] Finally, there are also people who simply enjoy eating fast food. They love the taste of foods like burgers, tacos, and pizza. For these people, a fast-food restaurant is the perfect place to go.

## The Minuses

Not everyone is in favor of fast-food restaurants spreading over the globe. In fact, a lot of people would prefer not to have the same fast-food chains in every country they visit. "Walking down the Champs-Elysées just isn't as romantic as it once was. When I see the same restaurants everywhere I go, I feel that the world is shrinking too much," complained one traveler. But there are more serious objections, too.

Nutritionists[3] point to the health consequences of eating fast foods since they are generally high in calories, fat, and salt, but low in fiber and nutrients. They blame the worldwide problem of obesity, in part, on eating fast food. Social critics condemn fast-food chains for introducing these unhealthy foods to other countries and for not paying their workers enough. Then there's the question of pollution. Those hamburgers come wrapped in a lot of paper and plastic, which creates waste that pollutes the air and water. It's a high price to pay for convenience.

It's obvious that people have strong opinions about fast food. Like it or not, it's easy to see that fast-food restaurants are a big part of our world. And one thing is certain—they are here to stay.[4]

1 *chains:* restaurants, hotels, or stores with the same name, appearance, products, and owner
2 *costing an arm and a leg:* being extremely expensive
3 *nutritionists:* experts on what people should eat
4 *here to stay:* permanent, continuing to exist for a long time

### Fast Facts

- French fries are the most popular fast food, followed by burgers, fried chicken, pizza, and tacos.

- Men tend to eat fast food more often than women.

- It's not unusual to get a drive-thru order in less than 3 minutes.

- The average American spends $100 a month on fast food.

- More than 13 million people around the world have jobs in fast-food restaurants.

# AFTER YOU READ

**A** VOCABULARY  **Complete the sentences with the words from the box.**

| appealing | consequence | convenience | globe | objection | reliability |
|---|---|---|---|---|---|

1. As a food writer, Ozawa travels all over the _____globe_____. Last year, he visited restaurants in forty countries.

2. I have no ____objection____ to the report about fast food. I agree with everything it says.

3. I love the ____convenience____ of eating at Burg's. It's open 24 hours a day!

4. People like the ____reliability____ of the restaurant information on Zagat.com. They know the site's research is carefully done.

5. A(n) ____consequence____ of the nutrition report was that some people stopped eating fast food.

6. The idea of low-cost, healthy food choices is very ____appealing____.

**B** COMPREHENSION  **Choose the word or phrase that best completes each sentence.**

1. Fast-food restaurants are _____.
   a. unpopular          b. expensive          c. everywhere

2. The article mentions _____ as a main reason for fast food's popularity.
   a. cleanliness        b. attractiveness     c. quick service

3. Many fast-food restaurants serve _____.
   a. fries              b. vegetable burgers  c. low-fat food

4. _____ happy to see fast-food chains all around the globe.
   a. Some people are    b. Everyone is        c. Nobody is

5. One big objection to fast food is that it is _____.
   a. cheap              b. unhealthy          c. bad-tasting

6. According to the article, workers at fast-food chains don't _____.
   a. eat well           b. make enough money  c. have enough family time

**C** DISCUSSION  **Work with a partner. Compare your answers in B. Why did you choose these words and phrases?**

## GERUNDS AND INFINITIVES

| Gerunds | Infinitives |
|---|---|
| **Gerund as Subject** | **It + Infinitive** |
| **Eating** fast foods is convenient. | *It*'s convenient **to eat** fast foods. |
| **Verb + Gerund** | **Verb + Infinitive** |
| They *recommend* **reducing** fats in the food. | They *plan* **to reduce** fats in the food. |
| **Verb + Gerund or Infinitive** | **Verb + Gerund or Infinitive** |
| She *started* **eating** fries every day. | She *started* **to eat** fries every day. |
| **Preposition + Gerund** | **Adjective + Infinitive** |
| We're tired *of* **reading** calorie counts. | We were *surprised* **to read** the number of calories. |
| **Possessive + Gerund** ~~Possessive + Gerund~~ | **Object Pronoun + Infinitive** ~~Pronoun + Infinitive~~ |
| I didn't like *his* **ordering** fries. | I urged *him* **to order** fries. |

## GRAMMAR NOTES

### 1  Gerunds as Subjects

| | |
|---|---|
| A **gerund** (base form + *-ing*) is a verb used as a noun. We often use a **gerund** as the **subject** of a sentence. | **Cooking** is a lot of fun. |
| A gerund can have a **negative** form (*not* + base form + *-ing*). | **Not exercising** leads to health problems. |
| **BE CAREFUL!** A gerund is often part of a phrase. When a **gerund phrase** is the **subject** of a sentence, make sure the following verb is in the **third-person singular**. | **Eating too many fries** *is* unhealthy.<br>NOT Eating too many fries ~~are~~ unhealthy. |
| **IN WRITING** There are often spelling changes when you add *-ing* to the base form of the verb. | **BASE FORM**     **GERUND**<br>waste       was**ting**<br>permit      permi**tting**<br>die         d**ying** |

## 2 Verb + Gerund

| | |
|---|---|
| A gerund often **follows certain verbs** as the **object** of the verb (*avoid, consider, discuss, dislike, enjoy, recommend*, etc.). | VERB + GERUND<br>My brother *avoids* **eating** fried food.<br>Many people *enjoy* **eating** fast food. |
| **USAGE NOTE** We often use *go* + gerund to describe activities such as *shopping, dancing, fishing, skiing*, and *swimming*. | People often eat fast food when they *go* **shopping**.<br>I'm always hungry after I *go* **swimming**. |
| Possessive + Gerund.<br>**USAGE NOTE** In **formal** English, you can use a **possessive** (*Anne's, the boy's, my, your, his, her, its, our, their*) before a gerund. In **informal** English, many people use **nouns** or **object pronouns** instead of possessives before a gerund. | I dislike *Julio's* **eating** fast foods. *(formal)*<br>I dislike *his* **eating** fast foods. *(formal)*<br>I dislike *Julio* **eating** fast foods. *(informal)*<br>I dislike *him* **eating** fast foods. *(informal)* |

## 3 Verb + Infinitive

| | |
|---|---|
| An **infinitive** is *to* + base form of the verb. We can use an infinitive **after the verb** in a clause. | They *hope* **to open** a new restaurant. |
| An infinitive can have a **negative** form (*not + to + base form*). | She *chose* **not to give up** meat. |
| An infinitive often follows certain verbs. There are three combinations:<br><br>• **verb + infinitive**<br>(*agree, can't wait, decide, deserve*, etc.)<br><br>• **verb + object (noun/pronoun) + infinitive**<br>(*cause, challenge, convince, encourage*, etc.)<br><br>• **verb + infinitive** or **verb + object + infinitive**<br>(*ask, expect, request, want*, etc.) | VERB + INFINITIVE<br>They *agreed* **to cook** with less fat.<br>My sister *can't wait* **to try** the low-fat burger.<br><br>VERB + OBJECT + INFINITIVE<br>She *convinced Max* **not to order** fries.<br>I *encouraged them* **to buy** the 2-for-1 special.<br><br>VERB + INFINITIVE<br>I *wanted* **to try** that new restaurant.<br>VERB + OBJECT + INFINITIVE<br>I *wanted my sister* **to try** it, too. |
| **BE CAREFUL!** We usually **do not repeat** *to* when there is **more than one infinitive**. | We plan **to stay** home, **watch** a movie, and **eat** pizza.<br>NOT We plan to stay home, ~~to~~ watch a movie, and ~~to~~ eat pizza. |

## 4 Verb + Gerund or Infinitive

| | |
|---|---|
| Some verbs are **followed by a gerund or an infinitive** (*begin, continue, hate, love*, etc.). The **meaning is the same.** | I **love** cooking with my friends.<br>I **love** to cook with my friends. |
| **BE CAREFUL!** When **two or more verbs** follow another verb, we use the **same form** of the verb. (In writing, this is called *parallel structure*.) | I **love** walking and doing yoga.<br>NOT I love walking and to do yoga.<br>I **love** to walk and do yoga.<br>NOT I love to walk and doing yoga. |
| **BE CAREFUL!** A few verbs (for example, *stop, remember,* and *forget*) can be followed by either a gerund or an infinitive, but the **meanings are very different.** | She **stopped** eating pizza.<br>*(She doesn't eat pizza anymore.)*<br>She **stopped** to eat pizza.<br>*(She stopped another activity in order to eat pizza.)*<br><br>He **remembered** meeting her.<br>*(He remembered that he had already met her in the past.)*<br>He **remembered** to meet her.<br>*(First he arranged a meeting with her. Then he remembered to go to the meeting.)*<br><br>I never **forgot** eating lunch at the Burg.<br>*(I ate lunch at the Burg, and I didn't forget the experience.)*<br>I never **forgot** to eat lunch.<br>*(I always ate lunch.)* |

## 5 Preposition or Phrasal Verb + Gerund

| | |
|---|---|
| A **gerund** is the only verb form that can **follow a preposition** (*about, against, at, between, by, for, from, in, of, on,* etc.). | PREP. + GERUND<br>I read an article **about** counting calories.<br>People save time **by** eating fast food. |
| A **gerund** follows these common combinations:<br>• **verb + preposition**<br>  (*advise against, approve of, worry about,* etc.)<br>• **adjective + preposition**<br>  (*excited about, famous for, interested in,* etc.) | VERB + PREP. + GERUND<br>I don't **approve of** eating fast food every day.<br><br>ADJECTIVE + PREP. + GERUND<br>We're very **interested in** trying different types of food. |
| **BE CAREFUL!** Use a **gerund**, not the base form of the verb, **after expressions with the preposition** *to* (*look forward to, be opposed to, object to,* etc.). | We **look forward to** having dinner with you.<br>NOT We look forward to have dinner with you. |
| A **gerund** is the only verb form that can follow a **phrasal verb** (*count on, end up, give up, keep on, put off,* etc.). | PHRASAL VERB + GERUND<br>My brother **gave up** drinking Coke.<br>My parents **kept on** eating fast food. |

## 6 Infinitives After Adjectives or Nouns

You can use an infinitive after **certain adjectives or nouns**:

- **adjective + infinitive**
  (*afraid*, *angry*, *curious*, *eager*, *easy*, *glad*, *possible*, etc.)

- **noun + infinitive**
  (*chance*, *decision*, *offer*, *price*, *reason*, *right*, *time*, etc.)

ADJECTIVE + INFINITIVE
They're **eager to try** the new taco.
She was **glad to hear** about the healthy menu.

NOUN + INFINITIVE
She has the **right to eat** what she wants.
I don't have **time to take** a break.

Sometimes *for* + **noun/pronoun** goes before the infinitive.

ADJ.        INFINITIVE
It's very **easy for students to eat** fast food.

NOUN      INFINITIVE
It's a high **price for them to pay**.

## 7 Infinitives of Purpose

You can use an infinitive to explain the **purpose of an action**.

An infinitive of purpose can explain the purpose of an action. It often **answers the question Why?**

A: **Why** does he always order fast food?
B: He does it **to save** time.

USAGE NOTE   In **conversation**, we often answer the question *Why?* with an incomplete sentence beginning with *to*.

A: **Why** did you stop eating fast food?
B: **To lose** weight.

USAGE NOTE   We can use *in order (not) to* in **formal speech** and **formal writing** when we explain the purpose of an action.

Older people should exercise regularly **in order to remain** healthy. *(medical report)*

USAGE NOTE   In everyday **conversation** and **informal writing**, we usually express a **negative purpose** with *because* + **a reason** or *so that* + **a reason**.

I sleep a lot **because I don't want to get sick**. *(conversation)*
I sleep a lot **so that I don't get sick**. *(email)*

## 8 Gerunds and Infinitives for General Statements

To make **general statements** you can use:

- **gerund as subject**

- *it* + **infinitive**

They have the **same meaning**.

**Cooking** is fun.

*It*'s fun **to cook**.

## REFERENCE NOTES

For **spelling rules for base form of verb + *-ing***, see Appendix 23 on page 463.

For a more complete list of **verbs that can be followed by gerunds**, see Appendix 10 on page 459.

For more complete lists of **verbs that can be followed by infinitives**, see Appendices 11 and 13 on pages 459 and 460.

For a more complete list of **verbs that can be followed by either gerunds or infinitives**, see Appendix 12 on page 459.

For a list of **verb + preposition combinations**, see Appendix 17 on page 460.

For a list of **adjective + preposition expressions**, see Appendix 16 on page 460.

For a list of **adjectives that can be followed by infinitives**, see Appendix 14 on page 460.

For a list of **nouns that can be followed by infinitives**, see Appendix 15 on page 460.

For a list of **phrasal verbs**, see Appendix 4 on page 455.

## STEP 3    FOCUSED PRACTICE

### EXERCISE 1   DISCOVER THE GRAMMAR

GRAMMAR NOTES 1–8   Read this questionnaire about fast-food restaurants. Underline the gerunds and circle the infinitives. (In Exercise 7 on page 149, you will complete the questionnaire with your own information.)

## FAST-FOOD QUESTIONNAIRE

It is increasingly common (to see) fast food in countries around the globe. Please complete this questionnaire about eating at fast-food restaurants. Check (✔) all the answers that apply to you.

1. In my opinion, eating fast food is _____ .
   ☐ healthy    ☐ unhealthy    ☐ convenient    ☐ inexpensive    ☐ fun

2. Which meals are you used to eating at a fast-food restaurant?
   ☐ breakfast    ☐ lunch    ☐ dinner    ☐ snacks    ☐ None

3. Which types of fast food do you like to eat?
   ☐ hamburgers    ☐ pizza    ☐ fried chicken    ☐ tacos    ☐ sushi
   ☐ Other: _____    ☐ None

4. To select a fast-food restaurant, what kind of information do you use?
   ☐ advice of friends    ☐ online menus    ☐ advertisements    ☐ prices    ☐ Other: _____

5. How often are you likely to eat at a fast-food restaurant?
   ☐ 1–3 times a week    ☐ 4–6 times a week    ☐ more than 6 times a week    ☐ Never

6. How much do you enjoy going to fast-food restaurants?
   ☐ I like it very much.    ☐ It's just OK.    ☐ I don't enjoy it.    ☐ I never go.

7. How do you feel about seeing the same fast-food restaurants all over the world?
   ☐ I like it.    ☐ I have no objections.    ☐ I don't like it.

8. Do you think the government should require fast-food restaurants to include healthy choices?
   ☐ Yes    ☐ No

# EXERCISE 2  GERUND OR INFINITIVE

GRAMMAR NOTES 1–8  Complete the information about fast-food favorites. Use the correct form—gerund or infinitive—of the verbs in parentheses. See Appendices 10–17 on pages 459–460 for help.

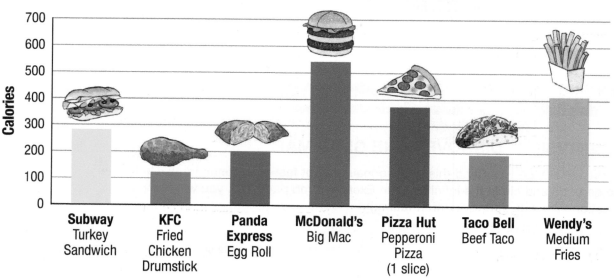

## Calorie Content of Fast-Food Favorites

People are starting ____to think____ about the consequences of ____going____ to
                        1. (think)                                2. (go)
fast-food restaurants, especially when they want ____to maintain____ a healthy lifestyle. If
                                                  3. (maintain)
you are one of these people, here are some facts ____to consider____ before you order.
                                                  4. (consider)

- ____Ordering____ a Big Mac will "cost" you about 540 calories.
    5. (order)

- ____Having____ a Taco Bell taco is much less fattening. One taco has only about
    6. (have)
  190 calories.

- If you want ____to lose____ weight, you should also consider ____getting____ a
                 7. (lose)                                      8. (get)
  Subway turkey sandwich. It contains around 280 calories.

- You'll probably end up ____gaining____ weight if you eat a lot of pepperoni pan pizza.
                          9. (gain)
  A single slice at Pizza Hut has about 370 calories.

- You should give up ____eating____ french fries! An order at Wendy's contains about
                      10. (eat)
  410 calories.

- Think about ____choosing____ an egg roll instead of fries. A Panda Express egg roll has
               11. (choose)
  just a little over 200 calories.

- Nutritionists advise people ____to avoid____ fried chicken. A drumstick at KFC contains
                               12. (avoid)
  about 120 calories—but people usually eat much more!

# EXERCISE 3 VERB + GERUND OR INFINITIVE

GRAMMAR NOTES 2–4  Read each conversation and complete the summary statement.
Use the correct form of a verb from the box followed by the gerund or infinitive form of the
verb in parentheses. See Appendices 10–12 on page 459 for help.

| admit | deserve | ~~forget~~ | recommend | remember | stop | try | volunteer |
|-------|---------|--------|-----------|----------|------|-----|-----------|

1. CUSTOMER: Uh, didn't I order fries, too?
   SERVER:   That's right, you did. I'll bring them right away.

   SUMMARY:  The server _____ *forgot to bring* _____ the fries.
                                (bring)

2. FATHER:   That Little Burg Meal isn't enough for you anymore. Have a Big Burg, OK?
   CHILD:    OK, but I really wanted the toy in the Little Burg Meal.

   SUMMARY:  The father _____ recommend ordering _____ a Big Burg.
                                (order)

3. MOM:   This car is a mess! Somebody, throw out all those fast-food containers!
   STAN:  I'll do it, Mom.

   SUMMARY:  Stan _____ volunteers to throw out _____ the fast-food containers.
                                (throw out)

4. PAT:    Hi, Renee. Want to go to Pizza Hut with us?
   RENEE:  Thanks, but I can't eat fast food now. I'm training for the swim team.

   SUMMARY:  Renee _____ has stoped / stops eating _____ fast food.
                                (eat)

5. EMPLOYEE: Thanks for the raise. I can really use it.
   MANAGER:  You've earned it. You're our best drive-through server.

   SUMMARY:  The employee _____ deserves to receive _____ a raise.
                                (receive)

6. MOTHER:  I think you should quit that fast-food job. Your grades are suffering.
   CAROL:   It's hard to decide. I need to save for college, but if my grades are bad . . .

   SUMMARY:  Carol _____ is trying / tries to decide _____ whether to keep her job.
                                (decide)

7. MOM:     You're not eating dinner. You had some fast food on the way home, didn't you?
   CHRIS:   Well, . . . actually, I stopped at Arby's, but I only had fries.

   SUMMARY:  Chris _____ admits going _____ to Arby's after school.
                                (go)

8. TIM:     I used to stay in the Burg's playground for hours when I was little.
   WANG:    Yeah, me too. My mother couldn't get me to leave.

   SUMMARY:  The boys _____ remember playing _____ in the Burg's playground.
                                (play)

# EXERCISE 4 GERUND OR INFINITIVE WITH AND WITHOUT OBJECT

GRAMMAR NOTES 1–7 Complete these letters to the editor of a school newspaper. Use the correct forms of the words in parentheses. See Appendices 10–17 on pages 459–460 for help.

## STUDENT NEWS

**TO THE EDITOR**

Yesterday, my roommate Andre _____*wanted me to have*_____ lunch with him in the
           **1.** (want / I / have)

dining hall. I was surprised about _____ there because last year
        **2.** (Andre / choose / go)

he and I had _____ the dining hall. It just wasn't appealing to
    **3.** (decide / not use)

us. But when we went in yesterday, instead of _____ the usual
        **4.** (find)

greasy fries and mystery meat, I was happy _____ the colorful
        **5.** (see)

Taco Bell sign. In my opinion, _____ to fast foods is really
        **6.** (change)

the thing _____. The administration made a great choice.
        **7.** (do)

I _____ fast food and I _____
  **8.** (support / they / sell)        **9.** (appreciate / my friend / encourage)

me to give campus food another try.

*M. Rodriguez*

**TO THE EDITOR**

I'm writing this letter _____ my anger and terrible
        **10.** (express)

disappointment at _____ fast-food chains in the dining halls.
        **11.** (have)

When a classmate and I went to eat yesterday, I _____ the
        **12.** (expect / find)

usual healthy choices of vegetables and salads. I _____ a
        **13.** (not expect / see)

fast-food court. In my opinion, it's simply wrong _____ fast food
        **14.** (bring)

into the college dining hall. The consequence of _____ the right
        **15.** (not eat)

food is bad health. As a commuter, I _____ the convenience of a
        **16.** (need / have)

healthy meal option every evening before class. But I usually _____
        **17.** (try / stay away)

from fast foods. I _____ a salad bar so that
  **18.** (urge / the administration / set up)

students like me can _____ meals on campus. I'm sure other
        **19.** (keep on / buy)

commuters will agree with my objections.

*B. Chen*

# EXERCISE 5 EDITING

**GRAMMAR NOTES 1–8**  Read these posts to an international online discussion group. There are eleven mistakes in the use of gerunds and infinitives. The first mistake is already corrected. Find and correct ten more. See Appendices 10–17 on pages 459–460 for help.

READ RESPONSES | POST A NEW RESPONSE | RETURN TO INDEX | PREVIOUS | NEXT

Re: love those tacos

*eating* **or** *to eat*

I love ~~eat~~ tacos for my lunch. I think they're delicious, convenient, nutritious, and inexpensive. I

don't mind to have the same thing every day! And I'm not worried about any health consequences.

What do you think?

Re: vegetarian travel

I'm a vegetarian. I stopped to eat meat two years ago to lose weight and improve my overall

health. I feel a little nervous about traveling to other countries. I'm interested in go to Ghana and

other countries in the region in September. Is it easy to find meatless dishes there?

Re: takoyaki

Hi! I am Paulo, and I come from Brazil. I travel a lot, and I enjoy to try different foods from all

over the globe. I hope I have a chance trying takoyaki (fish balls made with octopus) when I go to

Japan. Is there a takoyaki shop you can recommend my going to? I look forward to hear from you.

Re: Cheap and delicious in Seoul

Eat in Seoul is one of life's great pleasures. It's easy find delicious food at reasonable

prices. I suggest to try *kimbap*. It's made with steamed rice and fresh ingredients such as

carrots and spinach, rolled in seaweed—a little like Japanese sushi. I'd be happy to post

the recipe if you want having it.

Gerunds and Infinitives: Review and Expansion  **147**

## EXERCISE 6  LISTENING

09|02  (A) Two college students, Lily and Victor, are discussing their responses to a food-service survey. Listen to their conversation. Look at the list of possible changes. Listen again to the conversation. Check (✓) the possible changes that each student agrees with.

# School Food-Service Survey

**We're changing and you can help! Please complete the survey by checking (✔) the changes you want to see.**

| | name | Lily | Victor |
|---|---|---|---|
| **1.** Introducing Burger Queen fast foods | ☐ | ☐ | ☑ |
| **2.** Showing fat and calorie contents of each serving | ☐ | ☑ | ☐ |
| **3.** Providing more healthy choices | ☐ | ☑ | ☑ |
| **4.** Lowering prices | ☐ | ☐ | ☐ |
| **5.** Improving food quality | ☐ | ☑ | ☑ |
| **6.** Offering international foods | ☐ | ☑ | ☑ |
| **7.** Starting breakfast at 6:30 a.m. | ☐ | ☐ | ☑ |

09|02  (B) **Listen again to the conversation. Then work with a partner and discuss the questions.**

1. Did Lily follow Victor's advice about the meatloaf in the school cafeteria?

   EXAMPLE: A: I don't remember hearing anything about meatloaf. Do you?
   B: Victor told Lily not to eat it. But she decided to get it anyway, and it was terrible.

2. What is the purpose of the school-cafeteria survey?

3. What kinds of changes in the cafeteria is Lily most interested in?

4. What kinds of changes is Victor most interested in?

5. Is the food at Lily and Victor's school the same as or different from the food at your school?

(C) **Work with a partner. Take the survey. Then discuss your answers.**

EXAMPLE: A: Do you agree with Lily or Victor about having Burger Queen in the cafeteria?
B: I agree with Victor.
A: Me too. Lily's meat loaf sounds terrible. I'd prefer to have a burger!

## EXERCISE 7  IF YOU ASK ME . . .

**A** QUESTIONNAIRE  Give your opinions about fast food. Complete the fast-food questionnaire in Exercise 1 on page 143.

**B** Work with a partner. Compare your answers on the questionnaire.

EXAMPLE:  A: What's your answer to number 1?
        B: In my opinion, fast food is convenient and cheap. How do you feel about eating fast food?
        A: I agree. And it's not healthy, but it is fun!

**C** Have a class discussion about your answers. Tally the results.

EXAMPLE:  Fifteen students agree that eating fast food is convenient and fast.

## EXERCISE 8  A WORLD OF FAST FOOD

CROSS-CULTURAL COMPARISON  Work in a group. Describe popular fast food in your country. The food can be from an international fast-food restaurant or local fast food.

EXAMPLE:  A: In Germany, we like to order the Big Rösti at McDonald's. It's a burger with bacon, cheese, and a potato pancake on it. *Rösti* is the German word for potato pancake.
        B: The potato pancake is on the burger? I'm all for trying that! It sounds delicious.
        C: In addition to eating at fast-food restaurants, people in Mexico like to buy food from street vendors. My favorite is *elote*. It's . . .

## EXERCISE 9  HEALTHY CHOICES

**A** GROUP PROJECT  Work in a group. Use the websites of some popular fast-food restaurants to answer this question: Is it possible to have healthy food choices at a fast-food restaurant? Answer some of the questions below as you do your research.

EXAMPLE:  A: Let's go online now to get nutrition information.
        B: OK. We can start by looking at the salads.
        C: What do you think about the crispy chicken salad?
        D: I don't know. Some of the burgers seem to have fewer calories.

**Possible questions:**

- What is the total calorie count for a specific meal?
- How much salt does the meal have?
- What is the vitamin content of the food?

- Which menu items could replace a hamburger?
- What food sizes are available?
- How fresh is the food?

**B** Report back to your class. Compare your answers.

EXAMPLE:  A: We were surprised to see that some of the salads on this menu have more fat and calories than burgers.
        B: Right. But it depends on the size of the burger and what you eat with the burger.
        A: We decided to make our own combination meal of a hamburger with a side salad.
        B: Good choice!

# FROM GRAMMAR TO WRITING

**A** BEFORE YOU WRITE Think about the types of food that students can buy at your school (for example, pizza, burgers, salads, tacos, and sushi). Complete the outline.

| Types of Food | Plusses | Minuses |
|---|---|---|
| fast food. | | |
| | | |

**B** WRITE Use your outline to write two paragraphs. In the first paragraph, describe the food at your school. In the second paragraph, give your opinion about the food. Use gerunds and infinitives. Try to avoid the common mistakes in the chart.

EXAMPLE: I eat at school every day because I live on campus. I would like to describe my dining experience. The food here is . . .

## Common Mistakes in Using Infinitives and Gerunds

| | |
|---|---|
| Use a **gerund after certain verbs**, such as *dislike*, *enjoy*, and *suggest*. Do not use an infinitive. | I **suggest** making changes in the cafeteria food.<br>NOT I suggest to make changes in the cafeteria food. |
| Use a **gerund after a preposition** or a **phrasal verb**. Do not use an infinitive. | I object **to eating** so much fried food.<br>NOT I object to eat so much fried food.<br>Last semester, I **ended up** gaining weight.<br>NOT Last semester, I ended up to gain weight. |
| Use **parallel structure** when **two or more verbs** follow another verb. Use either infinitives or gerunds. Do not use infinitives and gerunds together. | The cafeteria should **continue** providing a salad bar and **serving** hot vegetarian meals.<br>NOT The cafeteria should continue providing a salad bar and to serve hot vegetarian meals. |

**C** CHECK YOUR WORK Read your paragraphs. Underline the gerunds. Circle the infinitives. Use the Editing Checklist to check your work.

## Editing Checklist

**Did you use . . . ?**

- [ ] gerunds as subjects
- [ ] correct verbs + gerunds
- [ ] correct verbs + infinitives
- [ ] prepositions (or phrasal verbs) + gerunds
- [ ] infinitives after certain adjectives or nouns
- [ ] *it* + infinitive for general statements
- [ ] parallel structure

**D** REVISE YOUR WORK Read your paragraphs again. Can you improve your writing? Make changes if necessary. Give your paragraphs a title.

# UNIT 9  REVIEW

**Test yourself on the grammar of the unit.**

**A** Complete the paragraph with the gerund or infinitive form of the verbs in parentheses.

Cost and convenience often persuade people _____ fast-food restaurants. If
                                              1. (use)

you are eating a fast-food lunch _____ money, think about _____
                                      2. (save)                              3. (order)

from the special value menu. A fast-food dinner can leave you free _____ or
                                                                          4. (relax)

_____ instead of _____ food. _____ for fast food is
      5. (study)                  6. (prepare)              7. (stop)

a cheap and convenient way _____ . But try _____ fast food too
                                 8. (eat)                    9. (not have)

often. _____ at home provides better quality food for less money.
          10. (cook)

**B** Read each conversation and complete the summary statement (S). Use the correct
form of the words in parentheses.

1. **DAD:** You used to love Taco Bell as a kid.      **S:** Tim _____
   **TIM:** I *did*? Did you take me there a lot?                        (remember / go)
                                                         to Taco Bell.

2. **AL:** I'm sick of eating fast food.              **S:** Nan _____
   **NAN:** You should take a cooking class.                            (want / Al / take)
                                                         a cooking class.

3. **CHU:** I ate in the cafeteria today.             **S:** Kay _____
   **KAY:** That's strange. You hate that food.                         (wonder about / Chu / eat)
                                                         in the cafeteria.

4. **DEB:** Would you like to have dinner now?        **S:** Tao _____
   **TAO:** Sure! I haven't eaten since breakfast.                      (stop / have)
                                                         lunch.

5. **IAN:** Did you mail that letter I gave you?      **S:** Liz _____
   **LIZ:** Oops. Sorry. I'll mail it tomorrow.                         (forget / mail)
                                                         Ian's letter.

**C** Find and correct five mistakes.

A: I was happy to hear that the cafeteria is serving salads now. I'm eager trying them.

B: Me too. Someone recommended to eat more salads to lose weight.

A: It was that TV doctor, right? He's always urging we to exercise more, too.

B: That's the one. He's actually convinced me to stop to eat meat.

A: Interesting! That would be a hard decision for us making, though. We love to barbecue.

**Now check your answers on page 477.**

**OUTCOMES**
- Describe how someone forces, causes, persuades, or allows someone else to do things
- Describe how someone makes things easier for someone else
- Identify key information and ideas in an opinion article and in a conversation
- Describe how someone has influenced one's life
- Research and discuss animals in captivity
- Write about keeping animals in captivity

STEP 1 GRAMMAR IN CONTEXT

## BEFORE YOU READ

Look at the photos. Discuss the questions.

1. How do you think the animals feel? Why do they feel that way?
2. Do you think people should use animals for entertainment?

### READ

▶ 10|01   Read this article about performance animals.

## That's Entertainment?

"Ooooh!" cries the audience as the orcas leap from the water in perfect formation. "Aaaah!" they shout as the trainer rides across the pool on the nose of one of the graceful giants. For years, dolphins, orcas, and other sea

mammals have been making audiences cheer at marine theme parks around the world. But how do trainers get nine-ton whales to do acrobatic tricks[1] or make them "dance"?

It's not easy. Traditional animal trainers controlled animals with collars and leashes and made them perform by using cruel punishments. Then, in the 1940s, marine theme parks wanted to have dolphins do tricks. The first trainers faced big problems. You can't get a dolphin to wear a collar. And you can't punish a dolphin—it will just swim away from you! This challenge made the trainers develop a kinder, more humane method to teach animals.

This method, positive reinforcement, uses rewards rather than punishments for training. To begin teaching, a trainer lets an animal act freely. When the trainer sees the "correct" behavior, he or she rewards the animal immediately, usually with food. The animal quickly learns that a reward follows the behavior. For complicated acts, the trainer breaks the act into many smaller parts and has the animal learn each part separately.

Positive reinforcement has completely changed our treatment of animals in zoos. Elephants, for example, need a lot of physical care. However, traditional trainers used force to make elephants "behave." Elephants sometimes rebelled and hurt or even killed their keepers. Through positive reinforcement, elephants at modern zoos have learned to stand at the bars of their cage and let keepers draw blood for tests and take care of their feet. Gary Priest, a former orca trainer, helped the keepers train the elephants at the San Diego Zoo. Do the elephants like the new system? "They love it! They'll do anything we ask," Priest said.

Unfortunately, not all trainers use positive reinforcement. Animal rights organizations have found abuses[2] of animal actors by circuses and other entertainment companies. And the question remains: Even with kind treatment, should we keep these animals captive[3] and have them perform just for our entertainment?

---

1 *acrobatic tricks:* the kind of acts that animals and people do at the circus (example: walking on a wire)
2 *abuses:* examples of cruel or violent treatment
3 *keep...captive:* keep animals or people in a place that they are not allowed to leave

## AFTER YOU READ

**A** VOCABULARY  **Match the words with their definitions.**

_b_ **1.** cruel
_d_ **2.** humane
_f_ **3.** reinforcement
_a_ **4.** physical
_e_ **5.** rebel
_c_ **6.** former

**a.** related to the body, not the mind
**b.** causing pain
**c.** having a position in the past, but not now
**d.** kind to people or animals
**e.** to fight against someone in power
**f.** a way of strengthening or encouraging an action

**B** COMPREHENSION  **Read the statements. Check (✓) True or False.**

|  | True | False |
|---|---|---|
| **1.** It's easy to train orcas and dolphins. | ☐ | ☑ |
| **2.** Many dolphins wear collars. | ☐ | ☑ |
| **3.** Methods of animal training have changed a lot since the 1940s. | ☑ | ☐ |
| **4.** Trainers give rewards so that animals will act freely. | ☑ | ☐ |
| **5.** Zoo elephants and their keepers have a better relationship now. | ☑ | ☐ |
| **6.** The author of the article is in favor of using animals for entertainment. | ☐ | ☑ |

**C** DISCUSSION  **Work with a partner. Compare your answers in B. Why did you check** *True* **or** *False*?

---

| STEP 2 | **GRAMMAR PRESENTATION** |
|---|---|

## MAKE, HAVE, LET, HELP, AND GET

### Make, Have, Let, Help

| Subject | Make/Have/Let/Help | Object | Base Form | |
|---|---|---|---|---|
| They | **make**<br>(**don't**) **have**<br>**let**<br>**help**\* | animals<br>them | learn | tricks. |

\* *Help* can also be followed by an infinitive.

### Get, Help

| Subject | Get/Help | Object | Infinitive | |
|---|---|---|---|---|
| They | (**don't**) **get**<br>**help** | animals<br>them | to learn | tricks. |

**154**    **Unit 10**

# GRAMMAR NOTES

## 1 Make, Have, and Get

Use *make*, *have*, and *get* to talk about things that someone **causes another person (or an animal) to do.**

| | |
|---|---|
| *Make*, *have*, and *get* show **how much choice** a person or animal has about doing an action. | |
| *Make* + object + **base form** of the verb means **to force** a person or animal to do something (there is **no choice**). | The trainer **made *the elephant* perform** tricks for the audience. *(The trainer forced the elephant to perform tricks.)*    NO CHOICE |
| *Have* + object + **base form** of the verb means **to cause** a person or animal to do something (there is **some choice**). | Some people **have *their pets* do** tricks. *(Some people cause their pets to do tricks.)* |
| *Get* + object + **infinitive** means **to persuade** a person or animal to do something by giving reasons or rewards (there is **a choice**). | Jan **got *her parents* to take** her to the zoo for a school assignment. *(Jan persuaded her parents to take her.)*    CHOICE |
| **BE CAREFUL!** *Get* is always followed by **object + infinitive**, not the base form of the verb. | INFINITIVE<br>You can't **get *a dolphin* to wear** a collar.<br>**NOT** You can't get a dolphin ~~wear~~ a collar. |
| *Make* can also mean **to have an effect** on someone or something. | The monkeys always **make *me* laugh**. *(They have this effect on me.)* |
| When the effect is a **feeling**, we often use *make* + object + adjective. | ADJECTIVE<br>Cruel treatment of animals **makes *me* angry**. *(Cruel treatment of animals causes me to feel angry.)* |

## 2 Let

| | |
|---|---|
| *Let* + object + **base form** of the verb means **to allow** a person or animal to do something. | Our teacher **let *us* leave** early after the test. *(Our teacher allowed us to leave early.)*<br>Some zoos **let *animals* interact** with humans. *(Some zoos allow animals to interact with humans.)* |
| **BE CAREFUL!** *Let* is always followed by **object + base form** of the verb, not an infinitive. | Zoos usually **let *people* take** photos.<br>**NOT** Zoos usually let people ~~to take~~ photos. |

## 3 Help

| | |
|---|---|
| *Help* means **to make something easier** for a person or an animal. | |
| *Help* can be followed by:<br>• **object + base form** of the verb<br>• **object + infinitive**<br>They have the **same meaning**. | She **helped *me* do** the homework.<br>She **helped *me* to do** the homework.<br>*(She made it easier for me to do the homework.)* |

## EXERCISE 1  DISCOVER THE GRAMMAR

GRAMMAR NOTES 1–3  **Read each numbered statement. Choose the sentence (*a* or *b*) that is similar in meaning.**

1. Ms. Bates got the principal to arrange a class trip to the zoo.
   a. Ms. Bates arranged the class trip.
   **b.** The principal arranged the class trip.

2. Mr. Goldberg had us do research about animals.
   a. Mr. Goldberg did the research for us.
   **b.** We did the research.

3. My teacher made me rewrite the report.
   **a.** I wrote the report again.
   b. I didn't write the report again.

4. She got me to do research on tropical birds.
   **a.** I agreed to do the research.
   b. I didn't agree to do the research.

5. The zoo lets small birds and animals wander freely inside the habitat.[1]
   **a.** They can go where they want.
   b. They have to stay in cages.

6. Chi was sick, so her teacher didn't let her go on the trip to the zoo.
   **a.** Chi stayed home.
   b. Chi went on the trip.

7. The homework was complicated, but Paulo helped Maria finish it.
   a. Paulo did Maria's homework for her.
   **b.** Both Paulo and Maria worked on her homework.

8. Their trip to the zoo made the students really appreciate animals.
   a. The trip forced the students to appreciate animals.
   **b.** The trip changed the students' opinions of animals.

---

1 *habitat:* in a zoo, a place outdoors or in a building that is like the natural environment of the animals

# EXERCISE 2 MEANING OF *MAKE, HAVE, LET, HELP,* AND *GET*

GRAMMAR NOTES 1–3 Students in a conversation class are talking about their experiences with authority figures.[1] Complete the sentences by circling the correct verb. Then match each situation with the person in authority.

**Situation**

_c_ 1. I was tired, so he didn't help / (have) me play in the second half of the game.

_h_ 2. I didn't really want to work overtime this week, but she (had) / let me work late because some of my co-workers were sick.

_e_ 3. I forgot to turn on my headlights before I left the parking lot a few nights ago. She (made) / got me pull over to the side of the road and asked to see my license.

_a_ 4. At first, we rebelled when he told us to write in our journals, but then he explained how important it was. Finally, he had / (got) us to try it.

_g_ 5. My check was delayed in the mail. I told him what had happened, and he made / (let) me pay the rent two weeks late.

_b_ 6. I needed to get a blood test for my physical exam. She got / (had) me roll up my sleeve and make a fist.

_i_ 7. We're a big family, and we all have our own chores. While she washed the dishes, she helped / (had) me dry. My brother, a former high school wrestling star, swept the floor!

_d_ 8. I'm an only child, and when I was young, I felt lonely. He (let) / got me sleep over at my friend's house.

_f_ 9. I wasn't paying attention, and I hit a parked car. He let / (helped) me to get the money for all of the repairs.

**Person in Authority**

a. my teacher

b. the doctor

c. my soccer coach

d. my father

e. a police officer

f. my insurance agent

g. my landlord

h. my boss

i. my mother

---

1 *authority figures:* people who are or seem powerful

# EXERCISE 3 AFFIRMATIVE AND NEGATIVE STATEMENTS

GRAMMAR NOTES 1–3 Read the conversations between a teacher, Ms. Allen, and her students. Complete the summary statements to show what Ms. Allen did. Use the correct form of the verbs in parentheses. Choose between affirmative and negative.

1. MS. ALLEN: Fernando, could you do me a favor and clean the board before you leave?
   FERNANDO: Sure.

   SUMMARY: Ms. Allen ___*had Fernando clean or had him clean*___ the board.
   (have / clean)

2. ANA: Could I work alone? I really don't like to work in a group.
   MS. ALLEN: You need to work in a group today. Don't look so sad. It's not a punishment!

   SUMMARY: She ___didn't let me work___ alone.
   (let / work)

3. PABLO: Ms. Allen, do I have to rewrite this paper on elephants?
   MS. ALLEN: Only if you want to.

   SUMMARY: She ___(didn't) make me rewrite___ his paper.
   (make / rewrite)

4. JUSTIN: What does *positive reinforcement* mean?
   MS. ALLEN: Why don't you see if one of your classmates can explain it to you?

   SUMMARY: She ___didn't have me guess___ the meaning.
   (have / guess)

5. MS. ALLEN: Rachel, I know you're busy, but I'd like you and Greta to research orcas. You're both so good at Internet research.
   RACHEL: Oh, OK!

   SUMMARY: She ___got us to research___ orcas on the Internet.
   (get / research)

6. RACHEL: We need some really great orca photos, and I can't find any.
   MS. ALLEN: Try the *National Geographic* site. They have fantastic nature photographs.

   SUMMARY: She ___helps us (to) find___ photographs of orcas.
   (help / find)

# EXERCISE 4 AFFIRMATIVE AND NEGATIVE STATEMENTS

GRAMMAR NOTES 1–3 **Read each conversation and complete the summary statement. Use** *make*, *have*, *let*, *help*, **or** *get* **plus the correct form of the verbs in parentheses. Choose between affirmative and negative.**

1. **MASAMI:** Can we use our dictionaries during the test?
   **MS. ALLEN:** No. You should be able to guess the meaning of the words from the context.

   **SUMMARY:** Ms. Allen _didn't let the students use_ **or** _didn't let them use_ their dictionaries.
   (use)

2. **MARÍA:** Mom, can I borrow the car?
   **MOM:** Only if you drive your sister to soccer.

   **SUMMARY:** María's mother _____ her sister to soccer.
   (drive)

3. **MARÍA:** John, the group wants you to read your report to the class.
   **JOHN:** No way! Sorry, but speaking in front of the class makes me nervous.

   **SUMMARY:** María _____ the report to the class.
   (read)

4. **JOHN:** Can I borrow your camera for our class trip to the zoo?
   **DAD:** Sure. I know you'll take good care of it.

   **SUMMARY:** John's father _____ his camera.
   (borrow)

5. **JOHN:** Excuse me, could I take pictures in here?
   **WORKER:** Yes, but don't use the flash. Light bothers these animals.

   **SUMMARY:** The zoo worker _____ the flash on his camera.
   (use)

6. **PAUL:** I don't know which movie to watch for my listening assignment.
   **TOM:** You might like *Free Willy*. It's about a captive orca.

   **SUMMARY:** Tom _____ a movie to watch.
   (choose)

## EXERCISE 5  EDITING

GRAMMAR NOTES 1–3  **Read this email petition about orcas. There are eight mistakes in the use of** *make, have, let, help,* **and** *get.* **The first mistake is already corrected. Find and correct seven more.**

# LET THEM GO!

*Blackfish*, a documentary film about orcas in captivity, made people ~~to think~~ *think* about the use of these magnificent mammals in marine theme parks. Public pressure even got SeaWorld to change the orca shows at its theme parks. But the orcas are still in captivity. So it's time for action.

In captivity, an orca can't have normal physical or emotional health. In the wild, an orca swims freely and has a complex social life in a large family group. However, marine theme parks and aquariums make this animal lives in a small, chemically treated pool where it may get sick and die. There are arguments that captive orcas have helped humans learned about them. However, orcas cannot behave naturally in captivity when trainers have them to perform embarrassing tricks for a "reward." How can watching tricks or seeing orcas in a small pool help we understand them?

Don't let these beautiful animals suffering this cruel treatment for human entertainment! First, help us end orca shows. Stop going to these shows, and get your friends and family stop also. Next, we must make marine theme parks and aquariums stop buying orcas. And they must let experts to retrain the orcas now in captivity and release them to a normal life. Write to your government officials and tell them how you feel.

Help us help the orcas! It's the humane thing to do. Sign this petition and send it to everyone you know.

## EXERCISE 6 LISTENING

▶10|02 **A** Listen to the conversation between a student and his writing teacher. Read the statements. Then listen again and check (✓) *True* or *False*.

|  | True | False |
|---|---|---|
| 1. Ms. Jacobson originally made Simon write about animals in zoos. | ☐ | ☑ |
| 2. She let him change the topic of his essay. | ☐ | ☐ |
| 3. She had him remove some details from his second paragraph. | ☐ | ☐ |
| 4. She got him to talk about his uncle. | ☐ | ☐ |
| 5. She helped him correct a grammar mistake. | ☐ | ☐ |
| 6. Simon got Ms. Jacobson to correct the gerunds in his essay. | ☐ | ☐ |
| 7. Ms. Jacobson made Simon look for the gerunds in his essay. | ☐ | ☐ |
| 8. She let Simon make an appointment for another conference. | ☐ | ☐ |

▶10|02 **B** Listen to the conversation again. Then work with a partner. Do you think Ms. Jacobson is a good writing teacher? Why or why not? Discuss your answers.

EXAMPLE: **A:** Ms. Jacobson let Simon explain why he was worried about his essay. That's good.
**B:** I agree. And she used positive reinforcement. However, she made him . . .

## EXERCISE 7  A HELPING HAND

CONVERSATION  **Work with a partner. Talk about a person who helped you learn something new (for example, a parent, other relative, teacher, or friend). Answer the questions below.**

EXAMPLE:  A: My older brother was a big help to me when I was a teenager.
B: Oh? What did he do?
A: Well, he got me to try a lot of new things. He even taught me . . .

1. What did the person get you to do that you had never done before?

2. How did this person help you?

3. How did it make you feel?

4. Did he or she let you make mistakes in order to learn?


## EXERCISE 8  FOR OR AGAINST?

Ⓐ DISCUSSION  **You are going to have a discussion about keeping animals in captivity for human entertainment. Use the Internet to research reasons for and against keeping animals in zoos and marine theme parks. Take notes.**

Ⓑ **Work in a group. Discuss whether you are for or against using animals for entertainment. Use** *make, have, let, help,* **and** *get.*

EXAMPLE:  A: I think it's cruel to make wild animals live in small habitats.
B: I'm not sure. Having them perform . . .
C: I think zoos can help us . . .
D: Zoos make me feel . . .

**A** BEFORE YOU WRITE Think about the arguments for and against keeping animals in zoos and marine theme parks. Then think about your own opinion. Complete the outline.

| Arguments For | Arguments Against | My Opinion |
|---|---|---|
| _____ | _____ | _____ |
| _____ | _____ | _____ |
| _____ | _____ | _____ |

**B** WRITE Use your outline to write three paragraphs. In your first paragraph, give the arguments for keeping animals in zoos and marine theme parks. In your second paragraph, give the arguments against. Give your own opinion in the third paragraph. Use *make*, *have*, *let*, *help*, and *get*. Try to avoid the common mistakes in the chart.

EXAMPLE: Many people believe that it is good to have animals live in captivity. They believe animals help . . .

On the other hand, other people want to let animals live freely in the wild. According to these people . . .

In my opinion . . .

### Common Mistakes in Using *Make, Have, Let, Help*, and *Get*

| | |
|---|---|
| Use the **base form** of the verb **after *make*, *have*,** and ***let***. Do not use an infinitive. | Should we **make** animals **live** in captivity?<br>NOT Should we make animals ~~to live~~ in captivity? |
| Use an **infinitive after *get***. Do not use the base form of the verb. | My friend **got** me **to agree** with his opinion.<br>NOT My friend got me ~~agree~~ with his opinion. |
| Use an **object pronoun after *make*, *have*, *let*, *help*,** and ***get***. Do not use a subject pronoun. | Most marine animal parks **have them** do tricks.<br>NOT Most marine animal parks have ~~they~~ do tricks. |

**C** CHECK YOUR WORK Read your paragraphs. Underline *make*, *have*, *let*, *help*, and *get* + object + verb. Use the Editing Checklist to check your work.

### Editing Checklist

**Did you use . . . ?**

- [ ] object + base form of the verb after *make*, *have*, and *let*
- [ ] object + base form or infinitive after *help*
- [ ] object + infinitive after *get*
- [ ] the correct verb to express your meaning

**D** REVISE YOUR WORK Read your paragraphs again. Can you improve your writing? Make changes if necessary. Give your paragraphs a title.

# UNIT 10 REVIEW

**Test yourself on the grammar of the unit.**

**A** Circle the correct words to complete the sentences.

1. I didn't know what to write about, so my teacher helped / made me choose a topic by suggesting ideas.

2. Before we began to write, she had / got us research the topic online.

3. At first, I was annoyed when my teacher let / made me rewrite the report.

4. She was fantastic. She always let / helped me ask her questions.

5. It was a good assignment. It really made / got me to think a lot.

**B** Complete the sentences with the correct form of the verbs in parentheses. Choose between affirmative and negative and use pronoun objects.

1. When I was little, my parents _____ a pet. They said I was too young.
   (let / have)

2. When I was ten, I finally _____ me a dog. His name was Buttons.
   (get / buy)

3. It was a lot of responsibility. My parents _____ him every day.
   (make / walk)

4. They _____ him, too. He ate a lot!
   (have / feed)

5. I was annoyed at my older brother. He _____ care of Buttons.
   (help / take)

6. Sometimes, I _____ Buttons a bath. Both enjoyed it.
   (get / give)

7. When I have children, I plan to _____ a pet. It's a great experience.
   (let / have)

**C** Find and correct eight mistakes.

Lately, I've been thinking a lot about all the people who helped me adjusting to moving here when I was a kid. My parents got me join some school clubs, so I met other kids. Then my dad helped me improved my soccer game so that I could join the team. And my mom never let me to stay home. She made me to get out and do things. My parents also spoke to my new teacher and had she call on me a lot, so the other kids got to know me quickly. Our next-door neighbors helped, too. They got I to walk their dog Red, and Red introduced me to all her human friends! The fact that so many people wanted to help me made me to realize that I was not alone. Before long, I felt part of my new school, my new neighborhood, and my new life.

**Now check your answers on page 477.**

# Phrasal Verbs: Review and Expansion
## TELEMARKETING

## STEP 1    GRAMMAR IN CONTEXT

### BEFORE YOU READ

Look at the cartoon. Discuss the questions.

1. Who do you think is calling the man? How does the man feel about the call?

2. Do you receive unwanted calls? How do you feel about them?

### READ

▶11|01  Read this magazine article about telemarketers.

# Welcome Home!

You just got back from a long, hard day at the office. You're exhausted. All you want to do is take off your jacket, put down your briefcase, and relax over a great dinner. Then, just as you're about to sit down at the table, the phone rings. You hesitate to pick it up. It's probably just another telemarketer trying to talk you into buying something you really don't need. But, what if it's not? It could be important family news that you don't want to miss out on. You have to find out!

"Hello?" you answer nervously.

"Good evening. Is this Mr. Groaner?" a strange voice asks. You know right away that it's a telemarketer. Your last name is Groden. "We have great news for you! You've been chosen to receive an all-expenses-paid trip to the Bahamas! It's an offer you can't afford to turn down!"

*"I just got home. Can you call back tomorrow when I'm still at work?"*

Telemarketing—the practice of selling products and services by phone—is spreading throughout the world as the number of phones goes up and phone rates come down. To most people, annoying calls from telemarketers are about as welcome as a bad case of the flu.

What can be done about this invasion of privacy?[1] Experts have come up with several tactics that you can try out.

- Sign up to have your phone number placed on a Do Not Call list. If you're on the list and telemarketers keep on calling, write down the date and time of the call, and find out the name of the organization calling you. You can then report the call to the proper authorities.

- Use Caller ID to help identify telemarketers. If an unfamiliar number shows up, don't pick up the phone. Even better, use the Block This Caller feature on your phone to prevent future calls from getting through.

- If you *have* answered the phone, say (firmly but politely!): "I'm hanging up now," and get off the phone.

- Ask the telemarketing company to take you off their list. But don't count on this happening immediately. You may have to ask several times before it takes effect.

None of these measures will eliminate all unwanted telephone solicitations,[2] but they should help cut down the number of calls that you receive.

Telemarketing, however, is part of a larger problem. We are constantly being flooded with unwanted offers and requests. Junk mail fills up our mailboxes (and later our trash and recycling cans when we throw it out). And the invasion is, of course, not limited to paper. When you turn on your computer and check your email, you have to deal with spam, the electronic equivalent of junk mail.

What's the solution? Leave home? Move to a desert island? Maybe not. They'll probably get to you there anyway!

---

1 *invasion of privacy:* interrupting or getting involved in another's personal life in an unwelcome way
2 *solicitations:* asking someone for something such as money or help

## AFTER YOU READ

Ⓐ VOCABULARY   **Circle the word or phrase that best completes each sentence.**

1. If you **eliminate** a problem, the problem disappears / gets better / gets worse.

2. The **authorities** are people that buy / control / write about things.

3. A useful **feature** of phones is text messaging / telemarketing / junk mail.

4. If two things are **equivalent**, they are the same / different / valuable.

5. Telemarketers' **tactics** are their products / sales methods / prices.

6. When you speak **firmly**, you show that you are worried / curious / certain.

**COMPREHENSION** **Read the statements. Check (✓) True or False.**

| | True | False |
|---|---|---|
| 1. Mr. Groden got a call from a telemarketer in the morning. | ☐ | ☐ |
| 2. Mr. Groden quickly figured out that it was a telemarketing call. | ☐ | ☐ |
| 3. More people now have phones, so telemarketing is becoming a global problem. | ☐ | ☐ |
| 4. If your name is on a Do Not Call list, you will not get telemarketing calls. | ☐ | ☐ |
| 5. You can do something to stop *all* of these unwanted calls. | ☐ | ☐ |
| 6. Telemarketing is just one example of an invasion of privacy. | ☐ | ☐ |

C **DISCUSSION** **Work with a partner. Compare your answers in B. Why did you choose** *True* **or** *False*?

---

## STEP 2    GRAMMAR PRESENTATION

## PHRASAL VERBS: REVIEW AND EXPANSION

### Separable Transitive

| Subject | Verb | Particle | Object (Noun) |
|---|---|---|---|
| She | **picked** | **up** | the phone. |

### Separable Transitive

| Subject | Verb | Object (Noun/ Pronoun) | Particle |
|---|---|---|---|
| She | **picked** | the phone it | **up**. |

### Inseparable Transitive

| Subject | Verb | Particle | Object (Noun/ Pronoun/Gerund) |
|---|---|---|---|
| He | **counts** | **on** | your calls. them. |
| They | **keep** | **on** | calling. doing it. |

### Intransitive

| Subject | Verb | Particle |
|---|---|---|
| They | **sat** | **down**. |

### Phrasal Verb + Preposition

| Subject | Verb | Particle | Preposition | Object (Noun/ Pronoun) |
|---|---|---|---|---|
| I | **hung** | **up** | **on** | the caller. him. |
| They | **came** | **up** | **with** | this idea. it. |

# GRAMMAR NOTES

## 1 Form of Phrasal Verbs

A **phrasal verb** (also called a *two-word verb*) has **two parts**: a verb and a particle.

* phrasal verb = verb + particle

VERB + PARTICLE
I **got off** the phone quickly.

These are some **common particles** that combine with verbs to form a phrasal verb:

* *in*     (call in, fill in, turn in)
* *out*   (find out, throw out, try out)
* *up*    (fill up, hang up, pick up)
* *down* (sit down, turn down, write down)
* *on*    (count on, put on, turn on)
* *off*   (get off, take off, turn off)

VERB + PARTICLE
I **turned in** the form.
I **throw out** my junk mail.
I don't **pick up** the phone.
I **write down** the date and time of each call.
I **turn on** my computer to check my email.
I **get off** the phone as soon as I can.

**Particles** look like prepositions, but they act differently. Particles often **change the meaning** of the verb, but prepositions do not.

VERB + PREPOSITION
I **looked up** and saw a large bird.
*(I looked toward the sky.)*
VERB + PARTICLE
I **looked up** his number online.
*(I tried to find his number.)*

## 2 Meaning of Phrasal Verbs

A **phrasal verb** has a **special meaning**. It is often very different from the meaning of its parts.

| PHRASAL VERB | MEANING |
| --- | --- |
| call in | hire |
| find out | discover |
| turn down | reject |

Let's **call in** an expert to help.
Did you **find out** who was calling you?
I **turned down** their offer.

USAGE NOTE Phrasal verbs are **less formal** than one-word verbs with similar meaning. They are very **common in everyday speech**.

They **set up** Do Not Call lists. *(less formal)*
They **established** Do Not Call lists. *(more formal)*

BE CAREFUL! Like other verbs, phrasal verbs often have **more than one meaning**.

Please **turn down** the radio. It's too loud.
*(Please lower the volume.)*
I **turn down** all telemarketing offers.
*(I reject all telemarketing offers.)*

BE CAREFUL! Use the **correct particle**. The particle often changes the meaning of the phrasal verb.

We **handed** *in* our homework.
*(We submitted our homework.)*
Then the teacher **handed** *out* our next assignment.
*(Then the teacher distributed our next assignment.)*

## 3 Separable Transitive Phrasal Verbs

Many phrasal verbs are **transitive**—they **take an object**. Most transitive phrasal verbs are **separable**.

| PHRASAL VERB | MEANING |
|---|---|
| *call off* something | cancel |
| *pick out* something | choose |
| *take off* something | remove |

PHRASAL VERB + OBJECT
Let's **call off** *the meeting*.
I **picked out** *the chair* I like best.
**Take off** *your coat*.

With a separable transitive phrasal verb, the **noun object** can go:

- **after** the particle

VERB + PARTICLE + OBJECT
I just **took off** *my coat*.

- **between** the verb and the particle

VERB + OBJECT + PARTICLE
I just **took** *my coat* off.

BE CAREFUL! When the **object** is a **pronoun**, it must go **between** the verb and the particle. Do not put the pronoun after the particle.

I **took** *it* **off**.
NOT I took off it.

USAGE NOTE When the **noun object** is part of a **long phrase**, we usually **do not separate** the verb and particle of a phrasal verb.

I **filled out** *the form from the Do Not Call registry*.
NOT I filled the form from the Do Not Call registry out.

With a small group of transitive phrasal verbs, the verb and particle **must be separated**.

| PHRASAL VERB | MEANING |
|---|---|
| *ask* someone *over* | invite to one's home |
| *see* something *through* | complete |

**Ask** *Ian* **over**. NOT Ask over Ian.
I **saw** *the job* **through**. NOT I saw through the job.

## 4 Inseparable Transitive Phrasal Verbs

**Some transitive** phrasal verbs are **inseparable**.

With inseparable transitive phrasal verbs, both **noun and pronoun objects** always go **after** the particle. Do not separate the verb from its particle.

I **ran into** *Ed* at work. NOT I ran Ed into at work.
I **ran into** *him* at work. NOT I ran him into.

A few phrasal verbs can have a **gerund** (verb + *-ing*) as an **object**. The gerund always comes **after** the particle.

They **kept on** *calling*.
Mike **put off** *reporting* the calls to the authorities.

## 5 Intransitive Phrasal Verbs

Some phrasal verbs are **intransitive**—they do **not take an object**.

| PHRASAL VERB | MEANING | |
|---|---|---|
| | | VERB + PARTICLE |
| *catch on* | become popular | The Do Not Call list has **caught on** everywhere. |
| *sign up* | register | Margaret **signed up** last month. |
| *show up* | appear | If an unfamiliar number **shows up**, don't answer. |

| | |
|---|---|
| With intransitive phrasal verbs, the verb and particle are **never separated**. | He's been away and just **got back** yesterday. |
| | NOT He's been away and just ~~got yesterday back~~. |

| | |
|---|---|
| USAGE NOTE Intransitive phrasal verbs are often action verbs and they occur frequently in the **imperative**. | Please **come in**. |
| | Don't **call back**! |

| | |
|---|---|
| IN WRITING Intransitive phrasal verbs are very **common in conversation**, but they are **rare in formal writing**. | Her efforts **paid off**. *(conversation)* |
| | Her efforts **were worthwhile**. *(formal writing)* |

## 6 Transitive or Intransitive Phrasal Verbs

| | |
|---|---|
| Like other verbs, some phrasal verbs can be **both transitive and intransitive**. The meaning is often the same. | He **called** *me* **back**. |
| | He **called back**. |
| | *(He returned my phone call.)* |

| | |
|---|---|
| BE CAREFUL! Some phrasal verbs have a completely **different meaning** when they are transitive or intransitive. | We **made up** *a story*. *(We invented a story.)* |
| | We **made up**. *(We ended a disagreement.)* |

## 7 Phrasal Verb + Preposition Combinations

Some **phrasal verbs** are used **in combination with a preposition** (such as *at, from, for, of, on, to,* or *with*).

A **phrasal verb + preposition combination** (also called a *three-word verb*) is usually **inseparable**. The **object** comes **after the preposition**.

| PHRASAL VERB + PREPOSITION | MEANING | |
|---|---|---|
| *come up with* something | invent | She **came up** *with* a way to stop junk mail. |
| *drop out of* something | quit | He **dropped out** *of* school and got a job. |
| *hang up on* someone | end a phone call suddenly | Why did you **hang up** *on* me? I was still talking. |

## REFERENCE NOTES

For a list of **separable phrasal verbs**, see Appendix 4 on page 455.

For a list of **inseparable transitive phrasal verbs**, see Appendix 4 on page 455.

For a list of **phrasal verbs that must be separated**, see Appendix 4 on page 455.

For a list of **phrasal verb + preposition combinations**, see Appendix 4 on page 455.

For a list of **intransitive phrasal verbs**, see Appendix 5 on page 457.

## EXERCISE 1  DISCOVER THE GRAMMAR

Ⓐ GRAMMAR NOTES 1–7  **Read this article about ways of dealing with telemarketers. Underline the phrasal verbs. Circle the objects. See Appendices 4 and 5 on pages 455 and 457 for help.**

# Getting the Last Laugh

Although your phone number is on the Do Not Call list, every night you still end up with calls from telemarketers. Lots of them. Why not have some fun then? We came up with these amusing tactics:

- When the telemarketer asks, "How are you today?"—tell her! Go over every detail. Don't leave anything out. Say, "I have a headache you wouldn't believe, and my back is acting up again. I ran into an old friend, and I couldn't remember her name! Now I can't figure out the instructions for downloading . . ."

- When a telemarketer calls during dinner, request his home telephone number so you can call him back. When he refuses, ask him to hold on. Put the phone down and keep on eating until you hear the dial tone.
  ＼ Continue.

- Ask the telemarketer to spell her first and last name and the name of the company. Tell her to speak slowly—because you're taking notes. Ask questions until she gives up answering and hangs up.          quit stop

- To credit card offers, say, "Thanks a lot! My company just laid me off, and I really need the money!"

Ⓑ **Write down a phrasal verb from the article next to its meaning.**

1. _acting up_ causing problems
2. _Go over_ review
3. _hangs up_ ends a phone call
4. _laid off_ ended employment
5. _came up with_ invented
6. _Call back_ return a call

7. _hold on_ wait
8. _leave out_ omit
9. _end up with_ have an unexpected result
10. _put down_ stop holding
11. _figure out_ understand
12. _ran into_ met accidentally

# EXERCISE 2  MEANING OF PHRASAL VERBS

GRAMMAR NOTE 2  A *scam* is a dishonest plan, usually to get money from people. Read about how to avoid some common scams. Complete the information with the correct forms of the phrasal verbs from the boxes. See Appendices 4 and 5 on pages 455 and 457 for help.

| end up with | hang up | let down | ~~throw out~~ |
|---|---|---|---|

I just _____ *threw out* _____ my first issue of *Motorcycle Mama*. I'm nobody's mama, and I

1.

don't own a motorcycle, so how did I _____ this subscription? Well, my

2.

neighbor's son was raising money for his soccer team, and I didn't want to _____ him

_____. It's easy to _____ on telemarketers, but it's hard to

3.                                                    4.

say *no* to your friends and neighbors.

| fall for | get to | help out | watch out for |
|---|---|---|---|

The magazine company _____ me through a friendship. It's one of the

5.

ways "persuasion professionals" get us to say *yes*. Of course it's OK to _____

6.

the local soccer team. But a lot of people _____ scams because of similar

7.

techniques. Learn to identify and _____ these common scams.

8.

| find out | give back | go along with | turn down |
|---|---|---|---|

When someone gives you something, naturally you want to _____ something

_____. This desire to return a favor can cost you money when a telemarketer

9.

announces you've won a vacation or a new car. Beware! These offers aren't free. When people

_____ them, they always _____ that there's a tax or a fee

10.                                          11.

to collect the "free" prize. Since they've accepted the offer, they feel obligated to pay. You should

_____ these offers _____. These are scams and they are illegal.

12.

| count on | fill out | pick out | put on | turn up |
|---|---|---|---|---|

A TV actor will _____ a doctor's white jacket and talk about cough

13.

medicine. In a magazine ad, a woman in a business suit will help you _____

14.

the best investment firm. Ads with fake "authority figures" are quite easy to identify, but there's an

Internet scam called *phishing* that's harder to recognize. For example, the phisher sends emails that

seem to be from well-known banks. They tell you that a problem with your account has

_____. Then they send you to an Internet site to _____

15.                                                    16.

forms with your account information. The *spoofed* site looks like the real thing, but a real bank will

never ask for your information over the Internet. You can _____ that!

17.

# EXERCISE 3 SEPARABLE PHRASAL VERBS AND PRONOUN OBJECTS

**A** GRAMMAR NOTE 3 Complete the conversations. Use the correct form of the phrasal verb from the first line of the conversation. Include a pronoun object.

1. **A:** Tell Ana not to pick up the phone. It's probably a telemarketer. They call constantly.

   **B:** Too late. She's already _picked it up_____.

2. **A:** You can't turn down this great offer for cat food!

   **B:** I'm afraid I have to _____turn it down___. I don't *have* a cat.

3. **A:** Did you fill out the online Do Not Call form?

   **B:** I _____filled it out_____ yesterday. I hope this will take care of the problem. I'm tired of these calls.

4. **A:** I left out my office phone and cell phone numbers on that form.

   **B:** Why did you ___leave them out_____?

5. **A:** Remember to call your mother back.

   **B:** I ___called her back___ last night.

6. **A:** Did you write down the dates of the calls?

   **B:** I ___wrote them down__, but then I lost the piece of paper.

7. **A:** Can you take my mother's name off your calling list?

   **B:** Sure. We'll ___take her off___ right away.

8. **A:** Let's turn the phone off and have dinner.

   **B:** I can't ___turn it off___. I'm expecting an important call.

▶11|02 **B** LISTEN AND CHECK **Listen to the conversations and check your answers in A.**

# EXERCISE 4  SEPARABLE AND INSEPARABLE PHRASAL VERBS

GRAMMAR NOTES 3–4, 7  Complete the ads from spam emails. Use the correct forms of the phrasal verbs and objects in parentheses. Place the object between the verb and the particle when possible. See Appendices 4 and 5 on pages 455 and 457 for help.

## LOSE Weight

_Take those extra pounds off_ fast! Love bread and cake?
**1.** (take off / those extra pounds)

Don't _give them up_ .
**2.** (give up / them)

No diet! No pills! No exercise! No worries! Just choose your target weight.

You'll _____ in no time. Our delicious
**3.** (get to / it)

drinks will _____ while you drop the
**4.** (fill up / you)

pounds. _____ at no cost. It's FREE
**5.** (try out / our plan)

for one month. _____ today!
**6.** (sign up for / it)

Want to know more? Click here for our information request form.

_____ to get our brochure.
**7.** (fill out / it)

Just _____ and watch those pounds come off! If you do not want to
**8.** (stick to / our plan)

receive emails from us, we will be more than happy to _____ our list.
**9.** (take off / you)

## MAKE $$$$! WORKING FROM HOME!

_turn your hobby into_ cash and increase your savings
**1.** (turn into / your hobby)

without leaving your home!

My home-based business _take $2000 in_ a day.
**2.** (take in / $2,000)

That's right—and I _turn work down_ every week.
**3.** (turn down / work)

Sure, I could _take employees on_ , but I'd rather
**4.** (take on / employees)

teach _you_ how to _go after those jobs_ . This is an
**5.** (go after / those jobs)

easy business, and you can _set it up_ in a few days. Click on the $, and I'll
**6.** (set up / it)

_Send the materials out_ right away. _check them out_ . If you
**7.** (send out / the materials)  **8.** (check out / them)

don't like them, _Send them back_ .
**9.** (send back / them)

It's as simple as that! Don't _put your decision off_ ! Act now! This offer is a money machine,
**10.** (put off / your decision)

so don't _pass it up_ . Start to _cash in on this great opportunity_ by
**11.** (pass up / it)  **12.** (cash in on / this great opportunity)

next week!

# EXERCISE 5 EDITING

GRAMMAR NOTES 1–7 Read this transcript of a phone call between a telemarketer (TM) and Janis Linder (JL). There are thirteen mistakes in the use of phrasal verbs. The first mistake is already corrected. Find and correct twelve more. See Appendices 4 and 5 on pages 455 and 457 for help.

JL: Hello?

TM: This is Bob Watson from *Motorcycle Mama*. I'm calling to offer you a 12-month subscription for the low price of just $15 a year. Can I ~~sign up you~~ *sign you up*?

JL: No thanks. I'm trying to eliminate clutter, so I'm not interested in any more magazine subscriptions. Besides, I just sat up for dinner.

TM: Why don't you at least try out it for six months? This is a great opportunity. Don't miss it out on!

JL: Sorry, I'm really not interested. I don't even have a motorcycle.

TM: Really? When I got on my first motorcycle, I didn't want to get off. Owning a motorcycle is great! You should look into it. And you can count *Motorcycle Mama* on. We'll tell you everything you need to know. Let me send you a free copy of our magazine, and you can look over it.

JL: I'll say this as firmly as I can. I'm not interested. And no matter what you say, I'm not going to fall it for. Please take my name out your list. If you keep on call, I'll notify the authorities. Goodbye.

TM: No, hold out! Don't hang up! Don't turn this great offer off! Chances like this don't come around every day!

JL: OK. I have an idea. Why don't you give me your phone number, and I'll call back you during *your* dinner?

*(The telemarketer hangs the phone.)*

JL: And good-bye to you, too!

## EXERCISE 6  LISTENING

⏵11|03  Ⓐ  Listen to the conversation between Mr. Chen and a telemarketer. Read the statements. Then listen again and check (✓) *True* or *False*.

| | True | False |
|---|:---:|:---:|
| 1. Mr. Chen hangs up immediately. | ☐ | ☑ |
| 2. The telemarketer says she wants to help Mr. Chen out with his phone rates. | ☐ | ☐ |
| 3. With the Get Together Program, Mr. Chen might run out of minutes. | ☐ | ☐ |
| 4. There's a charge for setting up the new phone plan. | ☐ | ☐ |
| 5. Mr. Chen figured out the cost of the Get Together Program cell phone. | ☐ | ☐ |
| 6. The telemarketer is going to give Mr. Chen some time to think over the plan. | ☐ | ☐ |
| 7. Mr. Chen is going to sign up for the service. | ☐ | ☐ |

⏵11|03  Ⓑ  Listen to the conversation again. Then work with a partner. Make a list of the advantages and disadvantages of the Get Together Program.

EXAMPLE:  A: Well, one advantage is that you can call up as many people as you want and talk for as long as you want because of the unlimited minutes.
 B: But I think the plan probably leaves out international calls. The telemarketer didn't say anything about international calls. That's a disadvantage.

## EXERCISE 7  TO PICK UP OR NOT TO PICK UP

Ⓐ  DISCUSSION  Work with a partner. Discuss these questions about telemarketing.

1. What do you think of telemarketing? Does it offer consumers anything positive? Or is it equivalent to junk mail?

EXAMPLE:  A: I think telemarketing is a terrible idea.
 B: It doesn't bother me. I just politely say I have to hang up, and then I get off the phone.

2. Should telemarketing be illegal? Do you go along with the idea of Do Not Call lists? Should some organizations be allowed to keep on calling you? If yes, what kind?

3. Do you think people should just hang up when telemarketers call? Or should they put them off with a polite excuse, such as, "Thanks. I'll think it over."?

Ⓑ  Work in a group. Compare your answers in A with those of your classmates.

EXAMPLE:  A: My partner and I don't agree about telemarketing, but we came up with...
 B: We both feel that telemarketing is a huge problem. We hang up, but the telemarketers call back the next day.
 C: Have you tried...?
 D: We think...

# EXERCISE 8  SELLING TACTICS

DISCUSSION  Work with a group. Bring in an ad from a magazine, a piece of junk mail, spam, or an ad from the Internet. Discuss the ads and the questions below. Use some of the phrasal verbs in the box in your discussion.

EXAMPLE:  A: I think this ad is trying to get to anyone who wants to make money fast.
B: I agree. It's not really aimed at a specific group of people.
C: It's probably a scam. When you click on OK, I bet they try to get money *from* you! Do you think people would fall for this?

- What group of people might want this product or service (children, teenagers, older people, men, women)?
- What tactics does the ad use to get people to want this product or service?
- Is this an honest offer or a scam? What makes you think so?

| | | | |
|---|---|---|---|
| cash in on s.t. | fall for s.t. | get to s.o. | miss out |
| catch on | fill s.t. out | go after s.o. | miss out on s.t. |
| count on s.t. | find s.t. out | help s.o. out | pay off |
| end up | get ahead | leave s.t. out | send s.t. back |
| end up with s.t. | get s.t. out of s.t. | make s.t. up | turn s.t. down |

# FROM GRAMMAR TO WRITING

**A** BEFORE YOU WRITE Think about an experience you have had on the phone. It could be a conversation with a friend, a wrong number, or a telemarketing call. Complete the outline.

**What Happened During the Phone Call**

_____

_____

_____

**What I Learned from the Experience**

_____

_____

_____

**B** WRITE Use your outline to write two paragraphs about the experience you had on the phone. In the first paragraph, describe what happened during the call. In the second paragraph, write about what you learned from the experience. Use phrasal verbs. Try to avoid the common mistakes in the chart.

EXAMPLE:    When I first got to this country, I had difficulty understanding English on the phone. Because I couldn't figure out what people were saying to me, I often ended up getting into trouble. One day, there was a message on my cell phone. It sounded important, so I called back. That's when I found out . . .

## Common Mistakes in Using Phrasal Verbs

| | |
|---|---|
| Use the **correct particle**. The wrong particle changes the meaning of the verb. | I **picked** *up* the phone when it rang. *(I answered the phone.)* <br> I **picked** *out* the phone because of its features. *(I selected the phone.)* |
| Put **pronoun** objects **between** the verb and the particle in transitive **separable** phrasal verbs. Do not put pronoun objects after the particle. | When the phone rang, I **picked** *it* up. <br> NOT I picked up it. |
| Put **pronoun** objects **after** the particle in transitive **inseparable** verbs. Do not put pronoun objects after the verb. | Think about this plan before you **settle on** *it*. <br> NOT before you settle it on. |

**C** CHECK YOUR WORK Read your paragraphs. Underline the phrasal verbs. Circle the objects. Use the Editing Checklist to check your work.

## Editing Checklist

**Did you use . . . ?**

☐ phrasal verbs

☐ the correct particles

☐ pronoun objects between the verb and the particle of separable phrasal verbs

☐ pronoun objects and noun objects after the particle of inseparable phrasal verbs

**D** REVISE YOUR WORK Read your paragraphs again. Can you improve your writing? Make changes if necessary. Give your paragraphs a title.

# UNIT 11 REVIEW

**Test yourself on the grammar of the unit.**

**A** Match each phrasal verb with its meaning.

| | | | |
|---|---|---|---|
| _____ | **1.** pick up | **a.** | remove |
| _____ | **2.** look into | **b.** | meet by accident |
| _____ | **3.** take off | **c.** | complete (a form) |
| _____ | **4.** fill out | **d.** | return |
| _____ | **5.** run into | **e.** | research |
| _____ | **6.** get back | **f.** | lift |
| _____ | **7.** give up | **g.** | quit |

**B** Complete each sentence with the correct form of the phrasal verb and object in parentheses. Place the object between the verb and particle when possible.

**1.** I had to _____ .
(get through with / my work)

**2.** The phone rang. I didn't want to _____ , but I did.
(pick up / it)

**3.** It was Ada. I can always _____ to call late!
(count on / her)

**4.** I asked her to _____ in the morning.
(call back / me)

**5.** Then I _____ .
(get off / the phone)

**6.** I _____ and went to bed.
(put on / my pajamas)

**7.** Finally, I _____ and fell asleep.
(turn off / the lights)

**C** Find and correct six mistakes.

I'm so tired of telemarketers calling up me as soon as I get back from work or just when I sit up for a relaxing dinner! It's gotten to the point that I've stopped picking the phone when it rings between 6:00 and 8:00 p.m. up. I know I can count on it being a telemarketer who will try to talk me into spending money on something I don't want. But it's still annoying to hear the phone ring, so sometimes I turn off it. Then, of course, I worry that it may be someone important. So I end up checking caller ID to find out. I think the Do Not Call list is a great idea. Who thought up it? I'm going to sign for it up tomorrow!

**Now check your answers on page 477.**

# Adjective Clauses

PART **5**

**OUTCOMES**
- Identify or give additional information about people, places, or things, using adjective clauses with correct subject relative pronouns
- Identify personality traits in a psychology article
- Identify the people described in a conversation
- Take a personality quiz and discuss the results
- Discuss personality traits
- Write about the qualities of a good friend

**OUTCOMES**
- Identify or give additional information about people, places, or things, using adjective clauses with correct object relative pronouns
- Identify key details in an online book review
- Identify the image described in a recording
- Describe your hometown or city
- Research a successful immigrant and report findings
- Write about a place from one's childhood

# Adjective Clauses with Subject Relative Pronouns

## PERSONALITY TYPES AND FRIENDS

**OUTCOMES**
- Identify or give additional information about people, places, or things, using adjective clauses with correct subject relative pronouns
- Identify personality traits in a psychology article
- Identify the people described in a conversation
- Take a personality quiz and discuss the results
- Discuss personality traits
- Write about the qualities of a good friend

---

**STEP 1**    **GRAMMAR IN CONTEXT**

that
who
whose
which.

## BEFORE YOU READ

Look at the cartoon and at the definitions. Discuss the questions.

1. What is the personality of an extrovert? An introvert?

2. Can people with very different personalities get along?

## READ

▶12|01   Read this article about extroverts and introverts.

# Extroverts and Introverts

**Extrovert:** someone who loves being in a group of people

**Introvert:** someone who avoids extroverts

Nadia, who needs to spend several hours alone each day, avoids large social gatherings whenever possible. She hates small talk, and at office holiday parties, which are "must-attend" events, she's always the first one to leave.

    You probably know someone like Nadia. Maybe you're even one of those people that nag[1] a friend like her to get out more. If so, stop! Nadia is an introvert, and there's really nothing wrong with that. Introverts are people that get their energy by spending time alone. Their opposites are extroverts, people whose energy comes from being around others. Neither type is better than the other. However, because there are so many more extroverts than introverts, there is a lot of misunderstanding about the introverts among us.

---

1 *nag:* keep telling someone, in way that is very annoying, to do something

First, people have a tendency to think that all introverts are shy. Not so. Shy people fear social situations, but many introverts just try to avoid the ones that drain² their energy. Nadia, who is great at leading big, noisy business meetings, isn't afraid of those meetings. But she needs a lot recovery time afterwards. Unlike extroverts, who love the small talk at those meetings, she prefers private conversations that focus on feelings and ideas.

Secondly, people also assume that you have to be an extrovert (or act like one) in order to succeed. However, every day the news is full of examples that contradict that belief. Microsoft's Bill Gates is one famous introvert who comes to mind. Another is successful businesswoman Andrea Jung. Jung, who grew up in a traditional Chinese family, considers herself "reserved," but not shy. A writer who has studied the personality traits of business leaders points out that the one trait which absolutely defines successful leaders is creativity. Introverts are known for being creative, so it shouldn't be a surprise to find many of them at the top of their professions.

What happens when an extrovert and an introvert become friends or fall in love? Opposites attract, but can first attraction survive really big personality differences? Yes, but only if both can accept the other person's needs—and it's not always easy. Extroverts, who have to talk through everything before they even know what they think, can drive an introvert crazy. Nadia, who always thinks before she speaks, doesn't always understand their need to talk. On the other hand, many extroverts, who reach for their cell phones after two minutes alone, can't see why an introvert like Nadia requires so much time by herself. (Is that really *normal?* they wonder.) However, if both people take the time to understand the other's personality type, the results can pay off. The introvert, who has a rich inner life, can help the extrovert become more sensitive to feelings. And the risk-loving extrovert can help the introvert develop a sense of adventure. As a result, each friend's personality becomes more complete.

It's important to remember that no one is a pure introvert or extrovert. In fact, we are probably all "ambiverts," people who act like introverts in some situations and extroverts in others. Like everyone else, you have a unique personality—your own special combination of traits that makes you *you!*

---

2 *drain:* use too much of something so that there is not enough left

# AFTER YOU READ

**Ⓐ VOCABULARY** Complete the sentences with the words from the box.

| contradict | require | sensitive | tendency | trait | unique |
| --- | --- | --- | --- | --- | --- |

1. Extroverts have a _____ to reach for their cell phones.

2. Rahul is so _____. He knows when I'm upset even when I hide my feelings.

3. Nadia hates to _____ people, even when they're obviously wrong.

4. Introverts _____ time alone. They get very unhappy without it.

5. No two people are exactly alike. Everyone is _____.

6. Creativity is a personality _____ of many introverts. It's part of who they are.

COMPREHENSION  Read each description. Check (✓) *Introvert* or *Extrovert*.

| Who . . . ? | Introvert | Extrovert |
|---|:---:|:---:|
| 1. gets energy from being alone | ☐ | ☐ |
| 2. gets energy from other people | ☐ | ☐ |
| 3. enjoys small talk | ☐ | ☐ |
| 4. likes to talk about ideas and feelings | ☐ | ☐ |
| 5. talks while thinking | ☐ | ☐ |
| 6. thinks before talking | ☐ | ☐ |
| 7. is sensitive to feelings | ☐ | ☐ |
| 8. likes to take risks | ☐ | ☐ |

**C** DISCUSSION  Work with a partner. Compare your answers in B. Why did you choose *Introvert* or *Extrovert*?

## STEP 2   GRAMMAR PRESENTATION

## ADJECTIVE CLAUSES WITH SUBJECT RELATIVE PRONOUNS

### Adjective Clauses After the Main Clause

| Main Clause | | | Adjective Clause | | |
|---|---|---|---|---|---|
| Subject | Verb | Noun/Pronoun | Subject Relative Pronoun | Verb | |
| I | read | a book | *that* *which* | discusses | **personality**. |
| An introvert | is | someone | *that* *who* | needs | **time alone**. |
| | | | *Whose* + Noun | | |
| I | have | a friend | *whose* personality | is | **like mine**. |

possession

## Adjective Clauses Inside the Main Clause

| Main Clause | Adjective Clause | | | Main Clause (cont.) | |
|---|---|---|---|---|---|
| Subject | Subject Relative Pronoun | Verb | | Verb | |
| The book | *that* *which* | **discusses** | **personality** | is | by Ruben. |
| Someone | *that* *who* | **needs** | **time alone** | may be | an introvert. |
| | *Whose* + Noun | | | | |
| Ana, | *whose* personality | is | **like mine,** | loves | parties. |

## GRAMMAR NOTES

### 1 Purpose of Adjective Clauses

Use **adjective clauses** to **identify** or give **additional information** about **nouns**. The nouns can refer to:

- **people**

I have a *friend* who avoids parties.
*(The clause who avoids parties identifies the friend.)*

- **places**

She lives in *Miami,* which is my hometown.
*(The clause which is my hometown gives additional information about Miami.)*

- **things**

She has a *job* that is very interesting.
*(The clause that is very interesting gives additional information about the job.)*

Adjective clauses can also identify or describe **indefinite pronouns** such as *one, someone, somebody, something, another,* and *other(s)*.

Nadia would like to meet *someone* who is funny.
*(The clause who is funny describes the person that Nadia would like to meet.)*

## 2 Sentences with Adjective Clauses

| You can think of **sentences with adjective clauses** as a **combination of two sentences**. | *I have a classmate. + He is an extrovert.* = I have a classmate **who is an extrovert.** |
|---|---|
| The **adjective clause follows the noun or pronoun** it is identifying or describing. The adjective clause can come: | |
| • **inside** the main clause | *My friend calls often. + She lives in Rome.* = My friend **who lives in Rome** calls often. |
| • **after** the main clause | *She has a son. + He is a successful doctor.* = She has a son **who is a successful doctor.** |
| **BE CAREFUL!** **Do not separate an adjective clause** from the noun or pronoun that it identifies or gives information about. | My friend **who lives in Berlin** seldom calls me. NOT My friend ~~seldom calls me who lives in Berlin.~~ |

## 3 Subject Relative Pronouns

Adjective clauses begin with **relative pronouns**. Relative pronouns can be **subjects**.

| Relative pronouns that can be the **subject** of the clause are *who, that, and which.* Use: | |
|---|---|
| • *who* or *that* for **people** | SUBJECT<br>I have a **friend** *who* loves spending time alone.<br>SUBJECT<br>I have a **friend** *that* loves spending time alone. |
| • *which* or *that* for **places** or **things** | SUBJECT<br>There's a **meeting** *which* starts at 10:00 a.m.<br>SUBJECT<br>There's a **meeting** *that* starts at 10:00 a.m. |
| **Relative pronouns** always have the **same form**. They do not change for singular and plural nouns or pronouns, or for males and females. | That's the **person** *that* gives great parties.<br>Those are the **people** *that* give great parties.<br>That's the **man** *who* gives great parties.<br>That's the **woman** *who* gives great parties. |
| **USAGE NOTE** In **conversation**, we use *that* more often than *who* and *which.* It's less formal. | Nadia is a person *that* avoids parties. *(less formal)*<br>Nadia is a person *who* avoids parties. *(more formal)* |
| **BE CAREFUL!** **Do not use a subject pronoun** (*I, you, he, she, it, we, they*) and a subject relative pronoun in the same adjective clause. | Scott is someone *who* **enjoys** parties.<br>NOT Scott is someone who ~~he~~ enjoys parties. |
| **BE CAREFUL!** **Do not leave out the subject relative pronoun** in an adjective clause. | Sarah is another person *who* **has** fun at parties.<br>NOT Sarah is another person ~~has fun at parties.~~ |

## 4 Whose

Some adjective clauses begin with the possessive form **whose**.

| | |
|---|---|
| Use **whose** + **noun** to show **possession** or **relationship**. | My friend has a son. + His name is Max. = My friend has a son **whose name** is Max. |
| Use **whose** to refer to: | |
| • **people** | **Friends whose** interests are different can help each other. |
| • **things** | I work at a **company whose** offices are in London. |
| **BE CAREFUL!** **Do not use who + possessive adjective (my, your, his, her, its, our, their) instead of whose.** | Deb is a woman **whose personality** is reserved. NOT Deb is a woman who her personality is reserved. |

## 5 Verbs in Adjective Clauses

| | |
|---|---|
| The **verb in the adjective clause** is **singular** if the subject relative pronoun refers to a singular noun or pronoun. The verb is **plural** if it refers to a plural noun or pronoun. | Ben is my **friend who lives** in Boston. Al and Ed are my **friends who live** in Boston. |
| **BE CAREFUL!** When **whose** + **noun** is the subject of the adjective clause, **the verb agrees with the noun subject** of the adjective clause. | Ed is a man **whose friends are** like family. NOT Ed is a man whose friends is like family. |

## 6 Identifying and Nonidentifying Adjective Clauses

There are two kinds of adjective clauses, **identifying** and **nonidentifying**.

| | |
|---|---|
| An **identifying** adjective clause is **necessary to identify** the noun it refers to. | I have a lot of good friends. My friend **who** lives in Chicago visits me often. *(The adjective clause is necessary to identify which friend.)* |
| A **nonidentifying** adjective clause gives **additional information** about the noun it refers to. It is **not necessary to identify** the noun. The noun is often **already identified** with an adjective such as *first*, *last*, *best*, or *most*, or the noun is the name of a person or place. | I have a lot of good friends. My **best** friend, **who** lives in Chicago, visits me often. *(The friend has already been identified as the person's best friend. The adjective clause gives additional information, but it isn't needed to identify the friend.)* |
| **BE CAREFUL!** **Do not use that to introduce nonidentifying adjective clauses. Use who for people and which for places and things.** | Ed, **who** introduced us at the party, called me last night. NOT Ed, that introduced us at the party, called me last night. My favorite city is **Miami, which** reminds me of home. NOT My favorite city is Miami, that reminds me of home. |

CONTINUED ▶

**CONTINUED ▶**

<table>
<tr>
<td>

Use **commas** to separate a nonidentifying adjective clause from the rest of the sentence.

</td>
<td>

NONIDENTIFYING ADJECTIVE CLAUSE
Bill Gates, **who is a well-known introvert,** founded Microsoft in 1975.

NONIDENTIFYING ADJECTIVE CLAUSE
I work at Microsoft, **which is located in Seattle.**

</td>
</tr>
<tr>
<td>

**Without commas**, an adjective clause has **a very different meaning** from an adjective clause with commas.

</td>
<td>

IDENTIFYING ADJECTIVE CLAUSE
My friends **who are extroverts** love parties.
*(My friends have different personalities. The adjective clause is necessary to identify which ones love parties.)*

NONIDENTIFYING ADJECTIVE CLAUSE
My friends, **who are extroverts,** love parties.
*(All of my friends are extroverts. They all love parties.)*

</td>
</tr>
</table>

## PRONUNCIATION NOTE

▶12|02  **Pronunciation of Identifying and Nonidentifying Adjective Clauses**

| | |
|---|---|
| In **writing**, we use **commas** around **nonidentifying adjective clauses**. | My sister Marie, **who lives in Seattle,** is an introvert. |
| In **speaking**, we **pause** briefly **before and after nonidentifying** adjective clauses. | My sister Marie [PAUSE] **who lives in Seattle** [PAUSE] is an introvert. |
| We **do not pause** before and after **identifying** adjective clauses. | My sister **who lives in Seattle** is an introvert. |

## EXERCISE 1 DISCOVER THE GRAMMAR

**GRAMMAR NOTES 1–6** Read this article about two other personality types. Circle the relative pronouns and underline the adjective clauses. Then draw an arrow from the relative pronoun to the noun or pronoun that it refers to.

# It's All How You Look at It

It's half empty!

It's half full!

Look at the photo. Do you see a glass (which) is half full or a glass which is half empty? For optimists, people who have a positive view of life, the glass is half full. For pessimists, people who have a negative view of life, the glass is half empty.

Most of us know people who have a strong tendency to be either optimistic or pessimistic. I have a friend whose life motto is "Things have a way of working out." Even when something bad happens, Cindi remains optimistic. Last year, she lost a job that was extremely important to her. She didn't get depressed; she just thought "Well, maybe I'll find a new job that's even better than this one!" But then there is the example of Monica, who always sees the dark side of every situation, even when something good happens. She recently won a lot of money in

a contest. Is she happy about this windfall? Not really. She worries that she won't know how to spend the money wisely. And now she's also worried that her friend Dan, who is struggling to start his own business, will be jealous of her. Cindi and Monica are women whose outlooks on life are as different as day and night.

Former U.S. president Harry Truman defined the two personalities very well: "A pessimist is one who makes difficulties of his opportunities, and an optimist is one who makes opportunities of his difficulties." However, people can learn to make these tendencies less extreme—even Cindi and Monica. Experts who study personality types agree: Half full or half empty, you may not be able to change how much water is in your glass, but you can often change how you view the situation and how you respond to it.

# EXERCISE 2 RELATIVE PRONOUNS AND VERBS

**GRAMMAR NOTES 3–6** Complete the statements in the personality quiz. Circle the correct words. (In Exercise 9, you will take the quiz.)

## Personality Quiz

Do you agree with the following statements? Check (✔) *True* or *False*.

|     |                                                                                      | TRUE | FALSE |
| --- | ------------------------------------------------------------------------------------ | ---- | ----- |
| 1.  | People (who) / which talk a lot tire me.                                              | ✔    | ☐     |
| 2.  | On a plane, I always talk to the stranger who take / (takes) the seat next to me.     | ☐    | ✔     |
| 3.  | I'm the kind of person (that) / which needs time to recover after a social event.    | ☐    | ✔     |
| 4.  | My best friend, (that) / who talks a lot, is just like me.                            | ☐    | ✔     |
| 5.  | I prefer to have conversations which (focus) / focuses on feelings and ideas.         | ✔    | ☐     |
| 6.  | I am someone whose favorite activities (include) / includes reading and doing yoga.   | ☐    | ✔     |
| 7.  | People (whose) / their personalities are completely different can be close friends.   | ✔    | ☐     |
| 8.  | I'm someone that always see / (sees) the glass as half full, not half empty.          | ✔    | ☐     |
| 9.  | Difficult situations are often the ones that (provide) / provides the best opportunities. | ✔ | ☐    |
| 10. | Introverts, (that) / (who) are quiet, sensitive, and creative, are perfect friends.   | ✔    | ☐     |

# EXERCISE 3 IDENTIFYING ADJECTIVE CLAUSES

**Ⓐ GRAMMAR NOTES 1–4, 6** We often use identifying adjective clauses to define words. First, match the words on the left with the descriptions on the right.

| _h_ | 1. difficulty | **a.** This situation gives you a chance to experience something good. |
| --- | --- | --- |
| ____ | 2. extrovert | **b.** This attitude shows your ideas about your future. |
| ____ | 3. introvert | **c.** This ability makes you able to produce new ideas. |
| ____ | 4. opportunity | **d.** This person usually sees the bright side of situations. |
| ____ | 5. opposites | **e.** This person requires a lot of time alone. |
| ____ | 6. optimist | **f.** This money was unexpected. |
| ____ | 7. outlook | **g.** This person usually sees the dark side of situations. |
| ____ | 8. pessimist | **h.** This problem is hard to solve. |
| ____ | 9. creativity | **i.** These people have completely different personalities. |
| ____ | 10. windfall | **j.** This person requires a lot of time with others. |

**B** Now write definitions with adjective clauses for the words on the left. Use the correct description on the right and an appropriate relative pronoun.

1. _A difficulty is a problem which is hard to solve. **or** A difficulty is a problem that is hard to solve._

2. _____

3. _____

4. _____

5. _____

6. _____

7. _____

8. _____

9. _____

10. _____

## EXERCISE 4 NONIDENTIFYING ADJECTIVE CLAUSES

GRAMMAR NOTES 1–6 **Combine the pairs of sentences. Make the second sentence in each pair an adjective clause. Use the correct punctuation. Make any other necessary changes.**

1. I'm attending English 101. It meets three days a week.

   _I'm attending English 101, which meets three days a week._

2. Sami is an optimist. He's in my English class.

   _Sami, who is in my English class, is an optimist._

3. He drives to school with his sister Jena. She wants to go to law school.

   _He drives to school with his sister Jena, who wants to go law school._

4. Jena is always contradicting him. She loves to argue.

   _Jena, who loves to argue, is alway contradicting him._

5. This personality trait never annoys cheerful Sami. He just laughs.

   _This personality trait never annoy ...., who just laughs._

6. Jena is going to have a great career. Her personality is perfect for a lawyer.

   _Jena, whose personality is perfect for a lawyer, is going to have a great career._

7. I always look forward to the class. The class meets three days a week.

   _I alway look forward to the class, which meets three days._

8. San Antonio has a lot of community colleges. San Antonio is in Texas.

   _San Antonio, which is in Texas, has a lot of ..._

9. My school has students from all over the world. It's one of the largest colleges in the country.

   _My school, which is one of the largest college in the country, has students from all over the world._

## EXERCISE 5 IDENTIFYING OR NONIDENTIFYING ADJECTIVE CLAUSES

GRAMMAR NOTES 1–6 **Read each conversation. Then use the first and last sentences in the conversation to help you write a summary statement. Use adjective clauses. Remember to use commas where necessary.**

**1.** A: This article is really interesting.
   B: What's it about?
   A: It discusses the different types of personalities.

   SUMMARY: *This article, which discusses the different types of personalities, is really interesting.*

**2.** A: The office party is going to be at the restaurant.
   B: Which restaurant?
   A: You know the one. It's across the street from the library.

   SUMMARY: _____

**3.** A: I liked that speaker.
   B: Which one? We heard several!
   A: I forget his name. He talked about optimists.

   SUMMARY: _____

**4.** A: Bill and Sue aren't close friends with the Swabodas.
   B: No. The Swabodas' interests are very different from theirs.

   SUMMARY: _____

**5.** A: I lent some chairs to the new neighbors.
   B: Why did they need chairs?
   A: They're having a party tonight.

   SUMMARY: _____

**6.** A: I'm watching an old video of Jason.
   B: Look at that! He was telling jokes when he was five!
   A: I know. This totally defines his personality.

   SUMMARY: _____

**7.** A: My boyfriend left me a lot of plants to water.
   B: How come?
   A: He's visiting Venezuela with some friends.

   SUMMARY: _____

## EXERCISE 6 IDENTIFYING OR NONIDENTIFYING ADJECTIVE CLAUSES

▶ 12|03 PRONUNCIATION NOTE **Listen to the sentences. Add commas if you hear pauses around the adjective clauses.**

**1.** My neighbor, who is an introvert, called me today.

**2.** My neighbor who is an introvert called me today.

3. My brother who is one year older than me is an extrovert.

4. My sister who lives in Toronto visits us every summer.

5. My friend who is in the same class as me lent me a book.

6. The book which is about personality types is really interesting.

7. The article that won a prize is in today's newspaper.

8. My boyfriend who hates parties actually agreed to go to one with me.

## EXERCISE 7  EDITING

GRAMMAR NOTES 1–6  **Read this student's essay about a friend. There are ten mistakes in the use of adjective clauses and their punctuation. The first mistake is already corrected. Find and correct nine more.**

# Good Friends

A writer once said friends are born, not made. In other words, we immediately

become friends with people who ~~they~~ are compatible with us. I have to contradict this

writer. Last summer, I made friends with someone which is very different from me.

In July, I went to Mexico City to study Spanish for a month. In our group, there were

twenty students and five adults, who was all language teachers. Two of the teachers

stayed with friends in Mexico City, and we saw those teachers only during the day. But

we spent a lot of time with the teachers, who stayed with us in the dormitory. They

were the ones who helped us when we had problems. After my first two weeks, I had

a problem it was getting me down. Mexico City, that is a very exciting place, was too

distracting. I'm a real extrovert—someone who he wants to go out all the time—and I

stopped going to my classes. As a result, my grades suffered. When they got really bad,

I wanted to leave. Bob Taylor, who was the most serious teacher in the dorm, was very

sensitive to those feelings. But he was also optimistic about my situation. He helped

me get back into my courses which were actually pretty interesting. I managed to do

well after all! After the trip, I kept writing to Mr. Taylor, who's letters are always friendly

and encouraging. Next summer, he's leading another trip what sounds great. It's a

three-week trip to Spain. I hope I can go.

## EXERCISE 8   LISTENING

▶12|04   **A**   Some friends are at a high school reunion. They haven't seen one another for twenty-five years. Listen to their conversation. Look at the picture. Then listen again to the conversation and write the correct name next to each person.

Ann     Asha     ~~Bob~~     Kado     Pat     Pete

▶12|04   **B**   Listen to the conversation again. Then work with a partner. Discuss your answers in A. Explain your choices.

EXAMPLE:   **A:** So, the man who is standing is Bob.
            **B:** Right. And what about Ann? Which person is Ann?
            **A:** She's the woman who . . .

## EXERCISE 9  GETTING PERSONAL

**A** CONVERSATION  Think about your own personality traits. Then take the quiz in Exercise 2 on page 190.

**B** Work with a partner. Talk about your answers to the quiz. What do you think your answers show about your personality?

EXAMPLE:  A:  Question 1. People who talk a lot tire me. That's true.
B:  I think that means you're probably an introvert. It isn't true for me. I talk a lot, and I enjoy people who talk a lot, too.

## EXERCISE 10  QUOTABLE QUOTES

DISCUSSION  Work in a group. Read these quotes about friends and personality types. Choose three quotes and discuss them. What do they mean? Do you agree with them? Why or why not? Give examples from your own experience to support your ideas.

1.  Show me a friend who will weep[1] with me; those who will laugh with me I can find myself.
—*Slavic proverb*

EXAMPLE:  A:  I think this means it's easier to find friends for good times than for bad times.
B:  I agree. A true friend is someone who is there for you during good *and* bad times.
C:  My best friend in high school was like that. She was someone who . . .

2.  An optimist is a guy that has never had much experience.
—*Don Marquis (U.S. writer, 1878–1937)*

3.  He is wise who can make a friend of a foe.[2]
—*Scottish proverb*

4.  A pessimist is one who makes difficulties of his opportunities, and an optimist is one who makes opportunities of his difficulties.
—*Harry Truman (U.S. president, 1884–1972)*

5.  Wherever you are, it is your own friends who make your world.
—*Ralph Barton Perry (U.S. philosopher, 1876–1957)*

6.  A true friend is somebody who can make us do what we can.
—*Ralph Waldo Emerson (U.S. writer, 1803–1882)*

---

1  *weep:* cry
2  *foe:* enemy

## EXERCISE 11 WHAT ARE FRIENDS FOR?

**A** QUESTIONNAIRE Complete the questionnaire. Check (✓) all the items that you believe are true. Then add your own ideas.

### A friend is someone who...

- [✓] **1.** always tells you the truth
- [ ] **2.** has known you for a very long time
- [✓] **3.** cries with you
- [ ] **4.** lends you money
- [ ] **5.** talks to you every day
- [✓] **6.** helps you when you are in trouble
- [✓] **7.** listens to your problems
- [ ] **8.** does things with you
- [✓] **9.** respects you
- [✓] **10.** accepts you the way you are
- [✓] **11.** is sensitive to your feelings
- [✓] **12.** gives you advice
- [✓] **13.** keeps your secrets
- [ ] **14.** never contradicts you

Other: _____

_____

_____

**B** Work with a partner. Compare your answers to the questionnaire. Discuss the reasons for your choices.

EXAMPLE: **A:** I think a friend is someone who always tells you the truth.
**B:** I don't agree. Sometimes the truth can hurt you.

**C** After your discussion, tally the results of the whole class. Discuss the results.

EXAMPLE: **A:** I'm surprised. Only three people said a friend is someone who always tells you the truth.
**B:** I'm not surprised. You want friends that are honest, but maybe not always.
**C:** I agree. The truth could be something that's painful. A friend might want to protect you.

**A** BEFORE YOU WRITE  Think about your friends. Complete the outline.

**A Good Friend Is Someone Who...**                **Description of My Best Friend**

_____                  _____

_____                  _____

**B** WRITE  Use your outline to write two paragraphs about your best friend. In the first paragraph, describe what a good friend should do. In the second paragraph, describe your best friend. Use adjective clauses with subject relative pronouns. Try to avoid the common mistakes in the chart.

EXAMPLE:     Ralph Waldo Emerson said, "A true friend is somebody who can make us do what we can." I completely agree. A friend is someone who . . .
        My best friend, whose name is Fran, is the perfect example of a true friend. She . . .

### Common Mistakes in Using Adjective Clauses with Subject Relative Pronouns

| | |
|---|---|
| Use an adjective clause **after a noun or pronoun** to **identify** or **give additional information** about a person, place, or thing. Do not separate the adjective clause and the noun or pronoun. | A **person who is a true friend** will always help you. <br> NOT A person ~~will always help you who is a true friend~~. |
| Use *who*, *which*, or *that* as the **subject relative pronoun** in an adjective clause. Do not use subject pronouns (*I, you, he, she, it, we, they*). | I have a friend *who* **is** always there for me. <br> NOT I have a friend ~~he~~ is always there for me. <br> NOT I have a friend who ~~he~~ is always there for me. |
| Use a **singular verb** in the adjective clause if the subject relative pronoun refers to a singular noun or pronoun. Use a **plural verb** if the relative pronoun refers to a plural noun or pronoun. | I have a **friend *who* understands** me. <br> NOT I have a friend who ~~understand~~ me. <br> Joe has **friends *who* understand** him. <br> NOT Joe has friends who ~~understands~~ him. |

**C** CHECK YOUR WORK  Read your paragraphs. Underline the adjective clauses. Circle the relative pronouns. Use the Editing Checklist to check your work.

### Editing Checklist

**Did you use . . . ?**

☐ *who / that* for people, *which / that* for places and things, *whose* for possession or relationship

☐ the correct verb form in adjective clauses

☐ identifying adjective clauses to identify a noun

☐ nonidentifying adjective clauses to give more information about a noun

☐ commas to separate nonidentifying adjective clauses

**D** REVISE YOUR WORK  Read your paragraphs again. Can you improve your writing? Make changes if necessary. Give your paragraphs a title.

# UNIT 12  REVIEW

**Test yourself on the grammar of the unit.**

**Ⓐ** Circle the correct words to complete the sentences.

1. I have a lot of friends who <u>is / are</u> introverts.

2. Maria is someone <u>whose / who</u> idea of a good time is staying home.

3. Ben, who always <u>think / thinks</u> carefully before he speaks, is very sensitive to people's feelings.

4. He lives in Los Angeles, <u>which / that</u> is a city I'd love to visit.

5. He wrote a book about personality types <u>that / it</u> is very interesting.

6. My friend <u>who / which</u> read it liked it a lot.

**Ⓑ** Complete each sentence with a relative pronoun (*who*, *which*, *that*, or *whose*) and the correct form of the verb in parentheses.

1. Thinkers and Feelers are types of people _____ very differently.
   (behave)

2. A Thinker, _____ facts to make decisions, is a very logical person.
   (use)

3. Emotions, _____ usually _____ a Feeler, are more important
   (convince)
   than facts to this personality type.

4. A Thinker is someone _____ always _____ fairly and honestly.
   (speak)

5. A Feeler avoids saying things _____ another person's feelings.
   (hurt)

6. I dislike arguments, _____ usually _____ me. I guess I'm a Feeler.
   (upset)

7. Ed, _____ personality _____ different from mine, loves to argue.
   (be)

**Ⓒ** Find and correct seven mistakes. Remember to check punctuation.

It's true that we are often attracted to people which are very different from ourselves. An

extrovert, which personality is very outgoing, will often connect with a romantic partner who

are an introvert. They are both attracted to someone that have different strengths. My cousin

Valerie who is an extreme extrovert, recently married Bill, whose idea of a party is a Scrabble

game on the Internet. Can this marriage succeed? Will Bill learn the salsa, that is Valerie's

favorite dance? Will Valerie start collecting unusual words? Their friends, that care about both

of them, are hoping for the best.

**Now check your answers on page 478.**

# UNIT 13

## Adjective Clauses with Object Relative Pronouns

### THE IMMIGRANT EXPERIENCE

**OUTCOMES**
- Identify or give additional information about people, places, or things, using adjective clauses with correct object relative pronouns
- Identify key details in an online book review
- Identify the image described in a recording
- Describe your hometown or city
- Research a successful immigrant and report findings
- Write about a place from one's childhood

---

## STEP 1   GRAMMAR IN CONTEXT

### BEFORE YOU READ

Look at the photo on page 200 and at the title of the reading. Discuss the questions.

1. Who is the man in the photo? Where is he?
2. How do you think he feels?

### READ

 13|01   Read this post from a class blog.

○ ○ ○

**Sociology 139**
# The Immigrant Experience

HOME      ABOUT THIS BLOG      POSTS

# Stories of a New Generation of Immigrants

Posted on March 21, 2016 by Alicia Arash — Leave a Comment

***Immigrant Voices: 21st-Century Stories*** is one of the best books that I've ever read. The stories which editors Achy Obejas and Megan Bayles selected for the anthology[1] are powerful. They offer a compelling view into the lives of the current generation of immigrants to the United States. Of the eighteen stories in the book, my personal favorite is "Absence."

"Absence" is about Wari, a painter from Lima, Peru. His experiences illustrate many of the issues immigrants encounter. As he walks on the streets of New York, Wari is excited about the newness around him. But he is alone. The people who he loves are in Lima,

---

1  *anthology:*  a book of stories or poems by different authors

and he is unable to communicate with almost everyone he meets because he doesn't speak English. Most importantly, he wonders if he is still an artist. After all, his paint, brushes, and pencils are among the things that he left in Peru.

Wari's problems began at the U.S. Embassy in Lima, where he went for a visa. Wari had an invitation from an American university to exhibit his paintings. His plan was to get a three-month visa, which he could use for a double purpose. He hoped to show his artwork and also to have enough time to make a decision about whether to remain in the United States. Instead of three months, he received a visa for only one month, but he continued preparing for the day when he would fly from Lima to Miami and on to New York. When he got to Miami, an immigration officer said Wari didn't have enough money to stay in the United States for one month and reduced his visa to just two weeks.

When "Absence" ends on the evening of Wari's art exhibit, the big questions remain unanswered. Is Wari ready for life outside of Peru? Will he lose his connection to the place where he grew up? Will he experience poverty and loneliness as he struggles with life in a new country?

My grandfather, with whom I have a close relationship, came to the United States as a young man. Maybe because of him, I feel connected to the people whose stories I read in *Immigrant Voices*. However, I'm certain this is a book that you'll be interested in, too. Once you start reading, you won't put it down!

# AFTER YOU READ

**A** VOCABULARY **Complete the sentences with the words from the box.**

| compelling | encounter | generation | issue | poverty | struggle |

1. Every day, I _____ new words in English, but I try to meet the challenge.

2. It's always interesting to hear the older _____ talk about how life used to be.

3. My grandfather was very poor. He left his country to escape from a life of _____.

4. The stories in the book are _____. I couldn't stop reading them.

5. The food in this country is a(n) _____ for me. I don't want to eat anything here.

6. Life can be difficult for immigrants, who often _____ to learn a lot in a very short time.

**B** COMPREHENSION **Check (✓) the boxes to complete the statements. Check all the true information from the blog post.**

1. Alicia Arash _____ the book *Immigrant Voices*.
   ☐ recommends ☐ has read ☐ selected stories for

2. Wari's experiences are _____ the experiences of many immigrants.
   ☐ similar to ☐ better than ☐ harder than

3. Wari _____ in the United States.
   ☐ speaks English with everyone ☐ has family and friends ☐ has nothing to paint with

4. Wari got his visa at the embassy in _____.
   ☐ Lima ☐ Miami ☐ New York

5. Wari wanted a three-month visa in order to _____, but he got a two-week visa instead.
   ☐ attend his art exhibit ☐ decide if he would immigrate ☐ learn English

6. Alicia Arash feels a connection to _____.
   ☐ Wari ☐ the immigrants in the book ☐ her grandfather

**C** DISCUSSION **Work with a partner. Compare your answers in B. Why did you check the boxes your checked?**

## ADJECTIVE CLAUSES WITH OBJECT RELATIVE PRONOUNS OR *WHERE* AND *WHEN*

### Adjective Clauses After the Main Clause

| Main Clause | | | Adjective Clause | | |
|---|---|---|---|---|---|
| Subject | Verb | Noun/Pronoun | (Object Relative Pronoun) | Subject | Verb |
| He | read | the book | *(that)* *(which)* | she | **wrote**. |
| She | is | someone | *(who[m])* | I | **respect**. |
| | | | Whose + Noun | | |
| That | is | the author | *whose* book | I | **read**. |
| | | | Where/(When) | | |
| She | loves | the city | *where* | she | **grew up**. |
| They | cried | the day | *(when)* | they | **left**. |

### Adjective Clauses Inside the Main Clause

| Main Clause | Adjective Clause | | | Main Clause (cont.) | |
|---|---|---|---|---|---|
| Subject | (Object Relative Pronoun) | Subject | Verb | Verb | |
| The book | *(that)* *(which)* | I | **read** | is | great. |
| Someone | *(who[m])* | **you** | **know** | was | there. |
| | Whose + Noun | | | | |
| The man | *whose* sister | **you** | **know** | writes | books. |

| Main Clause | Adjective Clause | | | Main Clause (cont.) | |
|---|---|---|---|---|---|
| Subject | Where/(When) | Subject | Verb | Verb | |
| The library | *where* | I | **work** | has | videos. |
| The summer | *(when)* | she | **left** | passed | slowly. |

# GRAMMAR NOTES

## 1 Object Relative Pronouns

| | |
|---|---|
| In Unit 12, you learned about adjective clauses in which the **relative pronoun** was the **subject** of the clause. | SUBJECT<br>*Achy Obejas is a writer.* + **She** *was born in Cuba.* =<br>SUBJECT<br>*Achy Obejas,* **who was born in Cuba**, *is a writer.* |
| A **relative pronoun** can also be the **object** of an adjective clause. | OBJECT<br>*Obejas is also a journalist.* + *I saw* **her** *on TV.*<br>OBJECT<br>*Obejas,* **who I saw on TV**, *is also a journalist.* |
| Like subject relative pronouns, **object relative pronouns** come at the **beginning** of the adjective clause. | SUBJECT<br>*Ben,* **who lives in California**, *is a journalist.*<br>OBJECT<br>*Ben,* **who we just met**, *reports on music.* |
| **Relative pronouns** (subject or object) always have the **same form**. They do not change for singular and plural nouns or pronouns, or for males and females. | *That's the* **student who** *I met.*<br>*Those are the* **students who** *I met.*<br>*That's the* **man who** *I met.*<br>*That's the* **woman who** *I met.* |
| The subject and the verb of the adjective clause follow the **object relative pronoun**. The **verb in the adjective clause** is singular if the subject of the clause is singular. It is plural if the subject of the clause is plural. | OBJ. + SUBJ. + VERB<br>*I like the blog posts* **which she writes**.<br>*I like the blog posts* **which they write**. |
| **BE CAREFUL!** **Do not use an object pronoun** (*me, you, him, her, it, us, them*) and an object relative pronoun in the same adjective clause. | *She is the writer* **who I saw** *on TV.*<br>NOT *She is the writer who I saw* ~~her~~ *on TV.* |

## 2 Identifying and Nonidentifying Adjective Clauses

| | |
|---|---|
| As you have seen in Unit 12, there are two kinds of adjective clauses:<br><br>• **identifying** | IDENTIFYING ADJECTIVE CLAUSE<br>*I read a lot of books. The book* **which I just finished** *was very powerful.*<br>*(The adjective clause is necessary to identify which book I mean.)* |
| • **nonidentifying** | NONIDENTIFYING ADJECTIVE CLAUSE<br>*I read a lot of books.* **This** *book,* **which I just finished**, *was very powerful.*<br>*(I'm pointing to the book, so the adjective clause isn't necessary to identify it. The clause gives additional information.)* |
| **IN WRITING** Use **commas** to separate a **nonidentifying** adjective clause from the rest of the sentence. In **speaking**, use short **pauses** to separate the **nonidentifying** adjective clause. | *The Rice Room,* **which I read last year**, *is a great book.*<br>*The Rice Room* [PAUSE] **which I read last year** [PAUSE] *is a great book.* |

**Relative pronouns** that can be the **object of the verb** in an adjective clause are *who(m)*, *which*, and *that*.

Use *whom*, *who*, or *that* for **people**:

- *whom*
- *who*
- *that*

You can also **leave out the object relative pronoun** in an **identifying** adjective clause.

VERB + OBJ.
*She's a woman.* + *I admire* **her**. =

She's a woman **whom** I admire.     MORE FORMAL

She's a woman **who** I admire.

She's a woman **that** I admire.

She's a woman I admire.     LESS FORMAL

Use *which* or *that* for **things**:

- *which*
- *that*

You can also **leave out the relative pronoun** in **identifying** adjective clauses.

VERB + OBJ.
*I read a book.* + *She wrote* **it**. =

I read a book **which** she wrote.     MORE FORMAL

I read a book **that** she wrote.

I read a book she wrote.     LESS FORMAL

**USAGE NOTE** In **conversation**, most people use *that* or **no relative pronoun** for the object of the verb in an **identifying** adjective clause.

IDENTIFYING ADJECTIVE CLAUSE
A: Did you read the article *that* **Alicia posted**?

B: Yes. I like all the articles **she puts on our blog**.

**BE CAREFUL!** Do not use *that* in a **nonidentifying** adjective clause.

NONIDENTIFYING ADJECTIVE CLAUSE
Alicia's post, *which* **we all read**, was interesting.

NOT Alicia's post, ~~that~~ we all read, was interesting.

**BE CAREFUL!** Do not leave out the relative pronoun in a **nonidentifying** adjective clause.

NONIDENTIFYING ADJECTIVE CLAUSE
I remember Wari, *who* **she described very clearly**.

NOT I remember Wari, ~~she described very clearly~~.

**Relative pronouns** that can be the **object of a preposition** in an adjective clause are *who(m)*, *which*, and *that*.

| | |
|---|---|
| Use *whom*, *who*, or *that* for **people**: | PREP. + OBJ.<br>*He's the writer.* + *I work for him.* = |
| • preposition + *whom* | He's the writer *for whom* I work.    MORE FORMAL |
| • *whom* . . . + preposition | He's the writer *whom* I work *for*. |
| • *who* . . . + preposition | He's the writer *who* I work *for*. |
| • *that* . . . + preposition | He's the writer *that* I work *for*. |
| You can also **leave out the object relative pronoun** in an **identifying** adjective clause. | He's the writer I work *for*.    LESS FORMAL |

| | |
|---|---|
| Use *which* or *that* for **things**: | PREP. + OBJ.<br>*This is a book.* + *I am interested in it.* = |
| • preposition + *which* | This is a book *in which* I am interested.   MORE FORMAL |
| • *which* . . . + preposition | This is a book *which* I am interested *in*. |
| • *that* . . . + preposition | This is a book *that* I am interested *in*. |
| You can also **leave out the relative pronoun** in **identifying** adjective clauses. | This is a book I am interested *in*.    LESS FORMAL |

| | |
|---|---|
| USAGE NOTE   In **conversation**, most people use *that* or **no relative pronoun** for the object of a preposition in an **identifying** adjective clause. The **preposition** comes at the **end of the clause**. | IDENTIFYING ADJECTIVE CLAUSE<br>A: Here's the story *that* she was talking *about*.<br>B: But it isn't the story I've been looking *for*! |

| | |
|---|---|
| BE CAREFUL!   Do not use *that* in a **nonidentifying** adjective clause. | NONIDENTIFYING ADJECTIVE CLAUSE<br>Wari's story, *which* I was impressed *by*, was powerful.<br>NOT Wari's story, ~~that~~ I was impressed by, was powerful. |

| | |
|---|---|
| BE CAREFUL!   Do not leave out the relative pronoun in a **nonidentifying** adjective clause. | NONIDENTIFYING ADJECTIVE CLAUSE<br>My grandmother, *who* I often write *to*, lives in Peru.<br>NOT My grandmother, ~~I often write to~~, lives in Peru. |

## 5 Whose

| | |
|---|---|
| Some adjective clauses begin with **whose** + **noun object** to show **possession** or **relationship**. | |
| **Whose** + **noun object** comes at the beginning of the adjective clause. You cannot leave out **whose**. | POSS. + NOUN OBJ.<br>*They're the immigrants.* + *We read **their stories**.* =<br>*They're the immigrants **whose stories** we read.* |
| The **noun** following **whose** can be the **object** of:<br>• the **verb** in the adjective clause | OBJECT    VERB<br>The professor ***whose class we like*** studies immigration. |
| • a **preposition** in the adjective clause | OBJECT                PREP.<br>She's an author ***whose*** book we're excited ***about***. |
| Use **whose** to refer to:<br>• **people** | I like **authors *whose*** books I can feel connected to. |
| • **things** | It's a **book *whose*** main character I love. |
| **BE CAREFUL!** Do not use **who** + possessive adjectives (*my, your, his, her, its, our, their*) instead of **whose**. | He's a writer ***whose*** stories I will never forget.<br>NOT He's a writer ~~who his~~ stories I will never forget. |

## 6 Where and When

| | |
|---|---|
| **Where** and **when** can also begin adjective clauses. | |
| Use:<br>• **where** for a **place**<br>• **when** (or **that**) for a **time** | That's the library ***where*** she works.<br>I remember the day ***when*** I met him.<br>I remember the day ***that*** I met him. |
| You can **leave out *when*** or ***that*** in **identifying** adjective clauses. | I remember the day **I met him**. |
| **USAGE NOTE** Instead of **where**, we sometimes use **preposition** + **which/that** to begin an adjective clause. | The building ***where*** I live is old.<br>The building ***in which*** I live is old.<br>The building ***which*** I live ***in*** is old.<br>The building ***that*** I live ***in*** is old. |
| We can also **leave out *which*** or ***that***.<br>**Preposition** + **which/that** is more formal than **where**. | The building **I live *in*** is old. |
| **BE CAREFUL!** Do not use a preposition with **where**. | The street ***where*** they live is quiet.<br>NOT The street where they live ~~on~~ is quiet. |
| **BE CAREFUL!** **Where** cannot be the subject of an adjective clause. | New York is a city ***that*** has many immigrants.<br>NOT New York is a city ~~where~~ has many immigrants. |

## REFERENCE NOTE

For more information on **identifying and nonidentifying adjective clauses**, see Unit 12 on page 187.

## EXERCISE 1 DISCOVER THE GRAMMAR

Ⓐ **GRAMMAR NOTES 1–6** Read a second blog post by Alicia Arash. Underline the adjective clauses and circle the relative pronouns, *where*, and *when*. Then draw an arrow from each relative pronoun to the noun or pronoun that it refers to.

---

**Sociology 139**
# The Immigrant Experience

HOME     ABOUT THIS BLOG     POSTS

# When Reality Hits Home

Posted on March 22, 2016 by Alicia Arash — Leave a Comment

**In the compelling story "Absence,"** author Daniel Alarcón explains what happens to most immigrants. Eventually, there is a day when the newness of a new country ends. Suddenly, the things that immigrants used to be interested in become annoying. Even worse, these things become problems for the immigrant. For example, the stores where they shop suddenly seem small, crowded, and expensive. Or they continue to struggle with English, which they have been studying for many months.

At this point, the list of things that immigrants miss from their home country begins to grow. They think about the boss whose name they once wanted to forget. Amazingly, they remember him as someone who they respected and admired. They have memories of quiet streets and beautiful parks where their children played without a care in the world. And the food back home was fresh and mouth-wateringly delicious. Most of all, they remember the warmth of the people, with whom they could always connect. They miss the feeling of fitting in and belonging.

Fortunately, 21st-century immigrants can call or Skype with friends and family who they've left behind. They can also use money that they've earned in their new country to travel back to their old country for a visit. Immigrants of previous generations didn't have these advantages.

**B** Read this conversation between Alicia and her classmate Ade. There are six adjective clauses without relative pronouns. The first one is already underlined. Find and underline five more. Then add appropriate relative pronouns.

ADE: The two articles ~~that or which~~ you posted on our class blog are great!

ALICIA: Thanks. I wrote the first one the day I finished reading *Immigrant Voices*. You can tell I was really excited about the book, can't you?

ADE: You're not alone. My sister loves immigrant literature. It's something she talks about all the time. In fact, the "birthday box" she sent me last week had a copy of *Immigrant Voices* in it.

ALICIA: Have you read it yet?

ADE: Not yet. But I will. It's on the list of things I'm going to do after midterm exams.

ALICIA: Well, as I said in my blog post, you'll love the book. By the way, you're from Nigeria, aren't you?

ADE: I was born in Nigeria. But this is the country I grew up in. I think of myself as Nigerian-American.

## EXERCISE 2 RELATIVE PRONOUNS AND VERBS

GRAMMAR NOTES 1–4, 6 Complete this interview from a high-school newspaper. Use *who(m)*, *that*, *which*, *where*, or *when* and the correct forms of the verbs in parentheses.

The **Grover** September 19, 2016
page 3

**MEET YOUR CLASSMATES**

**Maniya,** _____ who _____ a lot of our readers already

_____ know _____, has been at Grover High for three years
**1. (know)**

now. We interviewed Maniya, who is from the Philippines, about

her experiences as a new immigrant in the United States.

INTERVIEWER: How did your family choose Atlanta, Maniya?

MANIYA: My cousin, _____ we _____ with at first, lives here.
**2. (stay)**

INTERVIEWER: What were your first impressions?

MANIYA: At first, it was a lot of fun. We arrived here at the beginning of the summer,

_____ there _____ no school, so I didn't feel much
**3. (be)**

pressure to speak English.

INTERVIEWER: What problems did you encounter when you finally went to school?

MANIYA: Of course, the class in _____ I _____ the biggest
4. (have)

problems at first was English. I struggled to write compositions and to say the

things _____ I _____ to say. It was really a big issue
5. (want)

for me. Now it's much easier. I have a much stronger connection to English now.

INTERVIEWER: What was the biggest change for you when you got here?

MANIYA: We used to live in a big house, _____ there _____
6. (be)

always a lot of people. We were several generations under one roof. Here I live

with just my parents and sister, _____ I _____
7. (take care of)

after school.

INTERVIEWER: How did you learn English so quickly?

MANIYA: At night, I write words and idioms on a small piece of paper _____

I _____ in my pocket. Then I study them at school whenever I have
8. (put)

a chance between classes.

INTERVIEWER: Is there anything _____ you still _____ trouble with?
9. (have)

MANIYA: One thing _____ I still _____ hard to do is to make
10. (find)

jokes in English. Some things are funny in Tagalog but not in English.


# EXERCISE 3  IDENTIFYING ADJECTIVE CLAUSES

GRAMMAR NOTES 1–6  Complete the story. Use the sentences from the box. Change them
to identifying adjective clauses and use relatives pronouns, *where*, or *when*.

| I drank coffee there every day. | I knew her sister from school. | Many students attended it. |
| I had to leave Cracow then. | ~~I loved it very much.~~ | We both felt very good about it. |

Cracow is a city in Poland _____ *that I loved very much or which I loved very much* _____.
1.

I lived there until I came to the United States. My parents owned a café in the town center

_____. One day, I met a woman
2.

there _____. Her sister and I were in
3.

a class together _____. The woman
4.

and I felt a strong connection _____.
5.

For me, the day _____ was very sad.
6.

# EXERCISE 4  NONIDENTIFYING ADJECTIVE CLAUSES

GRAMMAR NOTES 1–6  **Complete this article about Ben Fong-Torres. Use the sentences in parentheses to write nonidentifying adjective clauses with relative pronouns, *where*, or *when*. Don't forget to add commas.**

Ben Fong-Torres was born in Alameda, California, in 1945. He was the son of first-generation Chinese parents. To escape a life of poverty, his father immigrated to the Philippines and then to the United States _, where he settled down_____. His mother came to the
**1.** (He settled down there.)

United States ten years later _____.
**2.** (Their marriage was arranged by relatives then.)

Fong-Torres, along with his brother and sister, grew up in the city of Oakland, California

_____. His family owned a Chinese
**3.** (There was a large Chinese community there.)

restaurant _____ when they were not in school.
**4.** (All the children worked there.)

Young Ben was always an enthusiastic reader of cartoons and a huge fan of popular music

_____. At the age of twelve, Ben went with his
**5.** (He heard it on the radio.)

father to Texas _____. Ben encountered problems
**6.** (They opened another Chinese restaurant there.)

there because he was among people who had had no previous contact with Asians.

Back in Oakland, after the failure of the Texas restaurant, Ben got jobs writing for various

magazines and newspapers. His interviews with hundreds of rock stars included the Beatles and

the Rolling Stones _____. He also did an
**7.** (He loved their music.)

interview with Ray Charles _____. Fong-Torres
**8.** (He won an award for it.)

was a DJ for San Francisco radio station KSAN, which

plays rock music, and in 1976 he won an award for

broadcasting excellence.

Fong-Torres and his wife Dianne Sweet

_____
**9.** (He married her in 1976.)

still live in San Francisco. He hosts many events

for the Chinese-American community in that

city and continues to write about music for

publications such as the e-zine (Internet

magazine) www.AsianConnections.com.

**Dianne and Ben Fong-Torres**

# EXERCISE 5 IDENTIFYING AND NONIDENTIFYING ADJECTIVE CLAUSES

**GRAMMAR NOTES 1–6** Combine the pairs of sentences. Make the second sentence in each pair an adjective clause. Make any other necessary changes. Use relative pronouns, *where*, or *when* only when necessary.

1. That's the house. I grew up in the house.
   *That's the house I grew up in.* **or** *That's the house where I grew up.*

2. I lived with my parents and my siblings. You've met them.

3. I had two sisters and an older brother. I felt a close connection to my sisters.

4. My sisters and I shared a room. We spent nights talking there.

5. My brother slept on the living room couch. I hardly ever saw him.

6. It was a large old couch. My father had made the couch himself.

7. My best friend lived across the hall. I loved her family.

8. We went to the same school. We both studied English there.

9. Mr. Robinson was our English teacher. Everyone was a little afraid of Mr. Robinson.

10. After school, I worked in a bakery. My aunt and uncle owned it.

11. They sold delicious bread and cake. People stood in line for hours to buy the bread and cake.

12. My brother and sisters live far away now. I miss them.

13. When we get together, we like to talk about the old days. We all lived at home then.

## EXERCISE 6 EDITING

GRAMMAR NOTES 1–6  Read this student's book report. There are eleven mistakes in the use of adjective clauses with object relative pronouns and their punctuation. The first one is already corrected. Find and correct ten more.

Eva Hoffman spent her early childhood in Cracow, Poland, the city ~~that~~ *where* or *in which* she was born.

When she was thirteen, she moved with her family to Vancouver, Canada. Her autobiography,

*Lost in Translation: A Life in a New Language*, that she wrote in 1989, describes her

experiences as she leaves Cracow, the city which she called it home.

In spite of her family's poverty and small, crowded apartment, Ewa Wyda (Hoffman's

Polish name) loved her native city. It was a place when life was lived intensely. She used

to visit the city's many cafés with her father, that she watched in lively conversations with

his friends. Hoffman remembers her neighbors as people, who she spent many happy hours

with. Among them was Marek, who apartment she visited almost daily and who she always

believed she would one day marry.

Madame Witeszczak who Ewa took piano lessons from, was the last person which Ewa

said goodbye to before she left Poland. "What do you think you'll miss most?" her teacher

asked. "Everything. Cracow. The school . . . you. Everything . . ."

At her new school in Vancouver, Hoffman is given her English name, Eva, that her

teachers find easier to pronounce. Ewa, however, feels no connection to the name. In fact,

she feels no connection to the English name of anything what she feels is important. All her

memories are still in her first language, Polish.

The story of Eva as she grows up and comes to terms with her new identity and language

is fascinating and moving. It's a familiar story that all immigrants can relate to.

## EXERCISE 7   LISTENING

▶13|02   **A** Look at the pictures. Then listen to an author's description of her childhood room. Listen again and circle the number of the picture that the woman describes.

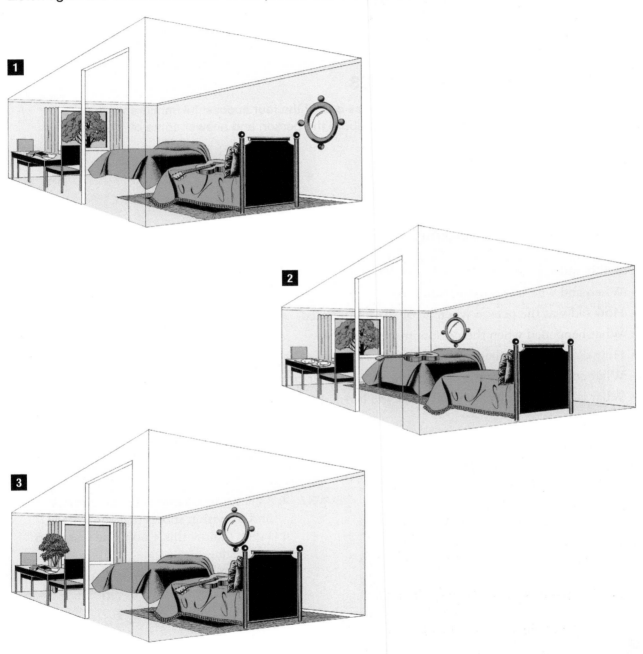

▶13|02   **B** Listen to the interview again. Then work with a partner. Discuss your answer in A. Why did you choose that picture? Why didn't you choose one of the other two pictures?

EXAMPLE:   A: How did you decide which room to choose?
        B: First of all, the bed that Maria's sister slept in . . .

## EXERCISE 8   HOME SWEET HOME

CONVERSATION   Work with a partner. Talk about the people and places in your hometown that are important to you. Use three of your own photos or pictures that you found on the Internet.

EXAMPLE:   A: I love my hometown. This is the street where we lived before we moved here.
B: Is that the house you grew up in?
A: Yes, it is. I lived there until I was fifteen.

## EXERCISE 9   SUCCESS STORIES

**A** GROUP PROJECT   Work in a group. Choose one of the four successful immigrants to the United States listed below. Do research about the person and answer some of the questions.

- José Hernández, astronaut
- Mila Kunis, actress
- Jhumpa Lahiri, author
- Jerry Yang, Internet entrepreneur

**Possible questions:**
- When and where was the person born?
- How old was the person when he or she immigrated?
- What happened when the person immigrated?
- How did the person become successful?
- What connection does the person have to his or her country of birth?
- What is the most interesting fact that you learned about the person?

EXAMPLE:   A: Mila Kunis is famous for the movies and television shows that she's made.
B: I didn't know this. Look. She was born in Ukraine.
C: Her family immigrated . . .
D: During the first months that she lived in the United States . . .

**B** Report back to your class. If your group chose the same person as another group, do you have the same information about that person? Compare answers.

EXAMPLE: **A:** Mila Kunis is famous for all the Hollywood movies that she's made.
**B:** Don't forget about television. Here's a list of the shows that she's appeared in.
**A:** She was born in Ukraine.
**B:** Right. But her family immigrated . . .
**A:** . . .

## EXERCISE 10 QUOTABLE QUOTES

DISCUSSION  Work in a group. Read these quotes about home. Choose three quotes and discuss them. What do they mean? Do you agree with them? Why or why not? Give examples from your own experience to support your ideas.

1. Home is where the heart is.
   —*Pliny the Elder (Roman soldier and encyclopedist, 23–79)*

   EXAMPLE: **A:** I think this means that home is not always a place.
   **B:** I agree. It's a feeling that you have.
   **C:** I think it can be a place or person that you love.

2. Home is where one starts from.
   —*T. S. Eliot (British poet, 1888–1965)*

3. Home is the place where you feel happy.
   —*Salman Rushdie (Indian author, 1947– )*

4. Home is a place you grow up wanting to leave, and grow old wanting to get back to.
   —*John Ed Pearce (U.S. journalist, 1917–2006)*

5. Home is not where you live but where they understand you.
   —*Christian Morgenstern (German poet, 1871–1914)*

6. Home is the place where, when you have to go there, they have to take you in.
   —*Robert Frost (U.S. poet, 1874–1963)*

# FROM GRAMMAR TO WRITING

**A** BEFORE YOU WRITE Think about a place from your childhood. Complete the outline.

Place: _____

| Description of the Place | Why the Place Was Important to Me |
|---|---|
| _____ | _____ |
| _____ | _____ |

**B** WRITE Use your outline to write two paragraphs about an important place from your childhood. In the first paragraph, describe the place. In the second paragraph, explain why the place was important to you. Use adjective clauses with object relative pronouns, *where*, or *when*. Try to avoid the common mistakes in the chart.

EXAMPLE:     The town where I grew up was the perfect place for a child. Living there was like living in an earlier century. We didn't lock our doors, and my best friend, who I saw every day, could visit anytime she wanted to. The house that my family owned was . . .

## Common Mistakes in Using Adjective Clauses with Object Relative Pronouns

| | |
|---|---|
| Use *who(m)*, *which*, or *that* as **the object relative pronoun** in an adjective clause. Do not use an object pronoun (*me*, *you*, etc.) and an object relative pronoun in the same adjective clause. | I remember the big dinners *that* we had on holidays.<br>NOT I remember the big dinners that we had ~~them~~ on holidays. |
| Use *who(m)*, *which*, *whose*, *where*, or *when* to start **nonidentifying** adjective clauses. Do not use *that*. | My best friend, *who* I saw daily, lived nearby.<br>NOT My best friend, ~~that~~ I saw daily, lived nearby. |
| Use *where* or **preposition** + *which/that* to describe a place. Do not use *where* + preposition. | The town *where* I lived was quiet.<br>NOT The town where I lived ~~in~~ was quiet. |

**C** CHECK YOUR WORK Read your paragraphs. Underline the adjective clauses. Circle the relative pronouns, *where*, and *when*. Use the Editing Checklist to check your work.

## Editing Checklist

**Did you use . . . ?**

☐ adjective clauses with object relative pronouns *who(m)*, *which*, or *that*

☐ *whose* to show possession or relationship

☐ *where* to show place and *when* to show time

☐ the correct verb form in adjective clauses

☐ commas to separate nonidentifying adjective clauses from the rest of the sentence

**D** REVISE YOUR WORK Read your paragraphs again. Can you improve your writing? Make changes if necessary. Give your paragraphs a title.

# UNIT 13 **REVIEW**

**Test yourself on the grammar of the unit.**

**A** Circle the correct words to complete the sentences.

1. Mrs. Johnson, whom / whose dog I walk, lives next door.

2. She lives in an old house that / who her father built.

3. It's right next to the park where / when I run every morning.

4. She has a daughter which / who I went to school with.

5. We became best friends in 2005, where / when we were in the same class.

6. Ann, that / who I still call every week, moved to Canada last year.

**B** Complete each sentence with a relative pronoun, *where*, or *when*.

1. Today, I took a trip back to Brooklyn, _____ I grew up.

2. The emotions _____ I felt were very powerful.

3. I saw the house _____ my family lived in for more than ten years.

4. I saw some old neighbors _____ I remembered well.

5. Mrs. Gutkin, _____ son I used to do homework with, still lives next door.

6. It was wonderful to see Mrs. Gutkin, _____ I've always liked.

7. I'll never forget the day _____ I moved away from this neighborhood.

**C** Find and correct seven mistakes.

I grew up in an apartment building who my grandparents owned. There was a small

dining room when we had family meals and a kitchen in that I ate my breakfast. My aunt,

uncle, and cousin, in who home I spent a lot of my time, lived in an identical apartment on

the fourth floor. I remember the time that my parents gave me a toy phone set that we used it

so I could talk to my cousin. There weren't many children in the building, but I often visited

the building manager, who's son I liked. I enjoyed living in the apartment, but for me the day

where we moved into our own house was the best day of my childhood.

**Now check your answers on page 478.**

# Appendices

## 1 Irregular Verbs

When two forms are listed, the more common form is listed first.

| BASE FORM | SIMPLE PAST | PAST PARTICIPLE |
|---|---|---|
| arise | arose | arisen |
| awake | awoke | awoken |
| be | was or were | been |
| beat | beat | beaten/beat |
| become | became | become |
| begin | began | begun |
| bend | bent | bent |
| bet | bet | bet |
| bite | bit | bitten |
| bleed | bled | bled |
| blow | blew | blown |
| break | broke | broken |
| bring | brought | brought |
| build | built | built |
| burn | burned/burnt | burnt/burned |
| burst | burst | burst |
| buy | bought | bought |
| catch | caught | caught |
| choose | chose | chosen |
| cling | clung | clung |
| come | came | come |
| cost | cost | cost |
| creep | crept | crept |
| cut | cut | cut |
| deal | dealt | dealt |
| dig | dug | dug |
| dive | dove/dived | dived |
| do | did | done |
| draw | drew | drawn |
| dream | dreamed/dreamt | dreamed/dreamt |
| drink | drank | drunk |
| drive | drove | driven |
| eat | ate | eaten |
| fall | fell | fallen |
| feed | fed | fed |
| feel | felt | felt |
| fight | fought | fought |
| find | found | found |
| fit | fit/fitted | fit |
| flee | fled | fled |
| fling | flung | flung |
| fly | flew | flown |
| forbid | forbid/forbade | forbidden |
| forget | forgot | forgotten |
| forgive | forgave | forgiven |
| freeze | froze | frozen |
| get | got | gotten/got |
| give | gave | given |

| BASE FORM | SIMPLE PAST | PAST PARTICIPLE |
|---|---|---|
| go | went | gone |
| grind | ground | ground |
| grow | grew | grown |
| hang | hung*/hanged** | hung*/hanged** |
| have | had | had |
| hear | heard | heard |
| hide | hid | hidden |
| hit | hit | hit |
| hold | held | held |
| hurt | hurt | hurt |
| keep | kept | kept |
| kneel | knelt/kneeled | knelt/kneeled |
| knit | knit/knitted | knit/knitted |
| know | knew | known |
| lay | laid | laid |
| lead | led | led |
| leap | leaped/leapt | leaped/leapt |
| leave | left | left |
| lend | lent | lent |
| let | let | let |
| lie (lie down) | lay | lain |
| light | lit/lighted | lit/lighted |
| lose | lost | lost |
| make | made | made |
| mean | meant | meant |
| meet | met | met |
| pay | paid | paid |
| prove | proved | proven/proved |
| put | put | put |
| quit | quit | quit |
| read /rid/ | read /rɛd/ | read /rɛd/ |
| ride | rode | ridden |
| ring | rang | rung |
| rise | rose | risen |
| run | ran | run |
| say | said | said |
| see | saw | seen |
| seek | sought | sought |
| sell | sold | sold |
| send | sent | sent |
| set | set | set |
| sew | sewed | sewn/sewed |
| shake | shook | shaken |
| shave | shaved | shaved/shaven |
| shine (intransitive) | shone/shined | shone/shined |
| shoot | shot | shot |
| show | showed | shown |
| shrink | shrank/shrunk | shrunk/shrunken |

*hung = *hung an object such as a painting*
**hanged = *executed by hanging*

| BASE FORM | SIMPLE PAST | PAST PARTICIPLE | BASE FORM | SIMPLE PAST | PAST PARTICIPLE |
|-----------|-------------|-----------------|-----------|-------------|-----------------|
| shut | shut | shut | swear | swore | sworn |
| sing | sang | sung | sweep | swept | swept |
| sink | sank/sunk | sunk | swim | swam | swum |
| sit | sat | sat | swing | swung | swung |
| sleep | slept | slept | take | took | taken |
| slide | slid | slid | teach | taught | taught |
| speak | spoke | spoken | tear | tore | torn |
| speed | sped/speeded | sped/speeded | tell | told | told |
| spend | spent | spent | think | thought | thought |
| spill | spilled/spilt | spilled/spilt | throw | threw | thrown |
| spin | spun | spun | understand | understood | understood |
| spit | spit/spat | spat | upset | upset | upset |
| split | split | split | wake | woke | woken |
| spread | spread | spread | wear | wore | worn |
| spring | sprang | sprung | weave | wove/weaved | woven/weaved |
| stand | stood | stood | weep | wept | wept |
| steal | stole | stolen | win | won | won |
| stick | stuck | stuck | wind | wound | wound |
| sting | stung | stung | withdraw | withdrew | withdrawn |
| stink | stank/stunk | stunk | wring | wrung | wrung |
| strike | struck | struck/stricken | write | wrote | written |

## 2 Non-Action Verbs

**APPEARANCE**
appear
be
look *(seem)*
represent
resemble
seem
signify

**VALUE**
cost
equal
weigh

**EMOTIONS**
admire
adore
appreciate
care
detest
dislike
doubt
envy
fear
forgive
hate
like
love
miss
regret
respect
trust

**MENTAL STATES**
agree
assume
believe
consider
disagree
disbelieve
estimate
expect
feel *(believe)*
find *(believe)*
forget
guess
hesitate
hope
imagine
know
mean
mind
presume
realize
recognize
remember
see *(understand)*
suppose
suspect
think *(believe)*
understand
wonder

**POSSESSION AND RELATIONSHIP**
belong
come from *(origin)*
contain
have
own
possess

**SENSES AND PERCEPTIONS**
feel
hear
hurt
notice
observe
perceive
recognize
see
seem
smell
sound
taste

**WANTS AND PREFERENCES**
desire
hope
need
prefer
want
wish

## 3 Verbs and Expressions Used Reflexively

allow yourself
amuse yourself
ask yourself
avail yourself of
be hard on yourself
be pleased with yourself
be proud of yourself
be yourself

behave yourself
believe in yourself
blame yourself
buy yourself
cut yourself
deprive yourself of
dry yourself
enjoy yourself

feel proud of yourself
feel sorry for yourself
forgive yourself
help yourself
hurt yourself
imagine yourself
introduce yourself
keep yourself (busy)

kill yourself
look after yourself
look at yourself
prepare yourself
pride yourself on
push yourself
remind yourself

see yourself
take care of yourself
talk to yourself
teach yourself
tell yourself
treat yourself
wash yourself

(s.o. = someone    s.t. = something)

**Separable phrasal verbs** show the object between the verb and the particle: **call** s.o. **up**.
**Verbs that must be separated** have an asterisk (*): **do** s.t. **over***.
**Inseparable phrasal verbs** show the object after the particle: **carry on** s.t.
Phrasal verbs that can have a **gerund as object** are followed by *doing*: **put off** doing s.t.

| PHRASAL VERB | MEANING |
|---|---|
| **ask** s.o. **over*** | *invite to one's home* |
| **block** s.t. **out** | *stop from passing through (light/noise)* |
| **blow** s.t. **out** | *stop burning by blowing air on it* |
| **blow** s.t. **up** | *make explode* |
| **bring** s.t. **about** | *make happen* |
| **bring** s.o. **or** s.t. **back** | *return* |
| **bring** s.o. **down*** | *depress* |
| **bring** s.t. **out** | *introduce (a new product/book)* |
| **bring** s.o. **up** | *raise (a child)* |
| **bring** s.t. **up** | *bring attention to* |
| **build** s.t. **up** | *increase* |
| **burn** s.t. **down** | *burn completely* |
| **call** s.o. **back*** | *return a phone call* |
| **call** s.o. **in** | *ask for help with a problem* |
| **call** s.t. **off** | *cancel* |
| **call** s.o. **up** | *contact by phone* |
| **calm** s.o. **down** | *make less excited* |
| **carry on** s.t. | *continue* |
| **carry** s.t. **out** | *complete (a plan)* |
| **cash in on** s.t. | *profit from* |
| **charge** s.t. **up** | *charge with electricity* |
| **check** s.t. **out** | *examine* |
| **cheer** s.o. **up** | *cause to feel happier* |
| **clean** s.o. **or** s.t. **up** | *clean completely* |
| **clear** s.t. **up** | *explain* |
| **close** s.t. **down** | *close by force* |
| **come from** s.o. **or** s.t. | *have been born in a particular family or place* |
| **come off** s.t. | *become unattached* |
| **come up with** s.t. | *invent* |
| **count on** s.t. **or** s.o. | *depend on* |
| **cover** s.o. **or** s.t. **up** | *cover completely* |
| **cross** s.t. **out** | *draw a line through* |
| **cut** s.t. **down** | *1. bring down by cutting (a tree)* *2. reduce* |
| **cut** s.t. **off** | *1. stop the supply of* *2. remove by cutting* |
| **cut** s.t. **out** | *remove by cutting* |
| **cut** s.t. **up** | *cut into small pieces* |
| **deal with** s.t. | *handle* |
| **do** s.t. **over*** | *do again* |
| **do** s.o. **or** s.t. **up** | *make more beautiful* |
| **draw** s.t. **together** | *unite* |
| **dream** s.t. **up** | *invent* |
| **drink** s.t. **up** | *drink completely* |
| **drop** s.o. **or** s.t. **off** | *take someplace in a car and leave there* |
| **drop out of** s.t. | *quit* |
| **empty** s.t. **out** | *empty completely* |
| **end up** doing s.t. | *do something you didn't plan to do* |
| **end up with** s.t. | *have an unexpected result* |
| **fall for** s.o. | *feel romantic love for* |

| PHRASAL VERB | MEANING |
|---|---|
| **fall for** s.t. | *be tricked by, believe* |
| **figure** s.o. **out** | *understand (the behavior)* |
| **figure** s.t. **out** | *solve, understand after thinking about it* |
| **fill** s.t. **in** | *complete with information* |
| **fill** s.t. **out** | *complete (a form)* |
| **fill** s.t. **up** | *fill completely* |
| **find** s.t. **out** | *learn information* |
| **fix** s.t. **up** | *redecorate (home)* |
| **follow through with** s.t. | *complete* |
| **get** s.t. **across** | *get people to understand an idea* |
| **get off** s.t. | *leave (a bus/train)* |
| **get on** s.t. | *board (a bus/train)* |
| **get out of** s.t. | *leave (a car/taxi)* |
| **get** s.t. **out of** s.t.* | *benefit from* |
| **get over** s.t. | *recover from* |
| **get through with** s.t. | *finish* |
| **get to** s.o. **or** s.t. | *1. reach s.o. or s.t.* *2. upset s.o.* |
| **get together with** s.o. | *meet* |
| **give** s.t. **away** | *give without charging money* |
| **give** s.t. **back** | *return* |
| **give** s.t. **out** | *distribute* |
| **give** s.t. **up** | *quit, abandon* |
| **give up** doing s.t. | *quit, stop* |
| **go after** s.o. **or** s.t. | *try to get or win, pursue* |
| **go along with** s.t. | *support* |
| **go on** doing s.t. | *continue* |
| **go over** s.t. | *review* |
| **hand** s.t. **in** | *give work (to a boss/teacher), submit* |
| **hand** s.t. **out** | *distribute* |
| **hand** s.t. **over** | *give* |
| **hang** s.t. **up** | *put on a hook or hanger* |
| **help** s.o. **out** | *assist* |
| **hold** s.t. **on** | *keep attached* |
| **keep** s.o. **or** s.t. **away** | *cause to stay at a distance* |
| **keep** s.t. **on*** | *not remove (a piece of clothing/ jewelry)* |
| **keep on** doing s.t. | *continue* |
| **keep** s.o. **or** s.t. **out** | *not allow to enter* |
| **keep up with** s.o. **or** s.t. | *go as fast as* |
| **lay** s.o. **off** | *end employment* |
| **lay** s.t. **out** | *1. arrange according to plan* *2. spend money* |
| **leave** s.t. **on** | *1. not turn off (a light/radio)* *2. not remove (a piece of clothing/ jewelry)* |
| **leave** s.t. **out** | *not include, omit* |
| **let** s.o. **down** | *disappoint* |
| **let** s.o. **or** s.t. **in** | *allow to enter* |
| **let** s.o. **off** | *1. allow to leave (from a bus/car)* *2. not punish* |

| PHRASAL VERB | MEANING |
|---|---|
| **light** s.t. **up** | *illuminate* |
| **look after** s.o. **or** s.t. | *take care of* |
| **look for** s.o. **or** s.t. | *try to find* |
| **look into** s.t. | *research* |
| **look** s.o. **or** s.t. **over** | *examine* |
| **look** s.t. **up** | *try to find (in a book/on the Internet)* |
| **make** s.t. **up** | *create* |
| **miss out on** s.t. | *lose the chance for something good* |
| **move** s.t. **around*** | *change the location* |
| **pass** s.t. **on** | *give to others* |
| **pass** s.t. **out** | *distribute* |
| **pass** s.o. **or** s.t. **over** | *decide not to use* |
| **pass** s.o. **or** s.t. **up** | *decide not to use, reject* |
| **pay** s.o. **or** s.t. **back** | *repay* |
| **pick** s.o. **or** s.t. **out** | 1. *choose* |
|  | 2. *identify* |
| **pick** s.o. **or** s.t. **up** | 1. *lift* |
|  | 2. *go get someone or something* |
| **pick** s.t. **up** | 1. *buy, purchase* |
|  | 2. *get (an idea/a new book)* |
|  | 3. *answer the phone* |
| **point** s.o. **or** s.t. **out** | *indicate* |
| **put** s.t. **away** | *put in an appropriate place* |
| **put** s.t. **back** | *return to its original place* |
| **put** s.o. **or** s.t. **down** | *stop holding* |
| **put** s.o. **off** | *discourage* |
| **put** s.t. **off** | *delay* |
| **put off** doing s.t. | *delay* |
| **put** s.t. **on** | *cover the body (with clothes/lotion)* |
| **put** s.t. **together** | *assemble* |
| **put** s.t. **up** | *erect* |
| **run into** s.o. | *meet accidentally* |
| **see** s.t. **through*** | *complete* |
| **send** s.t. **back** | *return* |
| **send** s.t. **out** | *mail* |
| **set** s.t. **up** | 1. *prepare for use* |
|  | 2. *establish (a business/ an organization)* |
| **settle on** s.t. | *choose after thinking about many possibilities* |
| **show** s.o. **or** s.t. **off** | *display the best qualities* |
| **show up on** s.t. | *appear* |
| **shut** s.t. **off** | *stop (a machine/light)* |
| **sign** s.o. **up (for** s.t.**)** | *register* |
| **start** s.t. **over*** | *start again* |

| PHRASAL VERB | MEANING |
|---|---|
| **stick with/to** s.o. **or** s.t. | *not quit, not leave, persevere* |
| **straighten** s.o. **out** | *change bad behavior* |
| **straighten** s.t. **up** | *make neat* |
| **switch** s.t. **on** | *start (a machine/light)* |
| **take** s.t. **away** | *remove* |
| **take** s.o. **or** s.t. **back** | *return* |
| **take** s.t. **down** | *remove* |
| **take** s.t. **in** | 1. *notice, understand, and remember* |
|  | 2. *earn (money)* |
| **take** s.t. **off/out** | *remove* |
| **take** s.o. **on** | *hire* |
| **take** s.t. **on** | *agree to do* |
| **take over** s.t. | *get control of* |
| **take** s.t. **up** | *begin a job or activity* |
| **talk** s.o. **into*** | *persuade* |
| **talk** s.t. **over** | *discuss* |
| **team up with** s.o. | *start to work with* |
| **tear** s.t. **down** | *destroy* |
| **tear** s.t. **off** | *remove by tearing* |
| **tear** s.t. **up** | *tear into small pieces* |
| **think about** doing s.t. | *consider* |
| **think back on** s.t. | *remember* |
| **think** s.t. **over** | *consider* |
| **think** s.t. **up** | *invent* |
| **throw** s.t. **away/out** | *put in the trash, discard* |
| **touch** s.t. **up** | *improve by making small changes* |
| **try** s.t. **on** | *put clothing on to see if it fits* |
| **try** s.t. **out** | *use to see if it works* |
| **turn** s.t. **around*** | *make it work well* |
| **turn** s.o. **or** s.t. **down** | *reject* |
| **turn** s.t. **down** | *lower the volume (a TV/radio)* |
| **turn** s.t. **in** | *give work (to a boss/teacher), submit* |
| **turn** s.o. **or** s.t. **into*** | *change from one form to another* |
| **turn** s.o. **off*** | *[slang] destroy interest in* |
| **turn** s.t. **off** | *stop (a machine/light), extinguish* |
| **turn** s.t. **on** | *start (a machine/light)* |
| **turn** s.t. **over** | *turn so the top side is at the bottom* |
| **turn** s.t. **up** | *make louder (a TV/radio)* |
| **use** s.t. **up** | *use completely, consume* |
| **wake** s.o. **up** | *awaken* |
| **watch out for** s.o. **or** s.t. | *be careful about* |
| **work** s.t. **off** | *remove by work or activity* |
| **work** s.t. **out** | *solve, find a solution to a problem* |
| **write** s.t. **down** | *write on a piece of paper* |
| **write** s.t. **up** | *write in a finished form* |

| PHRASAL VERB | MEANING |
|---|---|
| act up | cause problems |
| blow up | explode |
| break down | stop working (a machine) |
| break out | happen suddenly |
| burn down | burn completely |
| call back | return a phone call |
| calm down | become less excited |
| catch on | 1. begin to understand |
| | 2. become popular |
| cheer up | make happier |
| clean up | clean completely |
| clear up | become clear |
| close down | stop operating |
| come about | happen |
| come along | come with, accompany |
| come around | happen |
| come back | 1. return |
| | 2. become fashionable again |
| come by | visit |
| come down | become less (prices) |
| come in | enter |
| come off | become unattached |
| come on | 1. do as I say |
| | 2. let's go |
| come out | appear |
| come up | arise |
| dress up | wear special clothes |
| drop in | visit by surprise |
| drop out | quit |
| eat out | eat in a restaurant |
| empty out | empty completely |
| end up | reach a final place or condition |
| fall off | become detached |
| find out | learn information |
| fit in | be accepted in a group |
| follow through | complete |
| fool around | act playful |
| get ahead | make progress, succeed |
| get along | have a good relationship |
| get away | go on vacation |
| get back | return |
| get by | survive |
| get through | 1. finish |
| | 2. succeed in reaching s.o. by phone |
| get together | meet |
| get up | 1. get out of bed |
| | 2. stand |

| PHRASAL VERB | MEANING |
|---|---|
| give up | quit |
| go ahead | begin or continue to do something |
| go away | leave |
| go back | return |
| go down | become less (price, number), decrease |
| go off | explode (a gun/fireworks) |
| go on | continue |
| go out | leave |
| go over | succeed with an audience |
| go up | 1. be built |
| | 2. become more (price, number), increase |
| grow up | become an adult |
| hang up | end a phone call |
| help out | assist |
| hold on | 1. wait |
| | 2. not hang up the phone |
| keep away | stay at a distance |
| keep out | not enter |
| keep up | go as fast |
| lie down | recline |
| light up | illuminate |
| look out | be careful |
| make up | end a disagreement, reconcile |
| miss out | lose the chance for something good |
| pass away | die |
| pay off | be worthwhile |
| pick up | improve |
| play around | have fun |
| run out | not have enough |
| set out | begin an activity or a project |
| show up | appear |
| sign up | register |
| sit down | take a seat |
| slip up | make a mistake |
| stand up | rise |
| start over | start again |
| stay up | remain awake |
| straighten up | make neat |
| take off | depart (a plane) |
| tune in | 1. watch or listen to (a show) |
| | 2. pay attention |
| turn up | appear |
| wake up | stop sleeping |
| watch out | be careful |
| work out | 1. be resolved |
| | 2. exercise |
| | 3. understand |

## 6 Irregular Plural Nouns

| SINGULAR | PLURAL | | SINGULAR | PLURAL | | SINGULAR | PLURAL | | SINGULAR | PLURAL |
|---|---|---|---|---|---|---|---|---|---|---|
| analysis | analyses | | half | halves | | man | men | | deer | deer |
| basis | bases | | knife | knives | | woman | women | | fish | fish |
| crisis | crises | | leaf | leaves | | child | children | | sheep | sheep |
| hypothesis | hypotheses | | life | lives | | foot | feet | | | |
| | | | loaf | loaves | | tooth | teeth | | | |
| | | | shelf | shelves | | goose | geese | | | |
| | | | wife | wives | | mouse | mice | | | |
| | | | | | | person | people | | | |

## 7 Adjectives That Form the Comparative and Superlative in Two Ways

The more common form of the comparative and the superlative is listed first.

| ADJECTIVE | COMPARATIVE | SUPERLATIVE |
|---|---|---|
| common | more common/commoner | most common/commonest |
| cruel | crueler/more cruel | cruelest/most cruel |
| deadly | deadlier/more deadly | deadliest/most deadly |
| friendly | more friendly/friendlier | most friendly/friendliest |
| handsome | more handsome/handsomer | most handsome/handsomest |
| happy | happier/more happy | happiest/most happy |
| lively | livelier/more lively | liveliest/most lively |
| lonely | lonelier/more lonely | loneliest/most lonely |
| lovely | lovelier/more lovely | loveliest/most lovely |
| narrow | narrower/more narrow | narrowest/most narrow |
| pleasant | more pleasant/pleasanter | most pleasant/pleasantest |
| polite | more polite/politer | most polite/politest |
| quiet | quieter/more quiet | quietest/most quiet |
| shallow | shallower/more shallow | shallowest/most shallow |
| simple | simpler/more simple | simplest/most simple |
| sincere | more sincere/sincerer | most sincere/sincerest |
| stupid | stupider/more stupid | stupidest/most stupid |
| true | truer/more true | truest/most true |

## 8 Irregular Comparisons of Adjectives, Adverbs, and Quantifiers

| ADJECTIVE | ADVERB | COMPARATIVE | SUPERLATIVE |
|---|---|---|---|
| bad | badly | worse | the worst |
| far | far | farther/further | the farthest/furthest |
| good | well | better | the best |
| little | little | less | the least |
| many/a lot of | — | more | the most |
| much*/a lot of | much*/a lot | more | the most |

* *Much* is usually only used in questions and negative statements.

## 9 Participial Adjectives

| -ED | -ING | -ED | -ING | -ED | -ING |
|---|---|---|---|---|---|
| alarmed | alarming | disturbed | disturbing | moved | moving |
| amazed | amazing | embarrassed | embarrassing | paralyzed | paralyzing |
| amused | amusing | entertained | entertaining | pleased | pleasing |
| annoyed | annoying | excited | exciting | relaxed | relaxing |
| astonished | astonishing | exhausted | exhausting | satisfied | satisfying |
| bored | boring | fascinated | fascinating | shocked | shocking |
| confused | confusing | frightened | frightening | surprised | surprising |
| depressed | depressing | horrified | horrifying | terrified | terrifying |
| disappointed | disappointing | inspired | inspiring | tired | tiring |
| disgusted | disgusting | interested | interesting | touched | touching |
| distressed | distressing | irritated | irritating | troubled | troubling |

## 10 Verbs Followed by Gerunds (Base Form of Verb + -ing)

| | | | | | |
|---|---|---|---|---|---|
| acknowledge | delay | escape | imagine | postpone | report |
| admit | deny | excuse | justify | practice | resent |
| advise | detest | explain | keep *(continue)* | prevent | resist |
| allow | discontinue | feel like | keep on* | prohibit | risk |
| appreciate | discuss | finish | limit | propose | suggest |
| avoid | dislike | forgive | mention | put off* | support |
| ban | end up* | give up* | mind *(object to)* | quit | think about* *(consider)* |
| can't help | endure | go | miss | recall | tolerate |
| celebrate | enjoy | go on* | permit | recommend | understand |
| consider | | | | | |

*These phrasal verbs can be followed by a gerund.

*[handwritten]* go fishing
*[handwritten]* practice shooting baskets.

## 11 Verbs Followed by Infinitives (To + Base Form of Verb)

| | | | | | |
|---|---|---|---|---|---|
| afford | can't wait | grow | mean *(intend)* | pretend | threaten |
| agree | claim | help* | need | promise | volunteer |
| aim | choose | hesitate | neglect | refuse | wait |
| appear | consent | hope | offer | rush | want |
| arrange | decide | hurry | pay | seem | wish |
| ask | deserve | intend | plan | struggle | would like |
| attempt | expect | learn | prepare | swear | yearn |
| can('t) afford | fail | manage | | | |

* *Help* is often followed by the base form of the verb (example: *I helped paint the kitchen*).

*[handwritten]* I want to be free.

## 12 Verbs Followed by Gerunds or Infinitives

| | | | | | |
|---|---|---|---|---|---|
| begin | forget* | like | prefer | regret* | stop* |
| can't stand | hate | love | remember* | start | try |
| continue | | | | | |

*These verbs can be followed by either a gerund or an infinitive, but there is a big difference in meaning *(see Unit 9)*.

## 13 Verbs Followed by Object + Infinitive

| | | | | | |
|---|---|---|---|---|---|
| advise | choose* | get | order | promise* | tell |
| allow | convince | help** | pay* | remind | urge |
| ask* | encourage | hire | permit | request | want* |
| beg* | expect* | instruct | persuade | require | warn |
| cause | forbid | invite | prefer* | teach | would like* |
| challenge | force | need* | | | |

*These verbs can also be followed by an infinitive without an object (example: *ask to leave* or *ask someone to leave*).
** *Help* is often followed by the base form of the verb, with or without an object (example: *I helped (her) paint the kitchen*).

## 14 Adjectives Followed by Infinitives

| | | | | | |
|---|---|---|---|---|---|
| afraid | delighted | eager | happy | ready | sorry |
| alarmed | depressed | easy | hesitant | relieved | surprised |
| amazed | determined | embarrassed | likely | reluctant | touched |
| angry | difficult | encouraged | lucky | right | upset |
| anxious | disappointed | excited | pleased | sad | willing |
| ashamed | distressed | fortunate | prepared | shocked | wrong |
| curious | disturbed | glad | proud | | |

## 15 Nouns Followed by Infinitives

| | | | | | |
|---|---|---|---|---|---|
| attempt | desire | offer | plan | reason | time |
| chance | dream | opportunity | price | request | trouble |
| choice | failure | permission | promise | right | way |
| decision | need | | | | |

## 16 Adjective + Preposition Combinations

| | | | | | |
|---|---|---|---|---|---|
| accustomed to | bored with/by | disappointed with | happy about | responsible for | sorry for/about |
| afraid of | capable of | excited about | known for | sad about | surprised at/ |
| amazed at/by | careful of | famous for | interested in | safe from | about/by |
| angry at | certain about | fed up with | nervous about | satisfied with | terrible at |
| ashamed of | concerned about | fond of | opposed to | shocked at/by | tired of |
| aware of | content with | glad about | pleased about | sick of | used to |
| awful at | curious about | good at | ready for | slow at/in | worried about |
| bad at | different from | | | | |

## 17 Verb + Preposition Combinations

| | | | | | |
|---|---|---|---|---|---|
| admit to | believe in | dream about/of | pay for | succeed in | think about |
| advise against | choose between | feel about | plan on | talk about | wonder about |
| apologize for | complain about | insist on | rely on | thank someone for | worry about |
| approve of | decide on | object to | resort to | | |

# 18 Modals and Their Functions

## 1 SOCIAL MODALS AND EXPRESSIONS

| FUNCTION | MODAL OR EXPRESSION | TIME | EXAMPLES |
|---|---|---|---|
| Ability | can<br>can't | Present | Sam **can swim**.<br>He **can't skate**. |
| | could<br>couldn't | Past | We **could swim** last year.<br>We **couldn't skate**. |
| | be able to*<br>not be able to* | All verb forms | Lea **is able to run** fast.<br>She **wasn't able to run** fast last year. |
| Possibility | can<br>can't | Present or future | I **can help** you now.<br>I **can't help** you tomorrow. |
| Permission | can<br><br><br>can't<br>could<br>may<br><br>may not | Present or future | **Can** I **sit** here?<br>**Can** I **call** tomorrow?<br>Yes, you **can**.<br>No, you **can't**. Sorry.<br>**Could** he **leave** now?<br>**May** I **borrow** your pen?<br>Yes, you **may**.<br>No, you **may not**. Sorry. |
| Requests | can<br><br>can't<br>could<br>will<br>would | Present or future | **Can** you **close** the door, please?<br>Sure, I **can**.<br>Sorry, I **can't**.<br>**Could** you please **answer** the phone?<br>**Will** you **wash** the dishes, please?<br>**Would** you please **mail** this letter? |
| Advice | should<br>shouldn't<br>ought to<br>had better**<br>had better not** | Present or future | You **should study** more.<br>You **shouldn't miss** class.<br>We **ought to leave**.<br>We**'d better go**.<br>We**'d better not stay**. |
| Advisability in the Past<br>and<br>Regret or Criticism | should have<br>shouldn't have<br>ought to have<br>could have<br>might have | Past | I **should have become** a doctor.<br>I **shouldn't have wasted** time.<br>He **ought to have told** me.<br>She **could have gone** to college.<br>You **might have called**. I waited for hours. |
| Necessity | have to*<br><br><br>not have to* | All verb forms | He **has to go** now.<br>I **had to go** yesterday.<br>I **will have to go** soon.<br>He **doesn't have to go** yet. |
| | have got to*<br>must | Present or future | He**'s got to leave**!<br>You **must use** a pen for the test. |
| Prohibition | must not<br>can't | Present or future | You **must not drive** without a license.<br>You **can't drive** without a license. |

*The meaning of this expression is similar to the meaning of a modal. Unlike a modal, the verb changes for present tense third-person singular.
**The meaning of this expression is similar to the meaning of a modal. Like a modal, it has no -*s* for third-person singular.

**2** LOGICAL MODALS AND EXPRESSIONS

| FUNCTION | MODAL OR EXPRESSION | TIME | EXAMPLES |
|---|---|---|---|
| Conclusions and Possibility | must<br>must not<br>have to*<br>have got to* | Present | This **must be** her house. Her name is on the door.<br>She **must not be** home. I don't see her car.<br>She **has to know** him. They went to school together.<br>He**'s got to be** guilty. We saw him do it. |
| | may<br>may not<br>might<br>might not<br>could | Present or future | She **may be** home now.<br>It **may not rain** tomorrow.<br>Lee **might be sick** today.<br>He **might not come** to class.<br>They **could be** at the library.<br>It **could rain** tomorrow. |
| | may have<br>may not have<br>might have<br>might not have<br>could have | Past | They **may have left** already. I don't see them.<br>They **may not have arrived** yet.<br>He **might have called**. I'll check my phone messages.<br>He **might not have left** a message.<br>She **could have forgotten** to mail the letter. |
| Impossibility | can't | Present or future | That **can't be** Ana. She left for France yesterday.<br>It **can't snow** tomorrow. It's going to be too warm. |
| | couldn't | Present or future | He **couldn't be** guilty. He wasn't in town when the crime occurred.<br>The teacher **couldn't give** the test tomorrow. Tomorrow's Saturday. |
| | couldn't have | Past | You **couldn't have failed**. You studied too hard. |

*The meaning of this expression is similar to the meaning of a modal. Unlike a modal, the verb changes for present tense third-person singular.

## 19 Reporting Verbs

**STATEMENTS**

| | | | | |
|---|---|---|---|---|
| acknowledge | claim | explain | remark | state |
| add | comment | indicate | repeat | suggest |
| admit | complain | maintain | reply | tell |
| announce | conclude | mean | report | warn |
| answer | confess | note | respond | whisper |
| argue | declare | observe | say | write |
| assert | deny | promise | shout | yell |
| believe | exclaim | | | |

**INSTRUCTIONS, COMMANDS, ADVICE, REQUESTS, INVITATIONS**

| | |
|---|---|
| advise | invite |
| ask | order |
| caution | say |
| command | tell |
| demand | urge |
| instruct | warn |

**QUESTIONS**

ask
inquire
question

## 20 Time Word Changes in Indirect Speech

| DIRECT SPEECH | | INDIRECT SPEECH |
|---|---|---|
| now | → | then |
| today | → | that day |
| tomorrow | → | the next day **or** the following day **or** the day after |
| yesterday | → | the day before **or** the previous day |
| this week/month/year | → | that week/month/year |
| last week/month/year | → | the week/month/year before |
| next week/month/year | → | the following week/month/year |

## 21 Phrases Introducing Embedded Questions

I don't know ...
I don't understand ...
I wonder ...
I'm not sure ...
I can't remember ...
I can't imagine ...
It doesn't say ...

I'd like to know ...
I need to know ...
I want to know ...
I want to understand ...
I'd like to find out ...
We need to find out ...
Let's ask ...

Do you know ...?
Do you understand ...?
Can you tell me ...?
Could you explain ...?
Can you remember ...?
Would you show me ...?
Who knows ...?

## 22 Spelling Rules for the Simple Present: Third-Person Singular (*He, She, It*)

**1** Add *-s* for most verbs.

| | |
|---|---|
| work | work**s** |
| buy | buy**s** |
| ride | ride**s** |
| return | return**s** |

**2** Add *-es* for verbs that end in *-ch*, *-s*, *-sh*, *-x*, or *-z*.

| | |
|---|---|
| watch | watch**es** |
| pass | pass**es** |
| rush | rush**es** |
| relax | relax**es** |
| buzz | buzz**es** |

**3** Change the *y* to *i* and add *-es* when the base form ends in **consonant + y**.

| | |
|---|---|
| study | stud**ies** |
| hurry | hurr**ies** |
| dry | dr**ies** |

**4** Do not change the *y* when the base form ends in **vowel + y**. Add *-s*.

| | |
|---|---|
| play | play**s** |
| enjoy | enjoy**s** |

**5** A few verbs have **irregular forms**.

| | |
|---|---|
| be | **is** |
| do | **does** |
| go | **goes** |
| have | **has** |

## 23 Spelling Rules for Base Form of Verb + *-ing* (Progressive and Gerund)

**1** Add *-ing* to the base form of the verb.

| | |
|---|---|
| read | read**ing** |
| stand | stand**ing** |

**2** If the verb ends in a **silent** *-e*, drop the final *-e* and add *-ing*.

| | |
|---|---|
| leave | leav**ing** |
| take | tak**ing** |

**3** In **one-syllable** verbs, if the last three letters are a consonant-vowel-consonant combination (CVC), double the last consonant and add *-ing*.

```
C V C
↓ ↓ ↓
s i t          sit**ting**

C V C
↓ ↓ ↓
p l a n        plan**ning**
```

EXCEPTION: Do not double the last consonant in verbs that end in *-w*, *-x*, or *-y*.

| | |
|---|---|
| sew | sew**ing** |
| fix | fix**ing** |
| play | play**ing** |

**4** In verbs of **two or more syllables** that end in a consonant-vowel-consonant combination, double the last consonant only if the last syllable is stressed.

| | | |
|---|---|---|
| admít | admit**ting** | *(The last syllable is stressed, so double the *-t*.)* |
| whísper | whisper**ing** | *(The last syllable is not stressed, so don't double the *-r*.)* |

**5** If the verb ends in *-ie*, change the *ie* to *y* before adding *-ing*.

| | |
|---|---|
| die | d**ying** |
| lie | l**ying** |

**Stress**
′ shows main stress.

## 24 Spelling Rules for Base Form of Verb + *-ed* (Simple Past and Past Participle of Regular Verbs)

**1** If the verb ends in a **consonant**, add *-ed*.

| | |
|---|---|
| return | return**ed** |
| help | help**ed** |

**2** If the verb ends in *-e*, add *-d*.

| | |
|---|---|
| live | live**d** |
| create | create**d** |
| die | die**d** |

**3** In **one-syllable** verbs, if the last three letters are a consonant-vowel-consonant combination (CVC), double the last consonant and add *-ed*.

C V C
↓ ↓ ↓
h o p       hop**ped**

C V C
↓ ↓ ↓
g r a b    grab**bed**

EXCEPTION: Do not double the last consonant in **one-syllable** verbs that end in *-w*, *-x*, or *-y*.

| | |
|---|---|
| bow | bow**ed** |
| mix | mix**ed** |
| play | play**ed** |

**4** In verbs of **two or more syllables** that end in a consonant-vowel-consonant combination, double the last consonant only if the last syllable is stressed.

| | | |
|---|---|---|
| prefer′ | prefer**red** | *(The last syllable is stressed, so double the -**r**.)* |
| ′visit | visit**ed** | *(The last syllable is not stressed, so don't double the -**t**.)* |

**5** If the verb ends in **consonant + y**, change the *y* to *i* and add *-ed*.

| | |
|---|---|
| worry | worr**ied** |
| carry | carr**ied** |

**6** If the verb ends in **vowel + y**, add *-ed*. (Do not change the *y* to *i*.)

| | |
|---|---|
| play | play**ed** |
| annoy | annoy**ed** |

EXCEPTIONS:

| | |
|---|---|
| lay | la**id** |
| pay | pa**id** |
| say | sa**id** |

> **Stress**
> ′ shows main stress.

## 25 Spelling Rules for the Comparative (*-er*) and Superlative (*-est*) of Adjectives

**1** With **one-syllable** adjectives, add *-er* to form the comparative. Add *-est* to form the superlative.

| | | |
|---|---|---|
| cheap | cheap**er** | cheap**est** |
| bright | bright**er** | bright**est** |

**2** If the adjective ends in *-e*, add *-r* or *-st*.

| | | |
|---|---|---|
| nice | nice**r** | nice**st** |

**3** If the adjective ends in **consonant + y**, change *y* to *i* before you add *-er* or *-est*.

| | | |
|---|---|---|
| pretty | prett**ier** | prett**iest** |

EXCEPTION:

| | | |
|---|---|---|
| shy | shy**er** | shy**est** |

**4** In **one-syllable** adjectives, if the last three letters are a consonant-vowel-consonant combination (CVC), double the last consonant before adding *-er* or *-est*.

C V C
↓ ↓ ↓
b i g    big**ger**    big**gest**

EXCEPTION: Do not double the last consonant in adjectives that end in *-w* or *-y*.

| | | |
|---|---|---|
| slow | slow**er** | slow**est** |
| gray | gray**er** | gray**est** |

## 26 Spelling Rules for Adverbs Ending in *-ly*

**1** Add *-ly* to the corresponding adjective.

| | |
|---|---|
| nice | nice**ly** |
| quiet | quiet**ly** |
| beautiful | beautiful**ly** |

EXCEPTION:

| | |
|---|---|
| true | tru**ly** |

**2** If the adjective ends in **consonant + y**, change the *y* to *i* before adding *-ly*.

| | |
|---|---|
| easy | eas**ily** |

**3** If the adjective ends in *-le*, drop the *e* and add *-y*.

| | |
|---|---|
| possible | possib**ly** |

**4** If the adjective ends in *-ic*, add *-ally*.

| | |
|---|---|
| basic | basic**ally** |
| fantastic | fantastic**ally** |

## 27 Capitalization and Punctuation Rules

| | USE FOR . . . | EXAMPLES |
|---|---|---|
| **capital letter** | • the first-person pronoun *I* | Tomorrow **I** will be here at 2:00. |
| | • proper nouns | His name is **Karl**. He lives in **Germany**. |
| | • the first word of a sentence | **When** does the train leave? **At** 2:00. |
| **apostrophe (')** | • possessive nouns | Is that **Marta's** coat? |
| | • contractions | **That's** not hers. **It's** mine. |
| **comma (,)** | • after items in a list | He bought **apples, pears, oranges,** and **bananas**. |
| | • before sentence connectors *and, but, or,* and *so* | They watched TV**, and** she played video games. She's tired**, so** she's going to bed now. |
| | • after the first part of a sentence that begins with *because* | ***Because*** **it's raining,** we're not walking to the office. |
| | • after the first part of a sentence that begins with a preposition | ***Across from*** **the post office,** there's a good restaurant. |
| | • after the first part of a sentence that begins with a time clause or an *if*-clause | ***After*** **he arrived,** we ate dinner. ***If*** **it rains,** we won't go. |
| | • before and after a nonidentifying adjective clause in the middle of a sentence | Tony**, who lives in Paris,** emails me every day. |
| | • before a nonidentifying adjective clause at the end of a sentence | I get emails every day from Tony**, who lives in Paris.** |
| **exclamation point (!)** | • at the end of a sentence to show surprise or a strong feeling | You're here! That's great! Stop! A car is coming! |
| **period (.)** | • at the end of a statement | Today is Wednesday**.** |
| **question mark (?)** | • at the end of a question | What day is today**?** |

## 28 Direct Speech Punctuation Rules

Direct speech can either come **after or before** the reporting verb.

**1** When direct speech comes **after** the reporting verb:

EXAMPLES: He said, **"I had a good time."**
She asked, **"Where's the party?"**
They shouted, **"Be careful!"**

**a.** Put a comma after the reporting verb.

**b.** Use opening quotation marks (") before the first word of the direct speech.

**c.** Begin the quotation with a capital letter.

**d.** Use the appropriate end punctuation for the direct speech:
If the direct speech is a statement, use a period (.).
If the direct speech is a question, use a question mark (?).
If the direct speech is an exclamation, use an exclamation point (!).

**e.** Put closing quotation marks (") after the end punctuation of the quotation.

**2** When direct speech comes **before** the reporting verb:

EXAMPLES: **"I had a good time,"** he said.
**"Where's the party?"** she asked.
**"Be careful!"** they shouted.

**a.** Begin the sentence with opening quotation marks (").

**b.** Use the appropriate end punctuation for the direct speech:
If the direct speech is a statement, use a comma (,).
If the direct speech is a question, use a question mark (?).
If the direct speech is an exclamation, use an exclamation point (!).

**c.** Use closing quotation marks after the end punctuation for the direct speech (").

**d.** Begin the reporting clause with a lowercase letter.

**e.** Use a period at the end of the main sentence (.).

## 29 Pronunciation Table

▶ A|01   These are the pronunciation symbols used in this text. Listen to the pronunciation of the key words.

| VOWELS | | | | CONSONANTS | | | |
|---|---|---|---|---|---|---|---|
| SYMBOL | KEY WORD | SYMBOL | KEY WORD | SYMBOL | KEY WORD | SYMBOL | KEY WORD |
| i | beat, feed | ə | banana, among | p | pack, happy | z | zip, please, goes |
| ɪ | bit, did | ɚ | shirt, murder | b | back, rubber | ʃ | ship, machine, station, special, discussion |
| eɪ | date, paid | aɪ | bite, cry, buy, eye | t | tie | | |
| ɛ | bet, bed | aʊ | about, how | d | die | ʒ | measure, vision |
| æ | bat, bad | ɔɪ | voice, boy | k | came, key, quick | h | hot, who |
| ɑ | box, odd, father | ɪr | beer | g | game, guest | m | men |
| ɔ | bought, dog | ɛr | bare | tʃ | church, nature, watch | n | sun, know, pneumonia |
| oʊ | boat, road | ɑr | bar | ʤ | judge, general, major | ŋ | sung, ringing |
| ʊ | book, good | ɔr | door | f | fan, photograph | w | wet, white |
| u | boot, food, student | ʊr | tour | v | van | l | light, long |
| ʌ | but, mud, mother | | | θ | thing, breath | r | right, wrong |
| | | | | ð | then, breathe | y | yes, use, music |
| | | | | s | sip, city, psychology | t̬ | butter, bottle |

## 30 Pronunciation Rules for the Simple Present: Third-Person Singular (*He, She, It*)

**1** The third-person singular in the simple present always ends in the letter *-s*. There are, however, three different pronunciations for the final sound of the third-person singular.

| /s/ | /z/ | /ɪz/ |
|---|---|---|
| talk**s** | love**s** | dance**s** |

**2** The final sound is pronounced /s/ after the voiceless sounds /p/, /t/, /k/, and /f/.

| top | top**s** | take | ta**kes** |
|---|---|---|---|
| get | get**s** | laugh | lau**ghs** |

**3** The final sound is pronounced /z/ after the voiced sounds /b/, /d/, /g/, /v/, /m/, /n/, /ŋ/, /l/, /r/, and /ð/.

| describe | descri**bes** | remain | remai**ns** |
|---|---|---|---|
| spend | spen**ds** | sing | sin**gs** |
| hug | hu**gs** | tell | tel**ls** |
| live | li**ves** | lower | lowe**rs** |
| seem | see**ms** | bathe | ba**thes** |

**4** The final sound is pronounced /z/ after all **vowel sounds**.

| agree | agr**ees** | stay | st**ays** |
|---|---|---|---|
| try | tr**ies** | know | kn**ows** |

**5** The final sound is pronounced /ɪz/ after the sounds /s/, /z/, /ʃ/, /ʒ/, /tʃ/, and /dʒ/. /ɪz/ adds a syllable to the verb.

| miss | mis**ses** | massage | massa**ges** |
|---|---|---|---|
| freeze | free**zes** | watch | wat**ches** |
| rush | ru**shes** | judge | ju**dges** |

**6** *Do* and *say* have a change in vowel sound.

do /du/     does /dʌz/
say /seɪ/     says /sɛz/

## 31 Pronunciation Rules for the Simple Past and Past Participle of Regular Verbs

**1** The regular simple past and past participle always end in the letter *-d*. There are three different pronunciations for the final sound of the regular simple past and past participle.

| /t/ | /d/ | /ɪd/ |
|---|---|---|
| race**d** | live**d** | attend**ed** |

**2** The final sound is pronounced /t/ after the voiceless sounds /p/, /k/, /f/, /s/, /ʃ/, and /tʃ/.

| hop | ho**pped** | address | addre**ssed** |
|---|---|---|---|
| work | wor**ked** | publish | publi**shed** |
| laugh | lau**ghed** | watch | wa**tched** |

**3** The final sound is pronounced /d/ after the voiced sounds /b/, /g/, /v/, /z/, /ʒ/, /dʒ/, /m/, /n/, /ŋ/, /l/, /r/, and /ð/.

| rub | ru**bbed** | rhyme | rhy**med** |
|---|---|---|---|
| hug | hu**gged** | return | retur**ned** |
| live | li**ved** | bang | ban**ged** |
| surprise | surpri**sed** | enroll | enro**lled** |
| massage | massa**ged** | appear | appea**red** |
| change | chan**ged** | bathe | ba**thed** |

**4** The final sound is pronounced /d/ after all **vowel sounds**.

| agree | agr**eed** | enjoy | enj**oyed** |
|---|---|---|---|
| die | di**ed** | snow | sn**owed** |
| play | pl**ayed** | | |

**5** The final sound is pronounced /ɪd/ after /t/ and /d/. /ɪd/ adds a syllable to the verb.

| start | start**ed** | decide | decid**ed** |
|---|---|---|---|

# Glossary of Grammar Terms

**action verb** A verb that describes an action.

> Alicia **ran** home.

**active sentence** A sentence that focuses on the agent (the person or thing doing the action).

> **Ari kicked** the ball.

**addition** A clause or a short sentence that follows a statement and expresses similarity or contrast with the information in the statement.

> Pedro is tall, **and so is Alex.**
> Trish doesn't like sports. **Neither does her sister.**

**adjective** A word that describes a noun or pronoun.

> It's a **good** plan, and it's not **difficult.**

**adjective clause** A clause that identifies or gives additional information about a noun.

> The woman **who called you** didn't leave her name.
> Samir, **who you met yesterday**, works in the lab.

**adverb** A word that describes a verb, an adjective, or another adverb.

> She drives **carefully.**
> She's a **very** good driver.
> She drives **really** well.

**affirmative** A statement without a negative, or an answer meaning *Yes*.

> He **works.** *(affirmative statement)*
> **Yes**, he **does.** *(affirmative short answer)*

**agent** The person or thing doing the action in a sentence. In passive sentences, the word *by* is used before the agent.

> This article was written ***by* my teacher.**

**article** A word that goes before a noun.

The indefinite articles are *a* and *an*.

> I ate **a** sandwich and **an** apple.

The definite article is *the*.

> I didn't like **the** sandwich. **The** apple was good.

**auxiliary verb** (also called **helping verb**) A verb used with a main verb. *Be*, *do*, and *have* are often auxiliary verbs. Modals (*can, should, may, must . . .*) are also auxiliary verbs.

> I **am** exercising right now.
> **Do** you like to exercise?
> I **should** exercise every day.

**base form** The simple form of a verb without any endings (*-s, -ed, -ing*) or other changes.

> **be, have, go, drive**

**clause** A group of words that has a subject and a verb. A sentence can have one or more clauses.

> **We are leaving now.** *(one clause)*
> **If it rains, we won't go.** *(two clauses)*

**common noun** A word for a person, place, or thing (but not the name of the person, place, or thing).

> Teresa lives in a **house** near the **beach.**

**comparative** The form of an adjective or adverb that shows the difference between two people, places, or things.

> Alain is **shorter** than Brendan. *(adjective)*
> Brendan runs **faster** than Alain. *(adverb)*

**conditional sentence** A sentence that describes a condition and its result. The sentence can be about the past, the present, or the future. The condition and result can be real or unreal.

> If it **rains**, I **won't go.** *(future real)*
> If it **had rained**, I **wouldn't have gone.** *(past unreal)*

**continuous** See **progressive.**

**contraction** A short form of a word or words. An apostrophe (') replaces the missing letter or letters.

> **she's** = she is
> **can't** = cannot

**count noun** A noun that you can count. It has a singular and a plural form.

> one **book**, two **books**

**definite article** *the*

This article goes before a noun that refers to a specific person, place, or thing.

> Please bring me **the book** on **the table**.

**dependent clause** (also called **subordinate clause**) A clause that needs a main clause for its meaning.

> **When it's hot out,** I go to the beach.

**direct object** A noun or pronoun that receives the action of a verb.

> Marta kicked **the ball**. Ian caught **it**.

**direct speech** (also called **quoted speech**) Language that gives the exact words a speaker used. In writing, quotation marks come before and after the speaker's words.

> **"I saw Bob yesterday,"** she said.
> **"Was he in school?"** he asked.

**embedded question** A question that is inside another sentence.

> I don't know **where the restaurant is**.
> Do you know **if it's on Tenth Street**?

**formal** Language used in business situations or with adults you do not know.

> Good afternoon, Mr. Rivera. Please have a seat.

**gerund** A noun formed with verb + *-ing* that can be used as a subject or an object.

> **Swimming** is great exercise.
> I enjoy **swimming**.

**helping verb** See **auxiliary verb**.

**identifying adjective clause** (also called **restrictive adjective clause**) A clause that identifies which member of a group the sentence is about.

> There are ten students in the class. The student **who sits in front of me** is from Russia.

**if-clause** The clause that states the condition in a conditional sentence.

> **If I had known you were here,** I would have called you.

**imperative** A sentence that gives a command or instructions.

> **Hurry!**
> **Turn left on Main Street.**

**indefinite article** *a* or *an*

These articles go before a noun that does not refer to a specific person, place, or thing.

> Can you bring me **a book**? I'm looking for something to read.

**indefinite pronoun** A pronoun such as *someone, something, anyone, anything, anywhere, no one, nothing, nowhere, everyone,* and *everything*. An indefinite pronoun does not refer to a specific person, place, or thing.

> **Someone** called you last night.
> Did **anything** happen?

**indirect object** A noun or pronoun (often a person) that receives something as the result of the action of the verb.

> I told **John** the story.
> He gave **me** some good advice.

**indirect question** Language that reports what a speaker asked without using the exact words.

> He asked **what my name was**.
> He asked **if he had met me before**.

**indirect speech** (also called **reported speech**) Language that reports what a speaker said without using the exact words.

> Ann said **she had seen Bob the day before**.
> She asked **if he was in school**.

**infinitive** *to* + base form of the verb

> I want **to leave** now.

**infinitive of purpose** *(in order) to* + base form
This form gives the reason for an action.

> I go to school **(in order) to learn** English.

**informal** Language used with family, friends, and children.

> Hi, Pete. Sit down.

**information question** See *wh-* **question**.

**inseparable phrasal verb** A phrasal verb whose parts must stay together.

> We **ran into** Tomás at the supermarket.
> NOT We ~~ran Tomás into~~ . . .

**intransitive verb** A verb that does not have an object.

> She **paints**.
> We **fell**.

**irregular** A word that does not change its form in the usual way.

> good   →   well
> bad    →   worse
> go     →   went

**main clause** A clause that can stand alone as a sentence.

> **I called my friend Tom**, who lives in Chicago.

**main verb** A verb that describes an action or state. It is often used with an auxiliary verb.

> Jared is **calling**.
> Does he **call** every day?
> Paulo is **studying** in Barcelona this semester.
> Do you **know** him?

**modal** A type of auxiliary verb. It goes before a main verb or stands alone as a short answer. It expresses ideas such as ability, advice, permission, and possibility. *Can, could, will, would, may, might, should,* and *must* are modals.

> **Can** you swim?
> Yes, I **can**.
> You really **should** learn to swim.

**negative** A statement or answer meaning *No*.

> He **doesn't** work. *(negative statement)*
> **No**, he **doesn't**. *(negative short answer)*

**non-action verb** (also called **stative verb**) A verb that does not describe an action. It describes such things as thoughts, feelings, and senses.

> I **remember** that word.
> Chris **loves** ice cream.
> It **tastes** great.

**non-count noun** A noun you usually do not count (*air, water, rice, love . . .*). It has only a singular form.

> The **rice** is delicious.

**nonidentifying adjective clause** (also called **nonrestrictive adjective clause**) A clause that gives additional information about the noun it refers to. The information is not necessary to identify the noun. It is separated from the rest of the sentence by commas.

> My sister Diana, **who usually hates sports,** recently started tennis lessons.

**nonrestrictive adjective clause** See **nonidentifying adjective clause**.

**noun** A word for a person, place, or thing.

> My **sister, Anne,** works in an **office**.
> She uses a **computer**.

**object** A noun or a pronoun that receives the action of a verb. Sometimes a verb has two objects.

> Layla threw **the ball**.
> She threw **it** to **Tom**.
> She threw **him the ball**.

**object pronoun** A pronoun (*me, you, him, her, it, us, them*) that receives the action of the verb.

> I gave **her** a book.
> I gave **it** to **her**.

**object relative pronoun** A relative pronoun that is an object in an adjective clause.

> I'm reading a book **that** I really like.

**paragraph** A group of sentences, usually about one topic.

**particle** A word that looks like a preposition and combines with a main verb to form a phrasal verb. It often changes the meaning of the main verb.

> He looked the word **up**.
> *(He looked for the meaning of the word in the dictionary.)*

**passive causative** A sentence formed with *have* or *get* + object + past participle. It is used to talk about services that you arrange for someone to do for you.

> She **had the car checked** at the service station.
> He's going to **get his hair cut** by André.

**passive sentence** A sentence that focuses on the object (the person or thing receiving the action). The passive is formed with *be* + past participle.

> **The ball was kicked** by Ari.

**past participle** A verb form (verb + -*ed*). It can also be irregular. It is used to form the present perfect, past perfect, and future perfect. It can also be an adjective.

> We've **lived** here since April.
> They had **spoken** before.
> She's **interested** in math.

**phrasal verb** (also called *two-word verb*) A verb that has two parts (verb + particle). The meaning is often different from the meaning of its separate parts.

> He **grew up** in Texas. *(became an adult)*
> His parents **brought** him **up** to be honest. *(raised)*

**phrase** A group of words that form a unit without a main verb. Many phrases give information about time or place.

> **Last year**, we were living **in Canada**.

**plural** A form that means *two or more*.

> There **are** three **people** in the restaurant.
> **They are** eating dinner.
> **We** saw **them**.

**possessive** Nouns, pronouns, or adjectives that show a relationship or show that someone owns something.

> Zach is **Megan's** brother. *(possessive noun)*
> Is that car **his**? *(possessive pronoun)*
> That's **his** car. *(possessive adjective)*

**predicate** The part of a sentence that has the main verb. It tells what the subject is doing or describes the subject.

> My sister **works for a travel agency**.

**preposition** A word or phrase that goes before a noun or a pronoun to show time, place, or direction.

> Amy and I went **to** the cafeteria **on** Friday. She sits **next to** me **in** class.

**progressive** (also called **continuous**) The verb form *be* + verb + -*ing*. It focuses on the continuation (not the completion) of an action.

> She**'s reading** the paper.
> We **were watching** TV when you called.

**pronoun** A word used in place of a noun.

> That's my brother. You met **him** at my party.

**proper noun** A noun that is the name of a person, place, or thing. It begins with a capital letter.

> **Maria** goes to **Central High School**.
> It's on **High Street**.

**punctuation** Marks used in writing (period, comma, . . .) that make the meaning clear. For example, a period (.) shows the end of a sentence and that the sentence is a statement, not a question.

> "Come in**,**" she said**.**

**quantifier** A word or phrase that shows an amount (but not an exact amount). It often comes before a noun.

> Josh bought **a lot of** books last year.
> He doesn't have **much** money.

**question** See *yes/no* **question**, *wh-* **question**, **tag question**, **indirect question**, and **embedded question**.

**question word** See *wh-* **word**.

**quoted speech** See **direct speech**.

**real conditional sentence** A sentence that talks about general truths, habits, or things that happen again and again if a condition occurs. It can also talk about things that will happen in the future under certain circumstances.

> If it rains, he takes the bus.
> If it rains tomorrow, we'll take the bus with him.

**regular** A word that changes its form in the usual way.

> play   →   played
> fast   →   faster
> quick   →   quickly

**relative pronoun** A word that connects an adjective clause to a noun in the main clause.

> He's the man **who** lives next door.
> I'm reading a book **that** I really like.

**reported speech** See **indirect speech**.

**reporting verb** A verb such as *said*, *told*, or *asked*. It introduces direct and indirect speech. It can also come after the quotation in direct speech.

> Li **said**, "I'm going to be late." **or** "I'm going to be late," Li **said**. **or** "I'm going to be late," **said** Li.
> She **told** me that she was going to be late.

**restrictive adjective clause** See **identifying adjective clause**.

**result clause** The clause in a conditional sentence that talks about what happens if the condition occurs.

> If it rains, **I'll stay home**.
> If I had a million dollars, **I would travel**.
> If I had had your phone number, **I would have called you**.

**sentence** A group of words that has a subject and a main verb.

> **Computers are** very useful.

**separable phrasal verb** A phrasal verb whose parts can separate.

> Tom **looked** the word **up** in a dictionary.
> He **looked** it **up**.

**short answer** An answer to a *yes/no* question.

> A: Did you call me last night?
> B: **No, I didn't.** or **No.**

**singular** A form that means *one*.

> They have **a sister**.
> **She works** in **a hospital**.

**statement** A sentence that gives information. In writing, it ends in a period.

> Today is Monday.

**stative verb** See **non-action verb**.

**subject** The person, place, or thing that the sentence is about.

> **Ms. Chen** teaches English.
> **Her class** is interesting.

**subject pronoun** A pronoun that shows the person (*I, you, he, she, it, we, they*) that the sentence is about.

> **I** read a lot.
> **She** reads a lot, too.

**subject relative pronoun** A relative pronoun that is the subject of an adjective clause.

> He's the man **who** lives next door.

**subordinate clause** See **dependent clause**.

**superlative** The form of an adjective or adverb that is used to compare a person, place, or thing to a group of people, places, or things.

> Cindi is **the oldest** dancer in the group. *(adjective)*
> She dances **the most gracefully**. *(adverb)*

**tag question** A statement + tag. The **tag** is a short question at the end of the statement. Tag questions check information or comment on a situation.

> You're Jack Thompson, **aren't you?**
> It's a nice day, **isn't it?**

**tense** The form of a verb that shows the time of the action.

> **simple present:** Fabio **talks** to his friend every day.
> **simple past:** Fabio **talked** to his teacher yesterday.

**third-person singular** The pronouns *he, she,* and *it* or a singular noun. In the simple present, the third-person-singular verb ends in *-s*.

> Tomás **works** in an office. *(Tomás = he)*

**three-word verb** A phrasal verb + preposition.

> Slow down! I can't **keep up with** you.

**time clause** A clause that begins with a time word such as *when, before, after, while,* or *as soon as*.

> I'll call you **when I get home**.

**transitive verb** A verb that has an object.

> She **likes** apples.

**two-word verb** See **phrasal verb**.

**unreal conditional sentence** A sentence that talks about unreal conditions and their unreal results. The condition and its result can be untrue, imagined, or impossible.

> If I were a bird, I would fly around the world.
> If you had called, I would have invited you to the party.

**verb** A word that describes what the subject of the sentence does, thinks, feels, senses, or owns.

> They **run** two miles every day.
> She **loved** that movie.
> He **has** a new camera.

*wh-* question (also called **information question**) A question that begins with a *wh-* word. You answer a *wh-* question with information.

A: **Where** are you going?
B: To the store.

*wh-* word (also called **question word**) A word such as *who, what, when, where, which, why, how,* and *how much*. It can begin a *wh-* question or an embedded question.

**Who** is that?
**What** did you see?
**When** does the movie usually start?
I don't know **how much** it costs.

*yes/no* question A question that begins with a form of *be* or an auxiliary verb. You can answer a *yes/no* question with *yes* or *no*.

A: **Are** you a student?
B: **Yes**, I am. **or** **No**, I'm not.
A: **Do** you come here often?
B: **Yes**, I do. **or** **No**, I don't.

# Unit Review Answer Key

**Note:** In this answer key, where a short or contracted form is given, the full or long form is also correct (unless the purpose of the exercise is to practice the short or contracted forms).

## UNIT 1

**A**
1. studies
2. are coming
3. do
4. understand
5. use

**B**
1. 'm looking for
2. think
3. 's not **or** isn't carrying
4. need
5. see
6. 's standing
7. 's waiting
8. sounds
9. don't believe
10. wants

**C** Hi Leda,

How ~~do you do~~ [are you doing] these days? We're all fine. I'm writing to tell you that ~~we~~ [we're] not living in California anymore. We just moved to Oregon. Also, ~~we expect~~ [we're expecting] a baby! We're looking for an interesting name for our new daughter. Do you have any ideas? Right now, we're thinking about *Gabriella* because ~~it's having~~ [it has] good nicknames. For example, *Gabby*, *Bree*, and *Ella* all seem good to us. How ~~are~~ [do] those nicknames sound to you? We hope you'll write soon and tell us your news.

Love,
Samantha

## UNIT 2

**A**
1. met
2. was working
3. saw
4. had
5. When
6. was thinking
7. gave

**B**
1. were…doing
2. met
3. were waiting
4. met
5. were studying
6. noticed
7. entered

**C** It was 2005. I ~~studied~~ [was studying] French in Paris ~~while~~ [when] I met Paul. Like me, Paul was from California. We were both taking the same 9:00 a.m. conversation class. After class, we always ~~were going~~ [went] to a café with some of our classmates. One day, while we ~~was~~ [were] drinking café au lait, Paul ~~was asking~~ [asked] me to go to a movie with him. After that, we started to spend most of our free time together. We really got to know each other well, and we discovered that we had a lot of similar interests. When the course was over, we left Paris and ~~were going~~ [went] back to California together. The next year, we got married!

## UNIT 3

**A**
1. has been
2. took
3. has been reading
4. started
5. has gone
6. for
7. have become

**B**
1. has been working **or** has worked
2. discovered
3. didn't know
4. found out
5. got
6. has been going **or** has gone
7. hasn't found
8. has been having **or** has had

**C** A: How long ~~did~~ [have] you been doing adventure sports?
B: ~~I've gotten~~ [I got] interested five years ago, and I haven't stopped since then.
A: You're lucky to live here in Colorado. It's a great place for adventure sports. ~~Did you live~~ [Have you lived **or** Have you been living] here long?
B: No, not long. ~~I've~~ [I] moved here last year. I used to live in Alaska.
A: I haven't ~~go~~ [gone] there yet, but I've heard it's great.
B: It *is* great. When you go, be sure to visit Denali National Park.

## UNIT 4

**A**
1. had gotten
2. had been studying
3. had graduated
4. moved
5. hadn't given

**B** 1. had…been playing
2. joined
3. 'd decided
4. 'd been practicing
5. 'd taught
6. Had…come
7. 'd…moved
8. 'd…been living
9. hadn't been expecting

**C**     When five-year-old Sarah Chang enrolled in
the Juilliard School, she ~~has~~ *had* already been playing
the violin for more than a year. Her parents, both
musicians, had ~~been moving~~ *moved* from Korea to further
their careers. They had ~~gave~~ *given* their daughter a violin
as a fourth birthday present, and Sarah had been
~~practiced~~ *practicing* hard since then. By seven, she ^*had* already
performed with several local orchestras. A child
prodigy, Sarah became the youngest person to receive
the Hollywood Bowl's Hall of Fame Award. She
had already ~~been receiving~~ *received* several awards including
the Nan Pa Award—South Korea's highest prize for
musical talent.

## UNIT 5

**A** 1. turn
2. Are
3. doing
4. is
5. is going to
6. you're
7. finishes

**B** 1. will…be doing **or** are…going to be doing
2. 'll be leaving
3. 'll…be going
4. won't be coming **or** 're not going to be coming
5. Is…going to cause **or** Will…cause
6. No…it isn't. **or** No…it won't.
7. 'll be **or** 's going to be
8. 'll see

**C** A: How long are you going to ~~staying~~ *stay **or** be staying* in Beijing?

B: I'm not sure. I'll let you know as soon as ~~I'll~~ *I* find
out, OK?

A: OK. It's going to be a long flight. What will you
~~doing~~ *do **or** be doing* to pass the time?

B: I'll ~~be work~~ *work **or** be working* a lot of the time. And I'm going to try
to sleep.
A: Good idea. Have fun, and ~~I'm emailing~~ *I'll email* you all the
office news. I promise.

## UNIT 6

**A** 1. have been selling
2. we get
3. have been exercising
4. I'll have read
5. By

**B** 1. 'll have been living
2. 'll have been studying
3. 'll have graduated
4. graduate
5. 'll have found
6. 'll have made
7. 'll have earned

**C**     I'm so excited about your news! By the time you
read this, you'll already have ~~moving~~ *moved* into your new
house! And I have some good news, too. By the end
of this month, I'll have ~~save~~ *saved* $5,000. That's enough
for me to buy a used car! And that means that by this
time next year, ~~I drive~~ *I'll have driven* to California to visit you! I have
more news, too. By the time I ~~will~~ graduate, I will
have ~~been~~ started my new part-time job. I hope that
by this time next year, I'll also ~~had~~ *have* finished working
on my latest invention—a solar-powered flashlight.

    It's hard to believe that in June, we will have been
~~being~~ friends for ten years. Time sure flies! And we'll
have ~~been stayed~~ *stayed **or** been staying* in touch even though we are 3,000
miles apart. Isn't technology a great thing?

## UNIT 7

**A** 1. isn't
2. Didn't
3. You've
4. it
5. has
6. she
7. Shouldn't

**B** 1. have
2. No, I haven't
3. Aren't
4. No, I'm not
5. are
6. won't
7. Yes, you will

**C** A: Ken hasn't come back from Korea yet, has ~~Ken~~ *he*?

B: ~~No~~ *Yes*, he has. He got back last week. Didn't he call
you when he got back?

**A:** No, he didn't. He's probably busy. There are a lot of things to do when you move, ~~isn't~~ *aren't* there?

**B:** Definitely. And I guess his family ~~wanted~~ *will want* to spend a lot of time with him, won't they?

**A:** I'm sure they will. You know, I think I'll just call him. You have his phone number, ~~have~~ *don't* you?

**B:** Yes, I do. Could you wait while I get it off my phone? You're not in a hurry, ~~aren't~~ *are* you?

## UNIT 8

**A**
1. does
2. So
3. hasn't either
4. but
5. doesn't
6. too
7. either

**B**
1. I speak Spanish, and so does my brother.
   **or** ...my brother does too.
2. I can't speak Russian, and neither can my brother.
   **or** ...my brother can't either.
3. Jaime lives in Chicago, but his brother doesn't.
4. Chen doesn't play tennis, but his sister does.
5. Diego doesn't eat meat, and neither does Lila.
   **or** ...Lila doesn't either.

**C**  My friend Alicia and I have a lot in common. She comes from Los Angeles, and so ~~I do~~ *do I*. She speaks Spanish. I ~~speak~~ *do* too. Her parents are both teachers, and mine ~~do~~ *are* too. She doesn't have any brothers or sisters. ~~Either~~ *Neither* do I. There are some differences, too. Alicia is very reserved, but ~~I am~~ *I'm not*. I like to talk about my feelings and say what's on my mind. Alicia doesn't like sports, but I ~~don't~~ *do*. I'm on several school teams, ~~and~~ *but* she isn't. I think our differences make things more interesting, and so ~~do~~ *does* Alicia!

## UNIT 9

**A**
1. to use
2. (in order) to save
3. ordering
4. to relax
5. (to) study
6. preparing
7. Stopping
8. to eat
9. not to have **or** not having
10. Cooking

**B**
1. doesn't **or** didn't remember going
2. wants **or** wanted Al to take
3. wonders **or** wondered about Chu's **or** Chu eating
4. didn't stop to have
5. forgot to mail

**C**
**A:** I was happy to hear that the cafeteria is serving salads now. I'm eager ~~trying~~ *to try* them.

**B:** Me too. Someone recommended ~~to eat~~ *eating* more salads to lose weight.

**A:** It was that TV doctor, right? He's always urging ~~we~~ *us* to exercise more, too.

**B:** That's the one. He's actually convinced me to stop ~~to eat~~ *eating* meat.

**A:** Interesting! That would be a hard decision for us ~~making~~ *to make*, though. We love to barbecue.

## UNIT 10

**A**
1. helped
2. had
3. made
4. let
5. got

**B**
1. didn't **or** wouldn't let me have
2. got them to buy
3. made me walk
4. had me feed
5. didn't **or** wouldn't help me take
6. got him to give
7. let them have

**C**  Lately, I've been thinking a lot about all the people who helped me ~~adjusting~~ *adjust* **or** *to adjust* to moving here when I was a kid. My parents got me ~~join~~ *to join* some school clubs, so I met other kids. Then my dad helped me ~~improved~~ *improve* **or** *to improve* my soccer game so that I could join the team. And my mom never let me ~~to stay~~ *stay* home. She made me ~~to get~~ *get* out and do things. My parents also spoke to my new teacher and had ~~she~~ *her* call on me a lot, so the other kids got to know me quickly. Our next-door neighbors helped, too. They got ~~I~~ *me* to walk their dog Red, and Red introduced me to all her human friends! The fact that so many people wanted to help me made me ~~to realize~~ *realize* that I was not alone. Before long, I felt part of my new school, my new neighborhood, and my new life.

**A** 1. f     3. a     5. b     7. g
  2. e     4. c     6. d

**B** 1. get through with my work
  2. pick it up
  3. count on her
  4. call me back
  5. got off the phone
  6. put my pajamas on
  7. turned the lights off

**C**     I'm so tired of telemarketers ~~calling up me~~ *calling me up* as soon as I get back from work or just when I sit ~~up~~ *down* for a relaxing dinner! It's gotten to the point that I've stopped picking *up* the phone when it rings between 6:00 and 8:00 p.m. ~~up~~. I know I can count on it being a telemarketer who will try to talk me into spending money on something I don't want. But it's still annoying to hear the phone ring, so sometimes I ~~turn off it~~ *turn it off*. Then, of course, I worry that it may be someone important. So I end up checking caller ID to find out. I think the Do Not Call list is a great idea. Who ~~thought up it~~ *thought it up*? I'm going to ~~sign for it up~~ *sign up for it* tomorrow!

**A** 1. are     4. which
  2. whose     5. that
  3. thinks     6. who

**B** 1. who **or** that behave     5. that **or** which hurt
  2. who uses     6. which…upset
  3. which…convince     7. whose…is
  4. who **or** that…speaks

**C**     It's true that we are often attracted to people ~~which~~ *who* **or** *that* are very different from ourselves. An extrovert, ~~which~~ *whose* personality is very outgoing, will often connect with a romantic partner who ~~are~~ *is* an introvert. They are both attracted to someone that ~~have~~ *has* different strengths. My cousin Valerie, who is an extreme extrovert, recently married Bill, whose idea of a party is a Scrabble game on the Internet. Can this marriage succeed? Will Bill learn the salsa, ~~that~~ *which* is Valerie's favorite dance? Will Valerie start collecting unusual words? Their friends, ~~that~~ *who* care about both of them, are hoping for the best.

**A** 1. whose     4. who
  2. that     5. when
  3. where     6. who

**B** 1. where     5. whose
  2. that **or** which     6. who(m)
  3. that **or** which     7. when **or** that
  4. who(m) **or** that

**C**     I grew up in an apartment building ~~who~~ *that* **or** *which* **or** no relative pronoun my grandparents owned. There was a small dining room ~~when~~ *where* we had family meals and a kitchen in ~~that~~ *which* I ate my breakfast. My aunt, uncle, and cousin, in ~~who~~ *whose* home I spent a lot of my time, lived in an identical apartment on the fourth floor. I remember the time that my parents gave me a toy phone set that we used ~~it~~ so I could talk to my cousin. There weren't many children in the building, but I often visited the building manager, ~~who's~~ *whose* son I liked. I enjoyed living in the apartment, but for me the day ~~where~~ *when* **or** *that* **or** no relative pronoun we moved into our own house was the best day of my childhood.

**A** 1. get     6. to post
  2. may     7. must not
  3. 've got     8. be able to
  4. can't     9. might be
  5. help

**B** 1. 'd better not give **or** shouldn't give **or** ought not to give
  2. must register **or** 'd better register **or** 've got to register
  3. must not be
  4. must get **or** has to get **or** has got to get
  5. can't eat **or** must not eat
  6. may come **or** might come **or** could come

**C** 1. Could that ~~being~~ *be* Amelie in this photograph?
  2. With this site, I ~~must not~~ *don't have to* call to keep in touch with friends. It's just not necessary.

**3.** I don't know this person. I guess I'd ~~not better~~ *better not*

accept him as a friend on my Facebook page.

**4.** That doesn't look anything like Anton. It ~~doesn't~~ *can't*

~~have to~~ be him.

**5.** Were you able ~~remove~~ *to remove* that embarrassing photo?

## UNIT 15

**A**
1. have
2. ought
3. could
4. given
5. shouldn't
6. should I

**B**
1. I should've studied for the math test.
2. You could have shown me your class notes.
3. I shouldn't have stayed up so late the night before the test.
4. He ought to have called you.
5. You might've invited me to join the study group.

**C** I shouldn't have ~~stay~~ *stayed* up so late. I overslept and missed my bus. I ~~ought have~~ *ought to have* asked Erik for a ride. I got to the office late, and my boss said, "You might ~~had~~ *have* called." She was right. I ~~shouldn't have~~ *should've* called. At lunch, my co-workers went out together. They really could ~~of~~ *have* invited me to join them. Should ~~have I~~ *I have* said something to them? Then, after lunch, my mother called. She said, "Yesterday was Aunt Em's birthday. You could've ~~sending~~ *sent* her a card!" I really think my mother might ~~has~~ *have* reminded me. Not a good day! I ~~shouldn't have~~ *should've* just stayed in bed.

## UNIT 16

**A**
1. must
2. might not have
3. have
4. taken
5. may
6. have
7. couldn't

**B**
1. might not have gotten my message **or** may not have gotten my message
2. must not have studied
3. couldn't have forgotten our date **or** can't have forgotten our date
4. may have been at the movies **or** might have been at the movies **or** could have been at the movies
5. must have forgotten
6. must not have seen me

**C** Why did the Aztecs build their capital city in the middle of a lake? Could they ~~had~~ *have* wanted the protection of the water? They might have ~~been~~. Or the location may ~~has~~ *have* helped them to control nearby societies. At first, it must have ~~being~~ *been* an awful place, full of mosquitoes and fog. But it must ~~no~~ *not* have been a bad idea—the island city became the center of a very powerful empire. To succeed, the Aztecs had to have ~~became~~ *become* fantastic engineers quite quickly. When the Spanish arrived, they couldn't have ~~expect~~ *expected* the amazing palaces, floating gardens, and well-built canals. They must have been astounded.

## UNIT 17

**A**
1. Spanish is spoken in Bolivia.
2. They play soccer in Bolivia.
3. Reza Deghati took the photo.
4. The articles were translated into Spanish.
5. Quinoa is grown in the mountains.
6. They named the main street El Prado.

**B**
1. was discovered
2. is spoken
3. is grown
4. is exported
5. are employed **or** have been employed
6. was made
7. has been performed
8. is attended

**C** Photojournalist Alexandra Avakian was born and ~~raise~~ *raised* in New York. Since she began her career, she has covered many of the world's most important stories. Her work ~~have~~ *has* been published in many newspapers and magazines including *National Geographic*, and her photographs have ~~being~~ *been* exhibited around the world. Avakian has also written a book, *Window of the Soul: My Journey in the Muslim World*, which was ~~been~~ published in 2008. It has not yet been translated ~~by translators~~ into other languages, but the chapter titles appear in both English and Arabic. Avakian's book ~~have be~~ *has been* discussed on international TV, radio, and numerous websites.

## UNIT 18

**A** 1. done
2. be replaced
3. could
4. had
5. be
6. won't
7. has
8. handled

**B** 1. should be trained
2. have to be given
3. must be tested
4. can be experienced
5. will be provided
6. may be sent
7. could…be developed

**C**   The new spacesuits are going to be ~~testing~~ *tested* underwater today. They've got to ~~been~~ *be* improved before they can be used on the Moon or Mars. Two astronauts are going to be wearing them while they're working, and they'll *be*^ watched by the engineers. This morning, communication was lost with the Earth's surface, and all decisions had to be ~~make~~ *made* by the astronauts themselves. It was a very realistic situation. This crew ~~will got~~ *will have* **or** *has got* to be very well prepared for space travel. They're going to the Moon in a few years.

## UNIT 19

**A** 1. have it cut
2. done
3. get
4. your house painted
5. by

**B** 1. get it repaired
2. have them cleaned
3. have them shortened
4. get it colored
5. get it fixed
6. had it removed
7. get it renewed
8. 'll have it checked **or** 'm going to have it checked **or** 'm having it checked

**C**   I'm going on vacation next week. I'd like to have ~~done some work~~ *some work done* in my office, and this seems like a good time for it. Please have my carpet ~~clean~~ *cleaned* while I'm gone. And could you have my computer and printer looked at? It's been quite a while since they've been serviced. Ted wants to have my office painted ~~by a painter~~ while I'm gone. Please tell him any color is fine except pink! Last week, I ~~had designed some~~ *had some new brochures designed* ~~new brochures~~ by Perfect Print. Please call the printer and have them delivered directly to the sales reps. And could you also ~~get made up more business cards~~ *get more business cards made up*? When I get back, it'll be time to plan the holiday party. I think we should have it catered this year ~~from~~ *by* a professional. While I'm gone, why don't you call around and get some estimates from caterers? ~~Has~~ *Have* the estimates sent to Ted. Thanks.

## UNIT 20

**A** 1. do…do
2. are
3. is
4. shop
5. happens
6. doesn't stay
7. closes
8. go
9. feel
10. think

**B** 1. When **or** If it's 7:00 a.m. in Honolulu, what time is it in Mumbai?
2. If you love jewelry, you should visit an international jewelry show.
3. A tourist may have more fun if she tries bargaining.
4. If **or** When you're shopping at an outdoor market, you can always bargain for a good price.
5. But don't try to bargain if **or** when you're shopping in a big department store.

**C** 1. If I don't like something I bought online, then I ~~returned~~ *return* it.
2. Don't buy from an online site×if you don't know anything about the company.
3. When ~~he'll~~ *he* shops online, Frank always saves a lot of time.
4. I always ~~fell~~ *fall* asleep if I fly at night. It happens every time.
5. Isabel always has a wonderful time×when she visits Istanbul.

## UNIT 21

**A** 1. d   3. a   5. b
2. f   4. c   6. e

**B** 1. a. take
   b. 'll be **or** 'm going to be
2. a. will…do **or** are…going to do
   b. don't get
   c. 'll stay **or** 'm going to stay
   d. get

**3. a.** pass
  **b.** 'll celebrate **or** 'm going to celebrate

**C**  It's been a hard week, and I'm looking forward to
the weekend. If the weather ~~will be~~ *is* nice tomorrow,
Marco and I are going to go to the beach. The ocean
is usually too cold for swimming at this time of year,
so I probably ~~don't~~ *won't* go in the water unless it's really
hot outside. But I love walking along the beach and
breathing in the fresh sea air.

  If Marco has time, he might ~~makes~~ *make* some
sandwiches to bring along. Otherwise, we'll just get
some pizza. I hope it'll be a nice day. I just listened to
the weather report, and there may be some rain in
the afternoon. ~~Unless~~ *If* it rains, ~~we~~ *we'll* probably go to the
movies instead. That's our Plan B. But I really want to
go to the beach, so I'm keeping my fingers crossed!

## UNIT 22

**A** **1.** I'd feel          **5.** could
  **2.** were           **6.** weren't
  **3.** could          **7.** I'd
  **4.** you found

**B** **1.** would…do        **5.** would become
  **2.** found         **6.** put
  **3.** Would…take      **7.** made
  **4.** knew          **8.** would learn

**C** **1.** Pablo wishes he ~~can~~ *could* speak German.

  **2.** If he had the time, ~~he'll~~ *he'd* study in Germany. But he
    doesn't have the time right now.

  **3.** He could get a promotion ~~when~~ *if* he spoke another
    language.

  **4.** His company ~~may~~ *might* pay the tuition if he took a
    course.

  **5.** What would you do if you ~~are~~ *were* in Pablo's situation?

## UNIT 23

**A** **1.** hadn't told       **4.** If
  **2.** had          **5.** gone
  **3.** would have been

**B** **1. a.** would've been
    **b.** hadn't missed
    **c.** had been
    **d.** wouldn't have discovered
  **2. a.** hadn't accepted
    **b.** had taken
    **c.** wouldn't have met
  **3. a.** hadn't seen
    **b.** wouldn't have believed

**C**  Tonight, we watched the movie *Back to the Future*
starring Michael J. Fox. I might never ~~had~~ *have* seen it if I
hadn't read his autobiography, *Lucky Man*. His book
was so good that I wanted to see his most famous
movie. Now, I wish I ~~saw~~ *had seen* it in the theater when it first
came out, but I hadn't even been born yet! It would
have been better if we ~~would have~~ *had* watched it on a big
screen. Fox was great. He looked really young—just
like a teenager. But I would have recognized him even
~~when~~ *if* I hadn't known he was in the film.

  In real life, when Fox was a teenager, he was too
small to become a professional hockey player. But if
he hadn't looked so young, he ~~can't~~ *couldn't* **or** *wouldn't* have gotten his
role in the TV hit series *Family Ties*. In Hollywood,
he had to sell his furniture to pay his bills, but he kept
trying to find an acting job. If he ~~would have~~ *had* given up,
he might never have become a star.

## UNIT 24

**A** **1.** says          **5.** she'd cooked
  **2.** "I'd love to."      **6.** told
  **3.** planned         **7.** had been
  **4.** he           **8.** his

**B** **1.** (that) she always gets up early **or** she always got
    up early.
  **2.** (that) water boils at 100 degrees Celsius **or** water
    boiled at 100 degrees Celsius.
  **3.** (that) he liked my haircut **or** he likes my haircut.
  **4.** (that) she loved the pasta **or** she had loved
    the pasta.
  **5.** (that) it was his own recipe **or** it is his own recipe.
  **6.** (that) she mailed him the check **or** she had mailed
    him the check.
  **7.** (that) his boss had liked his work **or** his boss liked
    his work.

**C** 1. A psychologist I know often tells me ˣthat people today tell hundreds of lies every day.ˣ

2. Yesterday, Mia's boyfriend ~~said~~ *told* her that he liked her new dress.

3. When she heard that, Mia said she didn't really believe ~~you~~ *him*.

4. I didn't think that was so bad. I said that her boyfriend ~~tells~~ *told* **or** *had told* her a little white lie.

5. But Mia hates lying. She said that to ~~me~~ *her*, all lies were wrong.

## UNIT 25

**A** 1. was
2. I
3. take
4. might
5. today
6. would
7. could
8. there

**B** 1. (that) it was going to rain
2. (that) it could be the worst storm this year
3. (that) it was going to start soon
4. (that) they should buy water
5. (that) they had to leave right then
6. (that) she would call me the next day

**C** What a storm! They said it ~~is~~ *was* going to be bad, but it was terrible. They said it ~~will~~ *would* last two days, but it lasted four. On the first day of the storm, my mother called and told me that we should ~~have left~~ *leave* the house right ~~now~~ *then*. (I still can hear her exact words: "You should leave the house *right now!*") We should have listened to her! We just didn't believe it was going to be so serious. I told her last night that if we had known, we would ~~had~~ *have* left right away. We're lucky we survived. I just listened to the weather forecast. Good news! They said tomorrow should ~~have been~~ *be* sunny.

## UNIT 26

**A** 1. . (period)
2. give
3. "Please lie down."
4. not to
5. say
6. told
7. advised

**B** 1. He told **or** asked her to show him her license.
2. She advised **or** told him to get more exercise.

3. She invited **or** asked them to come to the English Department party.
4. He asked her to turn on the light.
5. She invited **or** asked them to hang out at her house.

**C** Too much stress is bad for your health. So, I asked my doctor ˌ*to* give me some tips on how to reduce everyday stress. First of all, she told me ~~exercising~~ *to exercise* every day. She also told me ~~to don't~~ *not to* work too long without taking a break. She advised me ~~doing~~ *to do* things to relax. For example, she said ~~that~~ to listen to music. She also ~~said~~ *told* me to sit with my eyes closed and to concentrate on my breathing. That helps lower blood pressure. She also advised me ~~no~~ *not to* drink too many beverages with caffeine. Finally, she said to ˣget enough sleepˣ—at least seven hours a night!

## UNIT 27

**A** 1. . (period)
2. if
3. their office was
4. I lived
5. I had

**B** 1. who the company had hired.
2. if **or** whether **or** whether or not I had taken the job.
3. if **or** whether **or** whether or not I liked my job.
4. how long I had worked there.
5. how many employees worked there.
6. why I wanted to work for them.
7. what the starting salary was.
8. if **or** whether **or** whether or not I could start soon.

**C** They asked me so many questions! They asked me where ~~did I work~~ *I worked*. They asked me who ~~was my boss~~ *my boss was*. They asked why I ~~did want~~ *wanted* to change jobs. They asked how much money I made. They ~~ask~~ *asked* me who I ~~have~~ *had* voted for in the last election. They even asked me what my favorite color was~~?~~ ˌ. Finally, I asked myself whether or ~~no~~ *not* I really wanted that job!

## UNIT 28

**A** 1. we should
2. our server is
3. . (period)
4. to
5. I should
6. ? (question mark)
7. whether

**B**  1. where the restaurant is?
2. if **or** whether the subway goes to the museum.
3. if **or** whether we should tip the porter.
4. why we didn't buy the book on tipping.
5. how much we should tip the tour guide.
6. if **or** whether you have any travel books.
7. what this sign says?

**C**  A: Hi. Is this a good time to call? I wasn't sure what
time you have dinner?
B: This is fine. I didn't know ~~were you~~ *if **or** whether you were* back from
your trip.

A: We got back two days ago. I can't remember if I
*emailed*
~~email~~ you some photographs.
                              *you took*
B: Yes. They were great. Can you tell me where ~~took~~
~~you~~ that picture of the lake? I want to go!
                           *that was*
A: Hmm. I'm not sure which one ~~was that~~. We saw a
lot of lakes in Switzerland.

B: I'll show it to you. I'd really like to find out where
*it is*
~~is it~~.

# Information Gaps, Student B

## EXERCISE 10  DR. EON'S CALENDAR

**A** INFORMATION GAP  Work with a partner. Student B will follow the instructions below. Student A will follow the instructions on page 83.

---

**STUDENT B**

- Complete Dr. Eon's calendar. Get information from Student A. Ask questions and fill in the calendar. Answer Student A's questions.

EXAMPLE:  A: What will Dr. Eon be doing on Sunday the first?
B: She'll be flying to Tokyo. What about on the second? Will she be taking the day off?
A: No, she'll be meeting with Dr. Kato.

### FEBRUARY 2077

| SUNDAY | MONDAY | TUESDAY | WEDNESDAY | THURSDAY | FRIDAY | SATURDAY |
|---|---|---|---|---|---|---|
| 1 fly to Tokyo | 2 meet with Dr. Kato | 3 attend World Future Conference | 4 | 5 | 6 | 7 |
| 8 | 9 | 10 | 11 | 12 fly to Denver | 13 visit Mom and Dad | 14 |
| 15 | 16 give speech at Harvard University | 17 meet with Dr. Rover | 18 | 19 | 20 | 21 |
| 22 relax! | 23 work at home | 24 | 25 | 26 | 27 | 28 |

---

**B** Now compare calendars with your partner. Are they the same?

# EXERCISE 11 LONDON AND VANCOUVER

**INFORMATION GAP** Work with a partner. Student B will follow the instructions below. Student A will follow the instructions on page 115.

STUDENT B

- Read about London and answer Student A's questions.

    EXAMPLE: A: London is the largest city in the United Kingdom, isn't it?
    　　　　　 B: Yes, it is.

## LONDON

London is the capital and largest city of the United Kingdom. It is also one of the oldest and largest cities in the world. Located in southeastern England, the city lies on the River Thames, which links it to shipping routes throughout the world. Because of its size, the city is divided into thirty-two "boroughs" or parts. With its many museums, palaces, parks, and theaters, tourism is a major industry. In fact, millions of tourists visit the city every year to take advantage of its many cultural and historical offerings. Unfortunately, like many great urban centers, London has problems such as traffic congestion, crime, and homelessness.

- Now look at the questions below. What do you know about Vancouver? Complete the questions by circling the correct words and writing the tags.

    1. Vancouver is / (isn't) the largest city in Canada, _is it_____?

    2. It lies / doesn't lie on the Atlantic Coast, _____?

    3. It has / doesn't have a very large port, _____?

    4. It is / isn't a very beautiful city, _____?

    5. Many / Not many tourists visit the city, _____?

    6. You can / can't hear many different languages there, _____?

    7. Movie production is / isn't an important industry in Vancouver, _____?

- Ask Student A the questions. Student A will read a paragraph about Vancouver and tell you if your information is correct or not.

    EXAMPLE: B: Vancouver isn't the largest city in Canada, is it?
    　　　　　 A: No, it isn't. It's the third largest city.

# EXERCISE 10 THE PHILIPPINES

**Ⓐ INFORMATION GAP** Work with a partner. Student B will follow the instructions below. Student A will follow the instructions on page 283.

---

**STUDENT B**

- The Philippines consists of many islands and has many natural resources. Look at the map of Mindanao and complete the chart. Write *Y* for *Yes* if Mindanao has a particular resource and *N* for *No* if it does not.

- Student A has the map of Luzon. Ask Student A questions about Luzon and complete the chart for Luzon.

  EXAMPLE: **B:** Is tobacco grown in Luzon?
  **A:** Yes, it is. It's grown in the northern and central part of the island.

- Student A doesn't have the map of Mindanao. Answer Student A's questions about Mindanao.

  EXAMPLE: **A:** Is tobacco grown in Mindanao?
  **B:** No, it isn't.

| | | | MINDANAO | LUZON |
|---|---|---|---|---|
| **G R O W** | 🍃 | tobacco | N | Y |
| | 🌽 | corn | | |
| | 🍌 | bananas | | |
| | ☕ | coffee | | |
| | 🍍 | pineapples | | |
| | 🌾 | sugar | | |
| **R A I S E** | 🐄 | cattle | | |
| | 🐖 | pigs | | |
| **M I N E** | ⬜ | gold | | |
| | ⬛ | manganese | | |
| **P R O D U C E** | 🌸 | cotton | | |
| | 🌿 | rubber | | |
| | 🪵 | lumber | | |

Mindanao

**Ⓑ** When you are finished, compare charts. Are they the same?

# Index

This index is for the full and split editions. All entries are in the full book. Entries for Volume A of the split edition are in black. Entries for Volume B are in blue.

Stative verbs. *See* Non-action verbs
Subject
    embedded *wh-* questions about,
        441–442
    gerunds as, 139
    indirect *wh-* questions about,
        423, 425
    relative pronouns as, 184–186
Subject pronouns, changes in
    indirect speech to, 380
Subject relative pronouns, 184–186

Tag questions
    answering, 108
    *be* in forming, 105, 108
    contractions in, 108
    difference between *yes/no*
        questions and, 107
    forms of, 105–106
    intonation of, 109
    uses of, 107–108
*Tell*, *say* contrasted, 379
*That*
    in indirect speech, 379, 398
    as object relative pronoun,
        202–206
    as subject relative pronoun,
        184–186, 188
*Then*, to emphasize results in real
    conditional sentences,
    319–320, 335
*This*, changing in indirect speech,
    398
Time clauses
    commas after, 22, 74, 91
    future, 74
    future perfect and future perfect
        progressive, 90
    future progressive, 74
    past perfect, 52
    past perfect progressive, 52
    past progressive, 21–22
    present progressive, 74
    simple past, 21–22, 52
    simple present, 74, 90–91
Time expressions
    changing in indirect speech, 397
    with present progressive, 7
*To*
    before gerunds, 141
    in infinitives, 140
*Too*, with additions of similarity,
    121, 122–124

Transitive phrasal verbs
    inseparable, 167, 169–170
    object of, 169
    separable, 167, 169
Transitive verbs, passive form of,
    273
Two-word verbs. *See* Phrasal verbs


*Unless*
    contrasted with *if*, 335
    to state negative condition, 335
Unreal conditional sentences. *See*
    Future unreal conditional
    sentences; Past unreal
    conditional sentences;
    Present unreal conditional
    sentences
*Until*, with simple past, 52
*Usually*, 6–7


Verbs. *See also* Auxiliary verbs;
    Gerund(s); Infinitives;
    Modals; Passive; Phrasal
    verbs
    agreement in adjective clauses,
        187, 203
    changes in indirect speech,
        379–380, 395–397, 424
    gerunds after, 140–141
    infinitives after, 140–141
    intransitive, 273
    non-action, 8, 21, 36, 51, 90
    reporting, 379–380, 396, 424
    transitive, 273


*Was/were (doing)*. *See* Past
    progressive
*Were*
    in future unreal conditional
        sentences, 348–349
    in present unreal conditional
        sentences, 348–349
*Wh-* questions
    direct, 423
    embedded, 439, 441
    indirect, 423, 424–425
*When*
    with adjective clauses, 202, 206
    with past perfect, 52
    with past perfect progressive, 52
    with past progressive, 21–22

    in present real conditional
        sentences, 320
    with simple past, 21, 52
*Where*, with adjective clauses, 202,
    206
*Whether*
    in embedded *yes/no* questions,
        441–442
    in indirect *yes/no* questions, 424
*Whether or not*
    in embedded *yes/no* questions,
        441
    in indirect *yes/no* questions, 424
*Which*
    as object relative pronoun,
        202–205
    as subject relative pronoun,
        184–186, 188
*While*, with past progressive, 21–22
*Who*
    as object relative pronoun,
        202–205
    as subject relative pronoun,
        184–186, 188
*Whom*, as object relative pronoun,
    202–205
*Whose*
    as object relative pronoun, 202,
        206
    as subject relative pronoun,
        184–187
*Will*
    for future, 72–73, 291
    with future progressive, 74
    in future real conditional
        sentences, 334
    in offers or promises, 73
    with passive, 290–291
    in quick decisions, 73
    to talk about facts, 72
*Will be (doing)*. *See* Future
    progressive
*Will have (done)*. *See* Future perfect
*Will have been (doing)*. *See* Future
    perfect progressive
*Wish*
    in past unreal conditional
        sentences, 363
    in present unreal conditional
        sentences, 349
Word order
    for additions, 123
    for embedded questions,
        441–442
    for indirect questions, 425
    for reporting direct speech, 379

haber.
he / hubo / hice.
habra.

Yo he visitado.
Yo he hecho
Yo hice.